More Praise for Harvey Karp

"I wish I had known Dr. Karp for my first two children. With the soothing, loving tips in this book, caring for my two most recent babies has been a dream." —Hunter Tylo, actress/founder of Hunter's Chosen Child

"Dr. Karp was exactly the doctor to see us through parenthood. He has the magic touch—not just with babies, but with new parents, too." —Robin Swicord and Nicholas Kazan, screenwriters of *Matilda, Practical Magic,* and *Reversal of Fortune*

"Dr. Karp is simply the best. Any time our kids have a problem, he guides us with warmth, wisdom, and humor. And that helps *us* sleep better at night." —Janet and Jerry Zucker, director of *Airplane, Ghost,* and *Rat Race*

"Harvey Karp's enlightened and creative approach has been a benefit not only to our children, but to my wife and me as parents." —Kristen and Lindsey Buckingham, photographer and singer/songwriter, Fleetwood Mac

"Harvey Karp would make my Big Mama proud! He is leading us back to age-old basics, back to motherwit." —Alfre Woodard, actress

"This beautifully written volume meets a tremendous need for a scientifically sound and effective parent guide to the care of persistently crying babies. Dr. Karp has written the best book that I've read on this challenging topic." —Morris Green, M.D., Perry W. Lesh Professor of Pediatrics, Indiana University School of Medicine

"The 'Karp Wrap' is a very powerful tool that can stop a baby's cries instantly! The mother's helpers I train say it calms babies faster than anything else." —Lynn Sullivan, R.N., Director, Newborn Nursing Services, SM-UCLA Hospital

"Dr. Karp offers doctors, therapists, and teachers practical new skills and a wonderfully clear approach to helping parents of fussy babies." —Dr. Carol Blake, Director, Early Childhood Center, Cedar-Sinai Medical Center

Parents Praise Dr. Karp

"I'll give you $100 if you teach me what you just did to calm my baby."
—Denise, Michael, Jacqueline, and Olivia

"Curtis' crying was loud and piercing. The only thing I have found to calm him were those "tricks" you teach in your office." —Carol, Don, Curtis, and Carter

"Our daughter cried terribly. Exhausted, I went to see Dr. Karp. After using his technique, we became believers. Incredibly, it always works for us." —Alise, Will, and Cameron

"We owe you our second born for teaching us "The Karp." It's a miracle cure for colic!" —Ana, Jeff, and Alexander

"We call it the "Harvey Shuffle." The first time I saw it I was astounded. In seconds, Ben stopped crying and my jaw was on the floor!"
—Christina, Jonah, and Ben

"My wife and I bought no less than ten baby books. But the things you showed us were not in the books." —Martin, Ann, and Madison

"Swaddling Theo made a huge difference. Now he is sleeping five to six hours straight at night. It even stopped his spitting up at night. We owe you." —Lisa, Evan, and Theo

"Dr. Karp's method was a lifesaver. With a simple 1, 2, 3—swaddle, shhhh, swing—our baby fell asleep and we received a round of applause." —Laurel, Atillio, Raffaella, and Rocco

"Colic hit us like a freight train. I called Dr. Karp and within two weeks, Emma was sleeping eight to ten hours a night. Dr. Karp changed our lives!" —Jody, Sam, and Emma

The Happiest Baby on the Block

The New Way to Calm Crying and
Help Your Baby Sleep Longer

Harvey Karp, M.D.

B a n t a m   B o o k s

THE HAPPIEST BABY ON THE BLOCK

PUBLISHING HISTORY
A Bantam Book / June 2002

Library of Congress Cataloging-in-Publication Data
Karp, Harvey.
The happiest baby on the block: the new way
to calm crying and help your baby sleep longer / Harvey Karp.
p.   cm.
Includes index.
ISBN 0-553-80255-0
1. Crying in infants.   2. Infants—Care.   3. Parent and child.
4. Infant—Sleep.   5. Child rearing.   I. Title
RJ253 .K37   2002
649'.122—dc21   2001056734

Published simultaneously in the United States and Canada

PRINTED IN THE UNITED STATES OF AMERICA

BVG   10 9 8 7

To the generous hearts
of new parents everywhere
and to our sweet babies
who come into the world
with such trust

Contents

PART TWO

Learning the Ancient Art of Soothing a Baby

Conclusion

The Rainbow at the End of the Tunnel   233

Appendices

Index
261

Acknowledgments

The real voyage of discovery consists, not in seeking out new lands, but in having a new vision.

Marcel Proust

I am a pediatrician—and I love it. I am privileged to practice a field of medicine where I get to be part-biologist, part-psychologist, part-anthropologist, part–animal impersonator, and most especially part-grandmother.

In this book, I also wear all those hats. I hope not only to show what the best parents in history have done to soothe their babies but also to explain why it works and how to have some fun, too! In doing this, my greatest goal is to teach parents, grandparents, and everyone who cares about babies how to translate their messages of love into the language all babies understand.

This book took a number of years to prepare and may never have been completed had it not been for the support and encouragement of a small group of people, to whom I owe my profound gratitude and appreciation:

- To all the kind mothers and fathers in my practice who allowed me to touch their wonderful children, to be a part of their families, and to learn along with them.

- To my beloved mother Sophie, who taught me to marvel at the beauty and order in the world, and to my father Joe, whose patience is my model and whose selfless generosity sheltered me and gave me the gift of education.

▪ To my extraordinary wife Nina, my soulmate, who opened my heart and eyes and is my greatest friend, teacher, and compass. To my mother-in-law Desa, who is a unique and courageous woman. And to my daughter Lexi, who graciously tolerated my long hours of work.

▪ To my teachers Arthur H. Parmelee, Jr., and T. Berry Brazelton. Their brilliant talent for making the complex seem simple helped me learn how to observe and understand children. To the curious minds of Ronald Barr, Julius Richmond, Tiffany Field, Barry Lester, and many other honest explorers of science whose road signs guided me on this wonderful path into the inner world of babies.

▪ To my colleagues who reviewed this book and so generously gave of their time and knowledge: Marty Stein, Jim McKenna, Neal Kaufman, Sandra Steffes, Constance Keeffer, and Stan Inkelis.

▪ To my friends who counseled and helped me during the long process of bookmaking: Toby Berlin and Michael Grecco, Laurie David, Eric Weissler, Peter Gardner, Bart Walker, Richard Grant, Sylvie Rabineau, Katy Arnoldi, Laurel and Tom Barrack, Jonathan Feldman, Dick and Lise Stolley, Carrie Cook, and to my partners and staff at Tenth Street whose support helped make this work possible.

▪ To the capable help of deputy publisher Nita Taublib, the sharp intellect and pencil of my editor Robin Michaelson, the witty imagination of Jennifer Kalis, and the savvy advice of my agent Suzanne Gluck.

Thank you all!

Introduction

How I Rediscovered the Ancient Secrets
for Calming Crying Babies

I certainly didn't realize how easy it was to calm crying babies when I began my pediatric studies in the early 1970s. During my medical-school training at Albert Einstein College of Medicine, my professors taught me that babies scream due to gas pains, so there were two valid approaches for soothing colic. First, try Grandmother's advice of holding, rocking, and pacifiers. If that failed, try medicine: *sedatives* (to push a baby into sleep), *anti-spasm medicines* (to treat stomach cramps), or *anti-gas drops* (to help get out burps).

By the late 1970s, however, these three medical approaches were called into question. Sedating babies was considered inappropriate. Doctors stopped using anti-spasm medicines after several babies treated with them lapsed into comas and died. And anti-gas drops lost their appeal when research proved them to be no more effective than water.

Although my medical education was excellent, I felt helpless when it came to caring for colicky newborns. As a resident, I worked for three years at Childrens Hospital of Los Angeles, one of the world's busiest pediatric hospitals. I was fully trained as a "baby doctor," yet I still couldn't help distraught parents soothe their babies' screams. In 1980, as a Fellow in Child Development at the UCLA School of Medicine, my frustration turned into shock and alarm. As a member of the UCLA Child Abuse Team, I treated several severely injured babies whose parents had committed horrible acts of abuse after being unable to calm their infants' persistent screaming.

I became outraged that our sophisticated medical system didn't have a single effective solution for babies with this common yet terribly disturbing problem. During the two years of my fellowship, I read everything I could about colic. I was determined to unearth every clue to explain why so many children were plagued by this mysterious condition.

I soon uncovered two facts that turned my alarm into hope.

First, I learned about the profound differences between the brain of a three-month-old baby and that of a newborn. A brilliant paper published in 1977 by one of America's preeminent pediatricians, Dr. Arthur H. Parmelee, Jr., described how sophisticated and complex the brains of babies become over the first months of life. He illustrated this point by showing pictures of two babies: a fussing newborn and a smiling three-month-old (shown below). Dr. Parmelee observed that most parents-to-be dreamed of giving birth to a smiling baby like the one on the left, while in reality they ended up with a fussy "fetus-like" newborn like the one seen on the right, at least for the first few months.

These pictures powerfully demonstrated the massive developmental leap babies make during the first

three months of life as well as the huge gap between how parents in our society expect new babies to look and act and their true behavior and nature.

My second pivotal discovery came when I read about child-rearing in other societies. As I explored the musty shelves of old books and journals stored at the UCLA Medical Library, I was shocked to learn that the colicky screaming that afflicted so many of my patients was *absent* in the babies of several cultures around the world!

The more I investigated this issue, the more it dawned on me that our culture, advanced in so many ways, was quite backward when it came to understanding the needs of babies. Somehow, somewhere, we had taken a wrong turn. Once I realized our ideas about babies' crying had been built upon centuries of myth and misconception, the solution to the prehistoric puzzle of why babies cry and how to soothe them suddenly became crystal clear. Our babies are born three months too soon.

I invite you to learn how your baby experiences the world, as well as my program of extremely effective techniques used to calm thousands of my patients over the last twenty years. These techniques may seem a little odd at first, but once you get the hang of them you'll see how wonderfully simple they are. Parents around the world have successfully used these methods to soothe their babies for thousands of years . . . and soon, you will, too!

—*Harvey Karp*

The Happiest Baby on the Block

PART ONE

Look Who's Squawking:
Why Babies Cry—
And Why Some Cry
So Much

1

At Last There's Hope:
An Easy Way
to Calm Crying Babies

Main Points:

- All babies cry, but most new parents have little experience soothing them
- The Basic Problem: In many ways, babies are born three months too soon
- The Calming Reflex: Nature's *Off* switch for a baby's crying
- The 5 "S's": How to turn on your baby's calming reflex
- The Cuddle Cure: Combining the 5 "S's" to help any fussy baby

---

Suzanne was worried and exhausted. Her two-month-old baby, Sean, was a nonstop screamer. He could cry for hours. One afternoon her sister came to watch the baby, and Suzanne bolted to the bathroom for a hot shower and a quick "escape." Forty-five minutes later she awoke, curled up in a ball on the blue tile floor, being sprayed with ice-cold water!

Meanwhile, half a world away in the rugged Kalahari plains of northern Botswana, Nisa gave birth to a tiny girl named Chuko. Chuko was thin and delicate but despite her dainty size, she, too, was a challenging baby who cried frequently.

Nisa carried Chuko in a leather sling everywhere she went. Unlike Suzanne, she never worried when Chuko cried, because like all mothers of the !Kung San tribe, she knew exactly how to calm her baby's crying—in seconds.

Why did Suzanne have such trouble soothing Sean's screams?

What ancient secrets did Nisa know that helped her calm her baby so easily?

As you are about to learn, the answers to these two questions will change the way you think about babies forever! They will show you the world through your baby's eyes and, most important, they will teach you how to calm your baby's cries in minutes and help prolong her sleep.

Your Baby Is Born

When perfectly dry, his flesh sweet and pure, he is the most kissable object in nature.
Marion Harland, *Common Sense in the Nursery,* 1886

Congratulations! You've done a great job already! You've nurtured your baby from the moment of conception to your baby's "birth"day. Having a baby is a wonderful—and wonder-full—experience that makes you laugh, cry, and stare in amazement . . . all at the same time.

Your top job as a new parent is to love your baby like crazy. After showering her with affection, your next two important jobs are to feed her and to calm her when she cries.

I can tell you from my twenty-five years as a pediatrician, parents who succeed at these two tasks feel proud, confident, on top of the world! They have the happiest babies and they feel like the best parents on the block. However, mothers and fathers who struggle with these tasks often end up feeling distraught.

Fortunately, feeding a baby is *usually* pretty straightforward. Most newborns take to sucking like they have a Ph.D. in chowing-down! Soothing a crying baby, on the other hand, can be unexpectedly challenging.

No couple expects their sweet newborn to be "difficult." Who really lis-

tens to horror stories friends and family share? We assume *our* child will be an "easy" baby. That's why so many new parents are shocked to discover how tough calming their baby's cries can be.

Please don't misunderstand me. I'm not saying crying is bad. In fact, it's brilliant! Leave it to nature to find such an effective way for helpless babies to get our attention. And once your baby has your attention, you probably zip down a checklist of questions and solutions:

- Is she hungry? Feed her.
- Is she wet? Change her diaper.
- Is she lonely? Pick her up.
- Is she gassy? Burp her.
- Is she cold? Bundle her up.

The trouble comes when *nothing* works.

Estimates are that one out of every five babies has repeated bouts of terrible fussiness—*for no apparent reason.* That adds up to almost one million sweet new babies born in the U.S. each year who suffer from hours of red-faced, eyes-clenched screaming.

This is why parents of unhappy babies are such heroes! A baby's scream is an incredibly heart-wrenching sound. Bone-tired and bewildered moms and dads lovingly cuddle their frantic babies for hours, trying to calm them, yet the continued crying can corrode their confidence: "Is my baby in pain?" "Am I spoiling her?" "Does she feel abandoned?" "Am I a terrible mother?"

Confronted by this barrage, sometimes the most loving parent may find herself pushed into frustration and depression. A baby's unrelenting shrieks can even drive desperate caregivers over the edge—into the tragedy of child abuse.

Exhausted parents are often told they must wait for their babies to "grow out of it." Yet most of us feel that can't be right. There must be some way to help our babies.

I'm going to show you how.

Help Wanted: Who Do New Parents Turn to When Their Baby Cries a Lot?

Although a network of clinics and specialists exists to help mothers solve their infant's feeding problems, there is little support for the parents of screaming babies. That's unfortunate because while the urge to quiet a baby is instinctual, the ability to do it is a skill that must be learned.

Today's parents have less experience caring for babies than any previous generation. (Amazingly, our culture requires more training to get a driver's license than to have a baby.)

That's not to say that inexperienced moms and dads are abandoned. On the contrary, they're bombarded with suggestions. In my experience, America's favorite pastime is not baseball but giving unasked-for advice to new parents. "It's boredom." "It's the heat." "Put a hat on him." Or "It's gas."

It can be so confusing! Who should you believe?

In frustration and concern, parents often turn to their doctor for help. Studies show that one in six couples visit a doctor because of their baby's persistent crying. When these babies are examined and found to be healthy, most doctors have little to offer but sympathy. "I know it's hard, but be patient; it won't last forever." Advice like this often sends worried parents to look for help in baby books.

Parents of colicky babies spend hours scanning books for "the answer" to their infant's distress. Yet, often the advice can be equally confusing: "Hold your baby—but be careful not to spoil him." "Love your baby—but let him cry himself to sleep."

Even these experts confess that for *really* fussy babies, they have nothing to offer:

> Very often, you may not even be able to quiet the screaming.
>
> What to Expect the First Year, Eisenberg, Murkoff, and Hathaway

> The whole episode goes on at least an hour and perhaps for three or four hours.
>
> Your Baby and Child, Penelope Leach

> It's completely all right to set the baby in the bassinet while trying to drown out the noise with the running water of a hot shower.
>
> The Girlfriend's Guide to Surviving the First Year of Motherhood, Vicki Iovine

But a hot shower is cold comfort for the parents of a screaming baby.

Many exhausted parents I meet have been persuaded, against their better judgment, that they can only stand by and endure their baby's screaming. But I tell them otherwise. Unhappy babies *can* be calmed—in minutes!

The Four Principles of Soothing Babies

In many ways, the people living in primitive cultures are backward compared to Western societies. However, in some areas their wisdom is great . . . and we are the "primitive" ones. This is particularly true when it comes to soothing crying newborns.

I teased out shreds of wisdom from the past and wove them with cutting-edge modern research and some unique observations made during my years of caring for more than five thousand infants. From this, I distilled four principles that are crucial for anyone who wants to understand babies better and be skillful at comforting them and improving their sleep:

- The Missing Fourth Trimester
- The Calming Reflex
- The 5 "S's"
- The Cuddle Cure

The Missing Fourth Trimester—Many Babies Cry Because They're Born Three Months Too Soon!

Did you ever see a baby horse or a baby cow? These newborn animals can walk, even run, on their very first day of life. In fact, they must be able to run—their survival depends upon it.

By comparison, our newborns are quite immature. They can't run, walk, or even roll over. One British mum told me her new daughter seemed so unready for the world she and her husband affectionately nick-named her "The Little Creature." They're not alone in seeing babies that way; the Spanish use the word *criatura,* meaning *creature,* to describe babies.

In many ways your new baby is more a fetus than an infant, spending most of her time sleeping and being fed. Had you delayed your delivery just three more months, your baby would have been born with the ability to smile, coo, and flirt. (Who wouldn't want *that* on their baby's first day of life!) However, I've never been able to talk a woman into keeping her infant inside for a fourth trimester . . . and for good reason. It's already a tight squeeze getting a baby's head out after nine months of pregnancy; by twelve months it would be impossible.

Why are our babies so immature at birth? The reason is simple. Unlike baby horses whose survival depends on their big strong bodies, a human baby's survival depends on big smart brains. In fact, our babies' brains are so huge we have to "evict" fetuses from the womb well before they're fully ready for the world to keep their heads from getting stuck in the birth canal.

Newborns have some abilities that demonstrate their readiness to be in the world, but these notwithstanding, for the first three months, our babies are so immature they would really benefit if they could hop back inside whenever they get overwhelmed. However, since we're not kangaroos, the least we can do as loving, compassionate parents is to make our little

criaturas feel at home by surrounding them with the comforting sensations they enjoyed twenty-four hours a day in the womb. However, in order to give babies a fourth trimester, parents need to answer one important question: What exactly was it like in there?

In your womb, your baby was packed tight into the fetal position enveloped by the warm wall of the uterus and rocked and jiggled for much of the day. She was also surrounded by a constant shushing sound a little louder than a vacuum cleaner!

For thousands of years, parents have known that mimicking conditions in the uterus comforts newborns. That's why almost every traditional baby-calming technique around the world imitates the sensations of the womb. From swaddling to swings to shushing, these methods return babies to a cuddly, rhythmic, womblike world until they are ready to coo, smile, and join the family. As helpful as this fourth-trimester experience is for calm babies, it is *essential* for fussy ones.

Most parents assume that this imitation soothes their baby simply by making her feel "back home." Actually, these experiences trigger a profound neurological response never before recognized or reported—until today. This ancient and very powerful baby reflex is *the calming reflex.*

The Calming Reflex: Nature's Brilliant "*Off* Switch" for Your Baby's Crying

This automatic reset switch stills a baby's crying and is truly a baby's (and parent's) best friend. Why did nature choose imitating the uterus as the trigger for this blessed reflex? The reason may surprise you: As important as it was for our ancestors to be able to quiet their babies, it was triply important for them to be able to quiet their *fetuses!*

Just imagine what it would feel like if your fetus threw a temper tantrum inside you. Not only could pounding fists and kicking feet make you sore, they could damage the fragile placenta or rip the umbilical cord, causing a fatal hemorrhage. Perhaps even more deadly than the risk of accidental injury was the chance that a squirming baby might get stuck sideways in the uterus and be unable to slide out, thus killing herself and her mother.

I'm convinced that the survival of our fetuses, and perhaps even the survival of our species, depended on this ancient calming reflex. Over millions of years, fetuses who became entranced by the sensations inside the uterus didn't thrash about and thus were most likely to stay alive. Our babies today are direct descendants of those "Zen" fetuses who were so easily pacified by the womb.

The 5 "S's": Five Steps to Turn On Your Baby's Calming Reflex

How is a vacuum cleaner like a lullaby? How is a Volvo like a flannel blanket? They all help switch on your baby's calming reflex by imitating some quality of your womb.

Although our ancient ancestors intuitively understood how to turn off their baby's crying and turn on their baby's calming, recognition of the calming reflex itself remained completely overlooked until I identified it during the mid-1990s while studying the characteristics of hundreds of crying babies in my practice.

I was struck by the fact that many traditional baby-calming methods failed to work unless they were done *exactly right.* I realized that, similar to a doctor setting off a knee reflex with a precise whack of a little hammer, the calming reflex could only be triggered by certain very specific actions. When presented correctly, however, the sounds and feelings of the womb had such a powerful effect that they could carry an infant from tears to tranquillity, sometimes even in mid-cry.

Parents and grandparents traditionally have used five different characteristics of the womb to soothe their babies. I refer to these time-honored "ingredients" of calm as the 5 "S's":

1. *S*waddling—tight wrapping
2. *S*ide/Stomach—laying a baby on her side or stomach
3. *S*hushing—loud white noise
4. *S*winging—rhythmic, jiggly motion
5. *S*ucking—sucking on anything from your nipple or finger to a pacifier

These five methods are extremely effective but only when performed *exactly* right. When done without the right technique and vigor, they do nothing. (Detailed descriptions of how to perform each "S" are in Chapters 8 through 12.)

The Cuddle Cure: Combining the 5 "S's" into a Perfect Recipe for Your Baby's Bliss

You don't have to be a rocket scientist to be a terrific parent, but there are some little tricks that can help you do your job better. Most infant-care books list these calming tips, but that's as unhelpful as listing the ingredients of a recipe without giving the instructions for how to combine and cook them.

Each individual "S" may be effective for soothing a mildly fussy baby. Your "easy" baby may only need to suck or to be danced around the room in order to be calmed. However, doing all five together can switch on the calming reflex so irresistibly that they soothe even the most frantic newborns. This layering of one "S" on top of another is so successful at making unhappy babies feel cozy and calm that one of my patients dubbed it "the Cuddle Cure."

If the Cuddle Cure were indeed a cake recipe made from the 5 "S's," I think it would be for a layer cake.

Swaddling is the first step of calming and the first layer in this comfort cake. Next is the Side/Stomach position. These initial "S's" prepare your baby to be calmed. Swaddling sets the stage for success by keeping her from flailing and accidentally overstimulating herself; the side or stomach position also stops the flailing, by taking away your baby's feeling that she's falling and by activating the calming reflex.

The next layer is Shhhh, followed immediately by Swinging. Both activate the calming reflex so your baby pays attention to you and the wonderful cuddling you're giving her. These get her more and more relaxed.

Last, but not least, Sucking is the icing on the cake! It works best after the other layers have calmed your baby down. It, too, triggers the calming reflex and keeps it turned on to make your baby feel deeply and profoundly at peace. (Of course, from your baby's point of view, you aren't making a cake, but she will feel like you have popped her back inside the "oven" for a little fourth-trimester time!)

A LAYER-CAKE OF COMFORT AND SOOTHING

The Cuddle Cure to the Rescue: The Story of Sean

These five principles form the most effective program for soothing agitated infants that has ever been discovered. It works on even the most challenging of babies, like Sean. . . .

Remember Sean? He's the boy whose crying so exhausted his mother that she fell asleep in the shower.

Don and Suzanne had expected that having a new baby might sometimes feel like motoring down a bumpy road, but they never imagined it would feel like driving off a cliff! Sean was a typical colicky baby, and his parents were the typical loving, bewildered, exhausted parents of a colicky child.

Here's how Suzanne described the early days with Sean:

"When I was growing up, my mother often told me what a colicky baby I had been. Shortly after Sean was born, I knew it was payback time. My handsome, dark-haired boy was born a week early but, like a racehorse, he was 'out of the gate' at a gallop!

"From almost the second week of his life, Sean had fits of uncontrollable screaming for hours every day. I felt like a terrible mother as I watched him writhe in pain. Nothing worked to settle him, and usually I ended up crying right along with him.

"Equally distressing was my secret fear that Sean's cries were the result of some injury he suffered at birth. His delivery was very difficult. After one and a half hours of hard pushing, the obstetrician yanked him out with a vacuum suction. My first memory is of Sean's poor head looking like a black and blue banana.

"For the first month, our pediatrician advised us that Sean's wailing was just his need to 'blow off some steam.' He warned that always responding to our baby could spoil him and accidentally teach him to cry even more! We thought his advice sounded logical, but leaving Sean to shriek made our baby even crazier—plus it was agonizing for us.

"Don and I read every baby book we could find. Day after day, we tried new approaches: swaddling—a failure; pacifier—useless; a change in my diet—futile; a swing—like waving to a jet thirty thousand feet overhead. We even tried a device that imitated a car's noise and vibration. This, too, was a bust.

"Exhausted and demoralized, we returned to our doctor. He was sympathetic but reiterated that we had no option other than to endure Sean's shrieking until he outgrew this phase. That afternoon, when Don and I got home, we agreed that it would be unbearable to wait, both for our suffering baby and for us.

"The next morning was terrible too. At our wit's end, we took our six-week-old baby to meet a new pediatrician. Dr. Karp asked us many questions, and once he was convinced that Sean's crying wasn't the sign of a serious medical condition, he taught us a technique he called the 'Cuddle Cure.'

"The Cuddle was a very specific mix of tight wrapping, vigorous rocking, and loud shushing. Dr. Karp explained that these sensations mimicked the baby's life in the womb. He said most babies cry because 'They're just not ready to be born. In a way they still need to be in the protected world of the uterus for another three months!'

"To be honest, my skeptical self thought, *This is too simple to be true.* After all, I had attempted wrapping, rocking, and white noise and ended up as squashed as a bug under a fly swatter. But after watching Dr. Karp's technique I realized I was doing them only halfway.

"Don and I decided to try the Cuddle. As incredible as it sounds, that afternoon was the last time Sean cried uncontrollably! The Cuddle cured Sean's crying. Whenever he began going berserk, we would do all the steps of the Cuddle, and within minutes his little body would relax and melt into our arms. We finally found the comfort Sean had been begging us for for so many weeks."

The Cuddle worked quickly for Suzanne and Don; however, like most techniques, it may take you some practice to get the hang of it. But don't worry: If you follow the advice in this book, step by step, you should master it within five to ten tries.

Some parents I speak with are hesitant to use the 5 "S's." They've been warned not to spoil their newborns and they fear that using the 5 "S's" will accidentally give their babies bad habits. Is that possible? Can young babies inadvertently be turned into brats who demand constant holding and attention?

Thankfully, the answer to that question is . . . *No!* During the first three months of life (the fourth trimester), it's impossible to spoil your baby by letting her suck or stay in your arms for hours. Does that surprise you? It really shouldn't when you remember that you were lavishing her with these sensations twenty-four hours a day—up until the moment of birth. Even if you hold your baby twelve hours a day now, it's a giant reduction from *her* point of view. What you will see is that by three to four months your baby will be increasingly able to calm herself with cooing, moving around, and sucking her hands. Since she will no longer need so much of your help, you will be able to rapidly wean her off the five "S's" at that time.

Parenting Crying Babies in the 21st Century

I hope you are beginning to get excited that there *are* fast and effective ways of soothing your baby when she gets fussy! My goal is to teach you the tricks that the best parents around the world have used for centuries.

The first part of the book will answer the questions:

- Why do babies cry?
- What is colic and how can you tell if your baby has it?
- Why are gas pains, anxiety, immaturity, and temperament rarely the causes of colic?
- What is the missing fourth trimester and why is it the *true* cause of colic?

The second part of the book will discuss:

- The calming reflex and how to trigger it by imitating the uterus
- The 5 "S's" and why they must be done vigorously to be effective
- Exact instructions to help you become an expert at swaddling, side/stomach position, shushing, swinging, and sucking
- The Cuddle Cure and how you can work wonders by doing all 5 "S's" together
- Other techniques that can help you soothe your fussy baby
- Tricks and tips to get your baby to sleep more at night
- Medical problems that can mimic colic

Once you understand your baby's need for a fourth trimester, the 5 "S's," and the Cuddle, you will be able to prevent countless hours of screaming. It is my sincere hope that once this knowledge is shared, *colic* will be found only in dictionaries.

You have been blessed with one of the most amazing experiences a person can ever have—the birth of a baby. It's an exciting ride, so strap yourself in . . . and enjoy. Please don't worry when your baby cries. Consider it an opportunity to perfect your new parenting skills as you learn how to turn your fussy infant into *the happiest baby on the block!*

2

Crying:
Our Babies' Ancient
Survival Tool

Main Points:

- The Crying Reflex: Your baby's brilliant attention-getting tool
- How a baby's crying can make you feel
- Do different baby cries have different meanings? Some babies scream even for little problems

At delivery, your baby's powerful wails are a welcome sign that you've given birth to a healthy child. However, if after the first week or two your infant continues to scream, his crying may become the last thing you want to hear! But we should be grateful for our babies' crying—it's one of their most wonderful abilities.

During the first few months of life, your baby will have no problem getting by without the foggiest idea of how to smile or talk, but he would be in terrible danger if he couldn't call out to you. Getting your attention is so important that your newborn can cry from the moment his head pops out of you. This great ability is called the "crying reflex."

The Crying Reflex: Nature's Brilliant Solution for Getting a Cavewoman's Attention!

A baby's cry . . . cries to be turned off.
Peter Ostwald, *Soundmaking: The Acoustic Communication of Emotion*

My guess is that millions of years ago, a Stone Age baby accidentally was born with a perfect way for getting his mother to come to him—screaming. Even if he yelped just because he had hiccups or had scared himself, his mom appeared in seconds.

Other baby animals also need to get their mother's attention quickly, but they would never *scream* for it. Loud crying could be fatal for a young rabbit or a monkey, because the sound might reveal his location to a hungry lion. For this reason, kittens meekly meow for help, squirrel monkeys make soft beeping sounds when they fall out of trees, and baby gorillas barely even whimper when they need their moms.

Baby humans, on the other hand, gave up such caution a long time ago. Whenever they needed their cavemom's attention, they wailed! Perhaps such brash, demanding babies were safe because their parents were able to fight off dangerous animals. Or perhaps a powerful cry was the only sound that could carry far enough for a baby's mom to hear him while working or chatting with friends outside the cave. Some scientists even believe that

Why are babies born with a cry reflex . . . but not a laugh reflex?

Wouldn't it be fun if babies were born laughing? Of course it would, but there are two very good reasons why newborns can cry up a storm yet can't giggle.

First, crying is easier than laughing. It takes less coordination, because it's one continuous sound made with each breath. Laughter, on the other hand, is a series of rapid, short sounds strung together like pearls on a single breath.

And while laughter is helpful for social play when your baby is older, crying is crucial for a baby's minute-to-minute survival, from his first day of life.

successive generations of babies began to shriek louder and louder because such noisy infants received more food and attention to keep them quiet, and thus were more likely to survive.

We may never know exactly when or how ancient human babies began to cry, yet it's clear that the cave babies who survived and passed their genes on to us were those who could "raise a ruckus."

Your baby's shrill cry is powerful enough to yank you out of bed or hoist you off the toilet with your pants down. (Not bad for a ten-pound weakling!) However, it is a mistake to think your baby is crying because he's *trying* to call you for help. During the first few months, trying to get your attention is the furthest thing from your crying baby's mind. In fact, your baby has absolutely no idea he's even sending you a message.

When you hear your two-week-old scream, you're not getting a communication from him; rather you're *accidentally eavesdropping* on his conversation . . . with himself. His cries are like agitated complaints he's muttering to himself, "Gosh, I'm hungry," or "Boy, I'm cold." Since you're right next to him, you hear his grumbles and want to lovingly respond, "What's the matter, sweetheart? You sound upset."

In a few months, your baby will begin to figure out that crying makes you come. By four to six months your baby will develop a vocabulary of

coos, bleats, and yells to communicate specific needs. This is when you may get the sense that your baby is beginning to make "phony" little shrieks to get you to come. But for now, don't worry that responding to his cries will teach him bad habits. Training your baby not to be manipulative will become an important lesson during the second six months of his life. For the moment you *want* him to learn that you'll come whenever he cries. This message of predictable, consistent love and support is *exactly* what will nurture his trust in you.

How a Baby's Cry Makes Us Feel

And, still Caroline cried, and Martha's nerves vibrated in extraordinary response, as if the child were connected to her flesh by innumerable invisible fibers.

Doris Lessing, *A Proper Marriage*

Just as your baby is born with certain automatic, built-in reflexes (like crying) you too are equipped with many automatic and irresistible feelings about your baby. Researchers proved years ago that adults are naturally attracted to an infant's face. Your baby's heart-shaped face, upturned nose, big eyes, and full forehead give you the urge to kiss and cuddle him for hours!

You also have special instincts to help you tell whether your infant is babbling or if he needs you urgently. Not only does your brain get the message but your body does too. That's why your baby's screams can really "get under your skin." You feel your nervous system snap into "red alert" as your heart begins to race, your blood pressure soars, your palms sweat, and your stomach tightens like a fist. Studies show that a baby's piercing cry can jolt a parent's nervous system like an electric shock. As you might expect, scientists have also demonstrated that parents experiencing other stresses—such as fatigue, isolation, marital discord, financial stress, hormonal imbalance, problems with family or neighbors, or other serious strains—are especially susceptible to feeling overwhelmed by their baby's cries.

It's not just the *sound* of your baby's cry that makes you want to help him, it's how he looks too. Seeing his little fists punching at the air and his face twist in apparent pain can penetrate your heart like an arrow. Every loving fiber in your body will compel you to comfort your crying baby. This powerful biological impulse is *exactly* why it feels so wrong to wait outside the nursery door and let your baby cry it out.

Not only parents tune in to a baby's cries. Single adults and children, too, find the sound of a baby crying upsetting. But new parents, especially ones without prior infant-care experience, find their baby's crying exceptionally disturbing.

Your baby's cry may even rekindle forgotten emotional trauma from your past. You may suddenly recall memories of prior failures or humiliations, like someone who was unfair to you, or remember people who criticized and attacked you. The crying may make you feel that you are being punished for some past misdeed. For some parents, this sense of helplessness is so intolerable that it makes them turn away from their babies' screams and ignore their needs. (See Appendix B for more practical advice about how to survive these difficult days.)

Of course, your baby isn't intentionally trying to make you feel guilty or inadequate. During the first few months of life, his cries are *never, never, never* manipulative, mean, rude, or critical. Nevertheless, those feelings may bubble up inside you when your baby screams on and on.

"Tell Mommy What's the Matter": Your Baby's Three-Word Vocabulary

Our tiny baby's first word to us wasn't Mama <u>or</u> Dada. It sounded more like ... well, a smoke alarm! She just <u>blasted</u>! It was scary because we had no idea exactly what she was trying to tell us.
Marty and Debbie, parents of two-week-old Sarah Rose

When you first bring your baby home from the hospital, every fuss can sound like a problem and every cry an urgent alarm. All parents dedicate themselves to meeting their newborn's needs, but when your baby cries, can you tell exactly what he needs? Should you be able to figure out why your baby is upset from the sound of his cry? Is the "I'm sleepy" cry of a one-month-old different from his "I'm starving" yell?

Some baby books tell parents that with careful observation they can decipher their baby's message from the way he cries; however, forty years of studies by the world's leading colic researchers have taught us that's not really true.

In a 1990 University of Connecticut study, mothers listened to the audiotaped yells of two different babies, a hungry one-month-old and a newborn who was just circumcised. They were asked if the babies were hungry, sleepy, in pain, angry, startled, or wet. Only twenty-five percent correctly identified the cry of the unfed baby as sounding like hunger (forty percent thought it was an overtired cry). Only forty percent of moms identified the cries of the recently circumcised baby as a pain cry (thirty percent thought he was either startled or angry).

You might wonder if these mothers would better understand their babies' cries if they were more experienced. However, the evidence shows that is not the case either. Researchers in Finland asked eighty experienced baby nurses to listen to the recorded sounds of babies at the moment of birth, when hungry, when in pain, and when gurgling in pleasure. Surprisingly, even these seasoned pros only correctly identified why the baby was crying about fifty percent of the time—barely better than by chance alone.

By three months your baby will learn to make many different noises, making it easier to decipher some messages from the sound of his cry alone. However, at birth, your infant's compact brain simply doesn't have enough room for a repertoire of grunts and whines. That's why during the first few months, most babies only make three simple but distinct sounds: whimpering, crying, and shrieking.

> **Whimpering:** This mild fussing sounds more requesting than complaining, like a call from a neighbor asking to borrow some sugar.
> **Crying:** This good strong yelp demands your attention, like when your kitchen timer goes off.
> **Shrieking:** This last "word" is a piercing, glass-shattering wail, as shrill and unbearable as a burglar alarm.

If asked what each sound signified, you'd probably guess that whimpering means a slight unhappiness like hunger pangs or getting sleepy;

crying indicates some greater distress like being very hungry, thirsty, or cold; and shrieking signals pain, fear, anger, or irritation (if earlier cries got no response).

If your baby is an easy, relatively calm child, your guesses are probably correct. As a rule, the more intense and shrill your baby's cry is—and the quicker it escalates to a shriek—the more likely he's in pain or needs your help right away.

And by adding a few more visual clues to the sound he's making, you'll increase your accuracy. For example:

- Is your baby opening his mouth and rooting? (This could indicate hunger.)
- Is he yawning, rubbing his eyes, moving his head from side to side, or staring out with droopy eyelids? (This could indicate fatigue.)
- Does he seem to be intentionally looking away from you or starting to hiccup? (This could indicate overstimulation.)
- Is he making facial grimaces and trying to bear down? (This could indicate intestinal discomfort.)

In short, when an *easy* baby is a little upset he whimpers, like a puppy whining outside the door. Usually his protests only get louder if his cries are ignored or if he is in great distress.

The needs of *fussy* babies, on the other hand, are often impossible to decipher from the sound of their cries alone. These little ones lack the self-control to proceed patiently through their three-"word" vocabulary, especially when tired or overstimulated. They blow by whimpering and crying, and shift immediately into loud, piercing shrieks that make it impossible to tell whether or not they have an urgent problem. These babies often get so upset by their own screaming that it snowballs and they are crying because they're crying! The gas or loud noise that started the wailin' and flailin' is almost forgotten.

Even when scientists use sophisticated acoustic analyzers to study the cries of fussy babies, they cannot find any differences between their shrieks of hunger, pain, overstimulation, boredom, startling, and even impatience. These intense babies blast out the same one-size-fits-all scream *regardless of what's bothering them.*

> Pam, the mother of two high-powered little boys, Matthew and Austin, told me when her boys were babies she joked with her husband that their screams were like the blasts of a smoke alarm. She said, "When you hear a smoke alarm go off, it's <u>impossible</u> to tell from the sound whether it's signaling a minor problem—burnt toast—or a calamity—your house is burning down. Likewise, with my boys, it was impossible for us to tell from the intensity of their cries if they were very ill or merely announcing a burp."

Most of the time, even a baby's most terrible shrieks are merely his way of telling you he's hungry, wet, soiled, or lonely, and he will quiet once you give him what he needs. But what if your baby's yelping persists even though his diaper is dry and you're holding him? What happens if you try *everything* and he still doesn't stop screaming?

That's when parents start to wonder if their baby has COLIC.

3

The Dreaded Colic:
A "CRYsis" for
the Whole Family

Main Points:

- What is colic?
- The top ten ancient theories about colic
- The Colic Clues: Ten universal facts about colic
- Today's top five colic theories

The sound of a crying baby is just about the most disturbing, demanding, shattering noise we can hear. In the baby's crying there is no future or past, only now. There is no appeasement, no negotiations possible, no reasonableness.

Sheila Kitzinger, *The Crying Baby*

Waaaa . . . waaaa . . . waaaaaa . . . WAAAAAAAAAAAAAAAAAAA!!!!!!!! The word *infant* derives from Latin and means "without a voice." However, many colicky babies wail so powerfully that their parents think a better name for them would be *mega*-fants or *rant*-fants!

There's no doubt that colicky infants can cry louder and longer than any adult. We would drop from exhaustion after five minutes of full-out screaming, but these little cuties can go and go, with the tenacity of the Energizer bunny.

The word *colic* derives from the Greek word *kolikos,* meaning "large intestine or colon." In ancient Greece, parents believed that intestinal pain caused their babies' crying. (While a gas twinge may start a baby's screaming fit, at other times these very same babies have gas and noisy stomachs yet they don't even make a peep. More on this in Chapter 4.)

All babies have short periods of crying that usually last for a few minutes, totaling about a half hour a day. These babies settle quickly once fed, picked up, or carried. However, once colicky babies start their frantic screaming, they can yell, on and off, for hours.

How Can You Tell If Your Baby Has Colic?

In 1982, Dr. T. Berry Brazelton asked eighty-two new mothers to record how much their normal, healthy infants cried each day during their first three months of life.

The results of this study are shown in the figure below. When Dr. Brazelton did the math, he discovered that at two weeks of age, twenty-

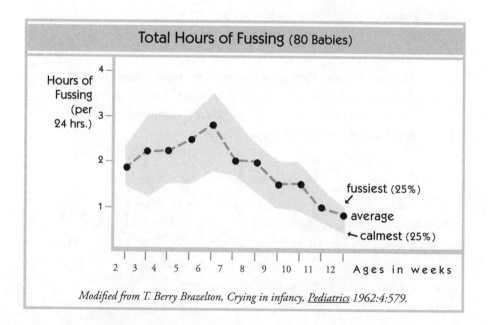

Modified from T. Berry Brazelton, Crying in infancy, <u>Pediatrics</u> 1962:4:579.

five percent of the babies cried for more than two hours each day. By six weeks, twenty-five percent cried for more than three hours each day. Reassuringly, he found that by three months almost all had recovered from their fussy period and few cried more than one hour a day. (Persistent crying tends to vanish after three months which is why some doctors refer to it as "three-month" colic.)

When a baby is brought to me because of crying fits, I first ask about the parents' family history and the baby's birth, feeding habits, and general behavior. Next I examine the baby to make sure she's healthy and thriving. Once I'm sure that the baby is well, I consider if her crying pattern fits the "Rule of Threes," the formal medical definition of colic first formulated by Dr. Morris Wessel, a private pediatrician from Connecticut.

The "Rule of Threes" states that a baby has colic if she cries at least: three hours a day . . . three days a week . . . three weeks in a row.

Some doctors call babies colicky even if they don't fit the "Rule of Threes" but still frequently scream uncontrollably for no obvious reason.

Some parents in my practice also think that the "Rule of Threes" should be revised. They say the true definition of colic is when a baby cries so much her poor mom needs three nannies, three margaritas, and . . . six hands! (Okay, there's an exception to every rule.)

Parents often ask me if there's a way to predict which babies will have colic. While many doctors have tried to find a pattern to this problem, no consistent association has been found between colic and a baby's gender, prematurity, birth order, or their parents' age, income, or education. Colic can happen to anybody's baby. It is truly an equal-opportunity parental nightmare!

What Really Causes Colic?

Nine times out of ten, parents of colicky babies believe that their infants are suffering from some kind of pain. This would seem to be a reasonable guess, since colicky babies:

- are not relieved by the comforts of feeding and holding
- often writhe and grunt

- may start and stop their screaming very abruptly
- have a shrill cry that resembles the sound they make when they're in pain (like after getting a shot)

Pain was what was on Sherry's mind when she brought her baby in to see me for a consultation about his incessant crying.

Charlie, a robust two-month-old, had a normal examination. This surprised his mother who was convinced that his daily frenzies must be the result of pain. When I asked her how she could be so sure, Sherry sheepishly admitted that she'd accidentally hit Charlie's head with the telephone receiver. She said, "When that happened, I realized that his cry after getting whacked sounded exactly the same as his normal afternoon screamfest. I thought, That proves it, he's been in pain this whole time."

Was Sherry right? Was Charlie's crying caused by pain? Or had she somehow misread the situation? As you can imagine, since time immemorial, parents of crying babies have been analyzing their child's shrieks, trying to come up with an explanation for why their contented little infant at times suddenly "morphs" into one of the unhappiest babies on the block.

The "Evil Eye" (and Other Theories): How Our Ancestors Explained Colic

Before I got married I had six theories about bringing up children; now I have six children and no theories.

John Wilmot

It wasn't so long ago that people believed leeches could cure diseases and babies were born blind. Likewise, our ancestors made many guesses about why some infants cried so much. Deciphering a Stone Age baby's cry may well have been one of the first multiple-choice questions in history:

Your cave baby is crying because:
a. She's hungry.
b. She's cold.
c. She needs a fresh loincloth.
d. A witch cast a spell on her.

Over the centuries, wild theories have abounded about the cause of prolonged crying. Here are a few:

The Top Ten Ancient Theories of the Cause of Colicky Crying
1. Someone who dislikes the mother gave the baby the "evil eye."
2. The baby caught a draft.
3. The baby's spirit is unhappy because her father denied the baby was his.
4. The baby is possessed by the devil.
5. The baby is communicating with the spirits of unborn babies.
6. The daytime is for adults to make noise, and at night it's the baby's turn.
7. The baby's crying is a punishment for Adam and Eve's original sin.
8. The mother's milk is too thin.
9. The mother's milk is too rich.
10. A trauma during pregnancy made the baby fearful.

Even Shakespeare tossed in his two cents about why babies cry. In *King Lear* he guessed: *When we are born, we cry that we are come to this great stage of fools.* Babies are amazing, but I'm afraid Shakespeare was giving them more credit than they deserve.

The Myth of "Blowing Off Steam"

Crying is good for the lungs the way bleeding is good for the veins!

Lee Salk

Parents have long noticed that fussy infants eventually cry themselves to sleep. Some experts have guessed that these babies *need* to scream to exercise their lungs or unwind from the day's thrills before they surrender to sleep.

I strongly disagree. The idea that screaming is good for babies is illogical from both a biological and evolutionary point of view. First, the lungs of calm babies are as healthy and strong as the lungs of colicky babies. Second, colicky prehistoric infants might well have put themselves in danger. Their screaming could have attracted enemies to their family's hiding place. And it might have enraged their Neanderthal parents, leading to abandonment, abuse, and even infanticide.

Now, I freely admit . . .

Yes . . . babies can get wound up by a full day's excitement.

Yes . . . some babies ignore their parents' best attempts to calm them.

Yes . . . screaming babies eventually conk out from sheer exhaustion.

But your baby is not a little pressure cooker that needs to "blow off steam" before cooling down. Letting your baby cry it out makes as little sense as closing your ears to your screeching car alarm while you wait for the battery to die.

At this point, you may be thinking, "But *I* often feel better after I have a good cry." Of course that's true; however, while adults may sob for minutes, colicky babies can wail for hours!

I believe that most parents who let their babies shriek until they collapse do this only because they feel desperate and exhausted. It's a last resort that goes against every parental instinct. Can it stop the crying? Yes. However, the real question is whether or not this climate of inconsistency—sometimes you answer her cry and sometimes you don't—is what you want to teach your baby to expect from you. Most parents answer that question with a resounding no.

All baby experts agree that our children do best when we are *consistent* in our responses. You know how frustrating it can be when some days you can calm your baby yet other days nothing works. Well, that's how your baby feels when her cry in the morning brings a prompt reward of touching and warm milk yet in the afternoon it's ignored.

Is it *ever* okay to let your baby yell? I don't believe it's a tragedy if your little one cries for ten minutes while you are in the bathroom or preparing dinner. The loving and cuddling you've been giving her all day easily outweighs that short-lived frustration. But fussy infants are not like toddlers. If your two-year-old screams because she wants to yank your earrings, you may have to let her cry so she can learn that when you say, "No!" you mean it. The time will come when lessons of discipline will become important, even lifesaving. But you're jumping the gun if you think you need to teach discipline to your two-month-old!

For the first few months, you should soothe your baby whenever she yells. Infants rarely cry unless they're upset about something, and it's our challenge and duty to figure out what they need and how to give it to them.

The Colic Clues—
Ten Universal Facts About Colic

In order to understand what causes colic, we first must agree on what it is. Researchers analyzing babies from all around the world have discovered ten fundamental traits of colic and colicky babies:

1. *Colicky crying usually starts at two weeks, peaks at six weeks, and ends by three to four months of age.*

2. *Preemies are no more likely to have colic than full-term babies. (And their colic doesn't start until they are about two weeks past their due date.)*

3. *Colicky babies have twisted faces and piercing wails, like a person in pain. Often, their cries come in waves (like cramps) and stop abruptly.*

4. *Their screams frequently begin during or just after a feeding.*

5. *They often double up, grunt, strain, and seem relieved by passing gas or pooping.*

6. *Colic is often much worse in the evening (the "witching hour").*

7. *Colic is as likely to occur with a couple's fifth baby as with their first.*

8. *Colicky crying often improves with rocking, holding, shhhhing, and gentle abdominal pressure.*

9. *Babies are healthy and happy between crying bouts.*

10. *In many cultures around the world, babies never get colic.*

Once scientists determined the colic clues, they compared them to the popular colic theories to determine which, if any, explained them best. The researchers immediately excluded many of the crazy old ideas and what remained are today's top five colic theories:

1. *Tiny Tummy Troubles*—babies suffer from severe discomfort caused by simple digestive problems (such as gas, constipation, cramps).
2. *Big Tummy Troubles*—babies suffer severe pain from true intestinal illness (such as food intolerance or stomach acid reflux).
3. *Maternal Anxiety*—babies wail because of anxiety they pick up from their mothers.
4. *Brain Immaturity*—immaturity of a baby's nervous system causes her to get overwhelmed and scream.
5. *Challenging Temperament*—a baby's intense or sensitive temperament makes her shriek even in response to minor upsets.

Each of these theories has its group of followers, but is any one of them the true cause of colic? Can any one of these theories explain all ten of the universal characteristics of colic?

4

The Top Five Theories
of Colic and Why
They Aren't Right

Main Points:

- Gas, constipation and overactive intestines: Why these Tiny Tummy Troubles are not the cause of severe crying
- Food sensitivities and stomach acid reflux: Why these Big Tummy Troubles are rarely the cause of persistent crying
- Why maternal anxiety isn't the cause of colic
- The ways in which a baby's brain is immature, and why that can't be the entire explanation for uncontrollable crying
- What is meant by challenging temperament and why it fails to explain why babies get colic

Theory #1: Do Tiny Tummy Troubles Cause Colic?

For thousands of years, many parents have had a "gut feeling" that their infants were crying from bad stomach pain. The three tummy-twisting problems that became the prime suspects of causing colic were intestinal "gas"; pooping problems; and "overactive" intestines.

Burping with the Best of Them

Babies often gulp down air during their feedings. Here are tips to help your baby swallow less air and to burp up what does get in:

1. Don't lay your baby flat during a feeding. (Imagine how hard it would be for you to drink lying down, without swallowing a lot of air.)

2. If your baby is a noisy eater, stop and burp him frequently during the meal.

3. Before burping your baby, sit him in your right hand, with your left hand cupped under his chin. Then bounce him up and down a few times. This gets the bubbles to float to the top of the stomach for easy burping. (Don't worry, it won't make him spit up.)

4. The best burping position: Sit down with your baby on your lap, with his chin resting comfortably in your cupped hand. (I never burp babies over my shoulder, because their spit-up goes right down my back.) Next, lean him forward so he's doubled over a little. Give his back ten to twenty firm thumps. Babies' stomachs are like glasses of soda, with little "bubblettes" stuck to the sides. So thump your baby like a drum to jiggle these free.

Let's examine each individually and then I will explain why none of these nuisances is the real cause of colic.

Do Babies Cry from Intestinal "Gas" . . .
or Is That Just a Lot of Hot Air?

Most infants have gas—often. I'm sure you've witnessed virtuoso performances of burping, tooting, and grunting several times a day. Many parents are convinced this intestinal grumbling causes their baby's cries.

Parents who think colic is a gas problem have two powerful allies: grandmas and doctors. For generations, grandmothers have advised new moms to treat their baby's colic by avoiding gassy foods, burping them well, and feeding them sips of tummy-soothing teas. For decades, doctors have suggested that mothers alter their diet or their child's formula, or give burping drops (simethicone) to reduce a baby's intestinal gas.

However, with all due respect to grandmothers and doctors, fussy newborns have no more gas in their intestines than calm babies. In 1954, Dr. Ronald Illingworth, England's preeminent pediatrician, compared the stomach X rays of normal babies with colicky babies and found *no* difference in the amount of gas the calm and cranky babies had at their peaks of crying. In addition, repeated scientific experiments have shown that simethicone burping drops (Mylicon and Phazyme) are no more helpful for crying babies than plain water. It turns out that the gas in your baby's intestine comes mostly from digested food, not from swallowed air.

Pooping Problems: Can Constipation Trigger
Colicky Crying?

Some parents worry that constipation is causing their baby's colic. Babies struggling to poop can look like they're in a wrestling match. However, constipation really means hard poop, and only a few, fussy, formula-fed babies suffer from that. Most infants who groan and twist usually pass soft or even runny stools.

If grunting babies aren't constipated, why are they straining so hard?

1. To poop, an infant has to simultaneously tighten his stomach and relax his anus. This can be hard for a young baby to do. Many accidentally clench both at the same time and try to force their poop through a closed anus.

Black Tar to Scrambled Eggs: What Are Normal Baby Poops Like?

Few new parents are prepared for how weird baby poops are. For starters, there's the almost extraterrestrial first poop—meconium. (Robin Williams described its tarry consistency as a cross between Velcro and toxic waste!) Within days, meconium's green-black color changes to light green and then to bright, mustard yellow with a seedy texture. (The seeds are miniature milk curds.)

In breast-fed babies, poops then turn into runny scrambled eggs that squirt out four to twelve times a day. Over the next month or two, the poop gradually becomes thicker, like oatmeal, and may only come out once a day or less. (The longest period I've ever seen a healthy, breast-fed baby go without a stool has been twenty-one days. However, if your baby is skipping more than three days without a stool, call your pediatrician to make sure he's okay.)

For bottle-fed babies, poop may be loose, claylike, or hard in the first weeks. The particular formula a baby drinks can affect this consistency. Some infants get constipated from cow's milk formula, while others get stopped up by soy. A few are even sensitive to whether the formula is made from powder or concentrate.

2. They're lying flat on their backs. Just think of the trouble you'd have trying to poop in that position!

Babies grunt and frown when they poop because they're working so hard to overcome these two challenges, *not* because they're in pain! (For more on infant constipation, see Chapter 14.)

"Overactive" Intestines—Crying, Cramps, and the Gastro-colic Reflex

Does your baby cry and double up shortly after you start a feeding? This twisting and grunting may look like indigestion, but it's usually just an overreaction to a *normal* intestinal reflex called the "gastro-colic reflex" (literally, the stomach-colon reflex).

This valuable reflex is the stomach's way of telling the colon: "Time to

How Your Baby's Tummy Works

A baby's digestive system is like a long conveyor belt. At one end, milk is loaded into the mouth five to eight times a day. It is quickly delivered to the stomach, and then is slowly carried through the intestines, where it is digested and absorbed. Whatever milk isn't absorbed gets turned into poop and is temporarily stored in the colon.

When the next meal begins, the stomach telegraphs a message to the lower intestines, commanding them to squeeze. The squeezing pushes the poop out, making room for the next load of food. This message from the stomach to the colon is to constrict the gastro-colic reflex.

get rid of the poop and make room for the new food that was just eaten!" If you've noticed that your baby poops during or after eating, this is why.

Most infants are unaware when this reflex is happening. Others feel a mild spasm after a big feeding or if they're frazzled at day's end. But for a few babies, this squeezing of the intestine feels like a punch in the belly! These infants writhe as if in terrible pain.

As you might imagine, the gastro-colic reflex can be even more uncomfortable if your baby is constipated and his colon must strain to push out firm poop. However, most babies who cry from this reflex have soft, pasty poops. They cry because they are overly sensitive to this weird sensation.

The Reasons Why Tiny Tummy Troubles Cannot Be the True Cause of Colic

It's not what we don't know that gets us into the most trouble, it's what we know . . . that just ain't so!
Josh Billings, *Everybody's Friend*, 1874

Despite the fact that many people think gas causes colic, it and the other Tiny Tummy Troubles (TTT's) don't explain this terrible crying because:

■ Most colicky babies burp and pass wind many times a day without a whimper.

Anti-Spasm Medicines: Soothing Crying Babies into a Stupor

From the 1950s to the 1980s, doctors armed parents with millions of prescriptions of anti-cramp medicine. Some doctors used Donnatal (a mix of anti-cramp medicine plus phenobarbitol) while others preferred Levisin (hyocyamine). Both are cramp-relieving and sedating, and both are still occasionally prescribed by doctors today.

However, of all the anti-spasm drugs recommended for colic, Bentyl was by far and away the most popular. In 1984, 74 million doses of it were sold in Britain alone. But Bentyl turned out to be the most dangerous of all the tummy drugs. In 1985, doctors were horrified to discover that a number of colicky babies being treated with it suffered convulsions, coma—even death.

In retrospect, it's likely that anti-cramp medicines work *not* because of any tummy effect, but because they induce sedation as an incidental side effect.

- Adults double up when they have stomachaches, but babies snap into this fetal position *whenever* they are upset, regardless of the cause.
- Many babies shriek even when they only are experiencing a minor discomfort.

The TTT's also fail to explain five of the ten universal characteristics of colic and colicky babies:

- *Colicky crying usually starts at two weeks, peaks at six weeks, and ends by three to four months of age.* Neither gas nor the gastro-colic reflex fit this clue because both are present from birth (before colic starts) and continue long past three months (when colic is over).

- *Colic in preemies doesn't start until two weeks after their due date.* Preemies have lots of gas and a vigorous gastro-colic reflex. If these sensations truly caused colic, crying in preemies would start immediately, not be delayed for months.

- *Colic is often much worse in the evening.* Babies poop and have stomach rumblings twenty-four hours a day, so if they caused colic, crying would be as common in the morning as it is at night.

- *Colicky crying often improves with rocking, wrapping, shhhhing, and tummy pressure.* It doesn't make any sense that rocking, wrapping, or shhhhing could stop bad stomach pain.

- *There are many cultures around the world where babies never get colic.* All babies around the world experience TTT's. So if they were the basis of colic, why would there be cultures where prolonged crying is virtually nonexistent?

Theory #2: Do Big Tummy Troubles Cause Colic?

Over the past thirty years, scientists have discovered several new problems that cause stomach pain in adults. I call these conditions "Big Tummy Troubles" because they are actual medical illnesses, not merely burps and hiccups.

As each new illness was reported, pediatricians carefully considered if it might occur in infants and explain the inconsolable crying that plagues so many of our babies. Two of these Big Tummy Troubles have been scrutinized as possible keys to the mystery of colic: food sensitivities and stomach acid reflux.

Food Sensitivity—Warning!
Some Foods May Be Hazardous to Your Baby's Smile

If you are breast-feeding, you may have been counseled to avoid foods that are too hot, too cold, too strong, too weak, as well as to steer clear of spices, dairy products, acidic fruit and "gassy" vegetables.

Likewise, mothers of colicky, bottle-fed babies are often advised to switch their child's formula to remove an ingredient that may cause fussiness.

Over the years, experts have considered three ways a baby's diet might trigger uncontrollable crying: indigestion, allergies, and caffeine-type stimulation.

Indigestion: Are Garlic and Onions Risky or the Spices of Life?

Passing up garlic, onions, and beans seems reasonable to most people. These foods can make *us* gassy. But if gassy foods are hard on a baby's tummy, why can breast-feeding moms in Mexico eat *frijoles* (beans) and those in Korea munch *kim chee* (garlic-pickled cabbage) without their babies ever letting out a peep?

Nevertheless, I do think it's reasonable for the mother of an irritable baby to avoid "problem" foods (citrus, strawberries, tomatoes, beans, cabbage, broccoli, cauliflower, brussels sprouts, peppers, onion, garlic) for a few days to see if her baby cries less. However, in my experience, only a handful of infants improve when these foods are eliminated. Studies even show that babies love tasting a smorgasbord of flavors. So don't be surprised if your little one sucks on your breast *more* heartily after you've had a plate of lasagna loaded with garlic!

Food Allergies: Why Couldn't Babies with Allergies Just Sneeze Instead of Scream?

Allergies are part of our immune system, protecting us from unfamiliar proteins (like inhaled pollen or cat dander) that try to enter our bodies.

As a rule, if you have an allergic reaction you'll sneeze, because the fight between your body and the allergens typically takes place in your nose. With infants, however, the battleground between their bodies' immune system and the foreign protein is usually in the intestines. Your baby's intestine is not yet fully developed. Her immature intestinal lining allows large, allergy-triggering molecules to enter her bloodstream like flies zooming through a torn screen door. Over the first year of life, your baby's intestinal lining gradually becomes a much better barrier to these protein intruders.

For many years, doctors believed babies could be allergic to their own mother's milk. In 1983, Swedish scientists proved this impossible. They demonstrated that babies whose colic improved when they were taken off their mother's milk were sensitive *not* to their mom's milk itself but to traces of cow's milk that had floated across the lining of the mother's intestines and snuck into her milk.

Please don't be overly concerned about your diet troubling your child. As a rule, babies rarely develop allergies to the foods their moms eat. The two biggest exceptions to that rule, however, are cow's milk, the proverbial eight-hundred-pound gorilla of baby allergies, and soy, coming in a not-too-distant second place (about ten percent of babies who are milk allergic are soy allergic as well).

I tell my patients it should come as no surprise that some babies develop an allergic reaction to cow's milk. After all, this food is lovingly made by cows for their own babies, and it was never intended to feed our hungry tots.

Cow's milk protein starts passing into your breast milk within minutes of drinking a glass. It reaches its peak level about eight to twelve hours later and it's out of your milk in twenty-four to thirty-six hours. Fortunately, most babies have no problem tolerating this tiny bit of milk protein. However, sensitive babies begin reacting to it within two to thirty-six hours of consuming it.

Milk-allergic babies may suffer from a number of bothersome symptoms besides severe crying. I have cared for infants whose milk allergy gave them skin rashes, nose congestion, wheezing, vomiting, and watery stools. The intestines of some of my patients have gotten so irritated by allergies that they produced strings of bloody mucous that could be seen mixed in with their stools. Although blood in your baby's diaper will raise your heart rate, it is usually no more ominous than finding blood in your mucous when you blow your nose. Be sure to contact your baby's doctor, however, to discuss the problem.

Stimulant Food: Is Your Baby on a Caffeine Jag?

Some babies are supersensitive. They jump when the phone rings and cry when they smell strong perfume. It should come as no surprise that some babies also get hyper from caffeine (coffee, tea, cola, or chocolate) or from stimulant medicines (diet pills, decongestants, and certain Chinese herbs) in their mom's milk.

While many babies are unfazed when their mothers drink one or two cups of coffee, even that small amount of caffeine can rev a sensitive baby up into the "red zone." The caffeine collects in a woman's breast milk over four to six hours and can make a baby irritable within an hour of being eaten.

Stomach Acid Reflux:
Do Colicky Babies Cry from "Heartburn"?

Pediatricians have also examined stomach acid reflux (also known as Gastro-Esophageal Reflux, or GER) as a possible colic cause. This condition—where acidic stomach juice squirts up toward the mouth, irritating everything it touches—is a proven cause of heartburn in adults.

Now, for most babies, a little reflux is nothing new. We just call it by a different name: "spit-up." Since the muscle that keeps the stomach contents from moving "upstream" is weak in most babies, a bit of your baby's last meal can easily sneak back out when she burps or grunts, especially if she was overfed or swallowed air.

Most newborns don't spit up much, but some babies "urp" up prodigious amounts of their milk. Fortunately, most of these babies don't suffer any ill effects from all this regurgitation. The greatest problem caused by their vomiting is often milk stains on your sofa and clothes.

On the other hand, infants with severe GER are plagued with copious amounts of vomiting, poor weight gain, and occasional burning pain. (In some babies, stomach acid travels just partially up the esophagus, causing heartburn *without* vomiting.)

When should you suspect reflux as the cause of your baby's unhappiness? Look for these telltale signs:

- She vomits more than five times a day and more than an ounce each time.
- Her crying occurs with most meals, during the day *and* night.
- She often wails right after a burp or a spit-up.
- The bouts of crying are no better by the time she's three months old.
- She may have episodes of back arching, hoarseness, wheezing, choking, and/or excessive and even painful hiccuping.

Big Tummy Troubles Strike Out as the Major Cause of Colic

Food sensitivity and acid reflux can make some babies scream, but do the Big Tummy Troubles (BTT's) explain most cases of colic or just a small number of ultrafussy babies?

In my experience, five to ten percent of very fussy infants cry due to food sensitivity from cow's milk or soy, and one to three percent of them cry from the pain of acid reflux. That notwithstanding, Big Tummy Troubles (BTT's) are *not* the cause of colic for the majority of fussy infants:

- If food allergies caused colic, a mother would only have to change her baby's formula or her diet and, *poof,* the crying would stop. But this rarely helps.

- If allergies caused colic, formula-fed babies should be especially fussy because they eat hundreds of times more cow's milk protein than do breast-fed babies. Yet colic is equally common in both groups.

- Doctors in Melbourne, Australia, examined twenty-four babies under three months of age who were so irritable they had to be hospitalized. All were checked for acid reflux; only one baby had it.

- Most babies with severe reflux have *no* pain. A review of 219 young babies sent to a hospital clinic because of severe reflux found that thirty-three percent had severe vomiting, thirty percent were not gaining weight, but very few had excessive crying.

The BTT's also fail to explain five of the ten universal characteristics of colic and colicky babies:

- *Colicky crying usually starts at two weeks, peaks at six weeks, and ends by three to four months of age.* Newborns are continually exposed to spit-up and allergens in their diet. If the BTT's caused colic, crying would start right away and continue well past three months. (Babies with cow's milk allergy have problems that last for at least six to twelve months, and serious reflux usually causes heartburn complaints for nine months or more.)

- *Colic in preemies doesn't start until two weeks after their due date.* A preemie born two months early rarely shows colic before she's two and a half months old, despite her daily exposure to spit-up and allergenic proteins.

- *Colic is often much worse in the evening.* If the BTT's caused colic, crying would occur at any time of the day, because babies eat the same food—and spit it up—from morning to night.

- *Colicky crying often improves with rocking, holding, shhhhing, and tummy pressure.* Why would these actions soothe inflamed intestines or heartburn? Indeed, rocking and pressure might even squirt *more* acid up from the stomach, worsening reflux pain.

- *There are many cultures around the world where babies never get colic.* All babies, regardless of where they live, occasionally spit up and drink breast milk containing tiny samplings from their mommy's last meal. Yet, despite this, infants in some cultures around the world *never* suffer from colic.

Theory #3: Does Maternal Anxiety Cause Colic?

Any mother who has felt fear and anxiety surrounding the birth of her new baby might wonder if these disquieting feelings could affect her newborn. This was Trina's concern. . . .

> With her ruby lips and lush, black hair, Tatiana was exquisite. But her delicacy in form was balanced by a strong and feisty temperament. She reflected her parents' passionate personalities, and Trina and Mirko could not have been more thrilled. However, as the weeks went by, they became more and more

frustrated as Tatiana's feistiness turned into prolonged periods of screaming.

Trina called one afternoon after her four-week-old daughter had been particularly cranky. She confided, "I'm a very sensitive and intuitive person. Is it possible that Tatiana is too? Is it possible she's upset because of all the stress I'm under?"

It seems that the joy Trina and Mirko had felt after Tatiana's birth was tempered by Trina's painful recovery from a cesarean section and then the destruction of their possessions from a flood in the apartment above theirs, days after they brought Tatiana home.

"The nest we created for our baby collapsed like a house of cards and we had to move into our friend's living room. When Tatiana developed colic at three weeks of age, I couldn't help but think her screams stemmed from all the anxiety she felt from me during this terribly upsetting time."

The birth of an infant brings with it such a wonderful but weighty responsibility that it's a rare parent who doesn't feel some anxiety and self-doubt. Many new mothers confide in me that they feel overwhelmed because:

- *Caring for their baby is unexpectedly stressful.*
  No matter how much you thought that you were prepared for your new baby, it still may hit you like a ton of bricks.

- *They have little baby experience.*
  Most of us have had very few opportunities to care for small babies. That's why our generation may well be the least experienced . . . in history!

- *They feel like everybody is criticizing them.*
  New parents are very vulnerable to everyone's advice and criticisms. "Pick her up!" "Don't pick her up!" "Feed on demand!" "Feed on a schedule!" Getting peppered by all these comments can whittle down your confidence and magnify your self-doubts.

■ *The responsibility falls predominantly upon their shoulders.*
Mothers feel a pressure to know what they're doing because
they are the ones who are expected to be able to soothe their
baby when no one else can.

A New Mom's Feelings of Inadequacy

Aye, aye, aaaaaye! Am I really ready for this?

Mothering a baby is a magnificent experience, but it's neither automatic
nor instinctive. Unless you've spent lots of time baby-sitting or helping
with younger siblings, don't be surprised if your new baby makes you feel
you need six arms—like a Hindu deity. For most women, mothering their
newborn is the toughest job they've ever had!

After talking to thousands of new mothers, I've made an "Aye, Aye,
Aye" list of the top ten stresses that can undermine a new mom's self-
confidence—and make even a goddess start to crumble:

1. *I*ntense fatigue
2. *I*nexperience
3. *I*solation from loving family and friends
4. *I*nsufficient isolation from intrusive family and friends
5. *I*nconsolable crying (the baby's, that is)
6. *I*rritating arguments with your spouse
7. *I*nstant loss of job income and gratification
8. *I*nsecurity about your body
9. *I*nstability of your hormones
10. *I*ndelible barf stains on every piece of clothing you own

Of course, these problems pale when compared to the vivid joy and feeling of purpose your baby brings into your life. However, new mothers enter
a vulnerable psychological space after giving birth, and fatigue and fear can
even further distort your perceptions. You're in the midst of one of life's
most intense experiences and, particularly if you have a colicky baby, waves
of anxiety and depression may repeatedly wash over you during these initial
months. (For more on postpartum depression, see Appendix B.)

Fortunately, the pressures you feel today will soon melt into a warm love that will probably be more powerful and profound than any other you have ever felt. In the meantime, please be tolerant of yourself, your husband, and, especially, your baby.

A Mom's Anxiety "Ain't" the Answer for Colic

Colicky infants are born, not made.
Dr. Martin Stein, *Encounters with Children*

It's common for mothers of irritable babies to feel jealous and self-critical when they see other moms with easy-to-calm infants. Those feelings can cast a shadow over a woman's confidence and make her wonder if her anxiety causes her baby's crying.

Fortunately, during the first few months of life babies aren't able to tell when their mothers are distressed and worried. Remember, *babies are just babies!* They are not born with the ability to read their mother's feelings as if they were messages written on her forehead in lipstick. These little prehistoric creatures even have trouble . . . burping. So don't worry about your baby being affected by your anxiety.

Also, new parents sometimes mistakenly assume their newborns are nervous because their hands tremble, their chins quiver, and they startle at sudden sounds or movements. However, those reactions are normal signs of a newborn's undeveloped nervous system and automatically disappear after about three months.

In my experience, however, there are a few ways a mother's anxiety about her fussy infant could unintentionally nudge her baby into more crying:

- Anxiety might lessen the mother's breast-milk supply or interfere with her milk letdown, thus frustrating a hungry baby. (See Chapter 14 to remedy these feeding problems.)

- A mother may be so distracted and depressed that she's emotionally unavailable to comfort her crying infant.

- An anxious mother may be afraid to handle her baby as vigorously as is necessary to calm the screaming. (See the discussion about "Vigor" in Chapter 7.)

The Top Five Theories of Colic and Why They Aren't Right   47

- Nervous moms tend to jump impatiently from one calming method to another. They can get so lost in their anxiety they don't notice they're upsetting their babies even more.

However, when you carefully study the issue of maternal anxiety, it's clear that it can't be making a million of our babies cry for hours every day. The nervous-mommy theory fails to explain three colic characteristics:

- *Colic in preemies starts about two weeks past their due date.* If a mother's anxiety caused her baby's colic, crying would occur earlier and more often in preemies. After all, these fragile babies can turn even calm parents into nervous wrecks.

- *Colicky babies seem to be in pain.* Even if your baby could sense your anxiety, why would she cry as if she had pain?

- *Colic is as likely to occur with a couple's fifth baby as with their first.* This is the most powerful argument against a connection between anxiety and colic. Since experienced parents are more confident, their fifth baby should be less prone to colic than their first, but that just isn't the case.

Trina didn't need to worry that her stress had invaded Tatiana's tender psyche. In reality, the opposite is usually the case. Your baby's wail can trigger red alert in *your* nervous system, making *you* feel tense and anxious!

Theory #4: Is a Baby's Immature Brain the Cause of Colic?

During medical school, I was taught colic was an intestinal problem. Soon thereafter, that theory was pushed aside by the concept of brain immaturity. As we discovered more about our babies' nervous systems, we came to believe colic resulted from their immature brains getting overstimulated by all the new experiences babies encountered after birth. It's no wonder this theory became popular because, let's face it, babies are so . . . immature!

Babies have the coordination of drunken sailors and the quick wits of, well, newborns. But what *exactly* is immature in your baby's brain, and how might that predispose him to uncontrollable crying?

Mental Abilities Your Baby Was Born With

Imagine you're taking a very long trip but can only bring one suitcase with you. Now imagine that your suitcase is tiny. In a funny way, that's the situation your baby was in as he was preparing for birth. He could only fit into his small brain the most basic abilities he would need to live outside the protection of your womb.

If you could have helped him pack, what abilities would you have considered important for him to be born with? Walking? Smiling? Saying "I love you, Mommy"?

Over millions of years, Mother Nature picked four indispensable survival tools to fit into our babies' apple-size brains:

1. *Life-support controls*—the ability to maintain blood pressure, breathing, etc.
2. *Reflexes*—dozens of important automatic behaviors that help newborns sneeze, suck, swallow, cry, and more.
3. *Limited control of muscles and senses*—once babies can breathe and eat, these very limited abilities allow them to touch, taste, look around, and interact with the world.
4. *State control*—after babies start interacting with their families and their exciting new world, state control helps them turn their attention on (to watch and learn) and off (to recover and sleep).

Of all of these abilities, state control is the most important in determining whether or not he gets colic.

State Control: Your Baby's Ability to Tune the World In . . . or Shut It Out

When doctors talk about your baby's state, we're not discussing whether you live in Ohio or Florida. State describes your baby's level of wakefulness or sleep—in other words, his state of alertness. States range from deep sleep to light sleep to fussiness to full-out screaming. Right in the middle

is perhaps the most magical state of all: quiet alertness. It's easy to tell when your baby is quietly alert: his eyes will be open and bright and his face peacefully relaxed as he surveys the sights around him.

Maintaining a state is one of the earliest jobs your baby's brain must accomplish. His ability to stop his crying, keep awake, or stay asleep is called his "state control." I like to think of state control as your baby's TV remote, which allows him to "keep a channel on" when something is interesting, to "change channels" when he gets bored, and to shut the "TV" off if it starts upsetting him or it's time to go to bed.

Many young infants have excellent state control. These "I can do it myself" babies focus intensely on something for a while then pull away whenever they want; they easily shift between sleeping, alertness, and crying. These self-calming babies are especially good at protecting themselves from getting overstimulated. When the world gets too chaotic, some stare into space, some rhythmically suck their lower lip, and others turn their heads as if to say, "You excite me sooo much, I just have to look away to catch my breath!"

You may also notice your baby settling himself by using an attention off-switch called "habituation." It is one of your baby's best tools for shielding himself from getting too much stimulation. Like a circuit breaker that cuts the electrical flow when the wires overload, habituation allows your baby to shut off his attention when his brain gets overloaded.

Habituation explains the extraordinary "sleep anywhere-anytime-despite-the-noise" ability that infants have. (It's also the tool baby boys use to help them sleep despite the pain of circumcision.)

You'll notice that your newborn follows a simple plan during his first few weeks of life: eating and sleeping! Then, as he acclimates to being out of your womb, he'll spend increasing time in quiet alertness. Unfortunately, many young babies can't handle the additional excitement that comes with this alertness. These babies are *poor* self-calmers with immature state control. They have trouble shutting off their alertness, so their circuits often overload. After a few weeks, as they begin to wake up to the world, their state control starts to get overwhelmed and fail.

These babies look exhausted but their eyes keep staring out, unable to close, as if held open by toothpicks. It's as if their remote control malfunctioned, stranding them on a channel showing a loud, upsetting movie.

One exasperated mom told me her colicky three-month-old, Owen, cried for several hours every day. He clearly needed to sleep, but he wouldn't close his eyes. She said, "I keep trying to get him off *The Crying Channel* and help him find the *Sleep Station* again."

When your little baby is locked into screaming, please don't despair. Much better state control will be coming to rescue you both in a few months. In the meantime, the second part of this book will teach you exactly how to soothe him when he's having a meltdown.

"Help Me . . . The World Is Too Big!" How *Overstimulation* Causes Crying

Avoid overstimulation with toys, lights, and colors; this fatigues the baby's senses.
Richard Lovell, *Essays on Practical Education*, 1789

Considering how exciting the world is, it's a wonder that all babies don't get overstimulated! Fortunately, most are great at shutting out the world when they need to. However, if your baby has poor state control, even a low activity level may push him into frantic crying. He may begin to sob because of a tiny upset, like a burp or loud noise, but then get so wound up—by his own yelling—that he's soon raging out of control.

These babies cry because they get overstimulated and then stuck in "cry mode." If we could translate their shrieks into English, we'd hear something like "Please . . . help me . . . the world is too big!"

"Help Me . . . I'm Stuck in a Closet!"
How *Understimulation* Causes Crying

Your baby is not crying to make you pick him up, but because you put him down in the first place.
Penelope Leach, *Your Baby and Child*

Our culture believes in the strange myth that a baby wants to be left in a quiet, dark room. But what is this stillness like for your new baby? Imagine you've been working in a noisy, hectic office for nine months. One morning you come to work and find yourself alone—no chatter, no ringing phones, no commotion. Soon, the stillness gets on your nerves. You begin pacing and muttering, until you lose it and scream, "Get me out of here!"

This scene is similar to the way babies experience the world when they come home from the hospital. Although *our* image of the perfect nursery is one where our little angel sleeps in serene quiet, to a newborn that feels a bit like being stuck in a closet.

As strange as it sounds, your baby doesn't want—or need—peace and quiet. What he yearns for are the pulsating rhythms that constantly surrounded him in his womb world. In fact, the understimulation and stillness of our homes can drive a sensitive newborn every bit as nuts as chaotic overstimulation can.

Does understimulation mean babies cry because they're bored? No. Unlike older children and adults, babies don't find monotonous repetition boring. (That's why your baby is happy drinking milk day after day.) Rather, they find the *absence* of monotonous repetition hard to tolerate. Their cries ask for a return to the constant, hypnotizing stimulation of the womb. Fussy babies often take three months before they become mature enough to cope with the world without this rhythmic reassurance.

Either understimulation or overstimulation can be terribly unsettling to young infants; however, even worse is to experience both at the same time. When an immature baby is subjected to chaos in the absence of calming, rhythmic sensations, it can drive him past his point of tolerance!

Is Immaturity the Long-Sought Cause of Colic? Close, but No Cigar!

Brain immaturity is a large piece of the colic puzzle. But this theory can't be the whole truth because it fails to explain two crucial colic clues:

- *Preemies are no more likely to have colic than full-term babies.* If brain immaturity were the underlying cause of a baby's screaming, preemies, with their superimmature brains, would be the fussiest of all babies. Yet these tiny babies never cry without a clear reason, and they stop promptly once their need is met.

- *There are many cultures around the world where babies never get colic.* This fact proves that brain immaturity cannot be the sole basis of persistent crying. There is no biological reason why the brains of infants in some cultures would be so much more mature than those in others.

Theory #5: Does Challenging Temperament Cause Colic?

> *A few years ago, I spoke at a Lamaze class. During the talk, a pregnant woman named Ronnie told the class about her plan to have an "easy" child. She said, "I have two friends with young children. Angela has twin two-year-olds who scream and fight like little savages, but Lateisha's child is an angel. I don't want to make the same mistakes Angela did; I want my baby to be like Lateisha's little princess!"*

Anyone who has been lucky enough to spend time around infants knows that some babies are as gentle as a merry-go-round while others are as wild as a roller coaster! What makes some children so volatile and challenging? Was Ronnie right? Is an error committed by their parents, or are some babies just natural-born screamers?

Nature Versus Nurture: What Determines Your Baby's Personality?

There's an old story that as a boy handed his father a report card of all F's, he lowered his head and asked quietly, "Father, do you think my trouble is my heredity . . . or my upbringing?"

For generations, people have debated what predicts a child's temperament. Is it determined by his hereditary gifts (nature) or is personality gradually molded by one's upbringing (nurture)?

A thousand years ago, baby experts believed temperament was transferred to babies in the milk they were fed. That's why ancient experts warned parents never to give their baby milk from an animal or from a wet nurse with a weak mind, poor scruples, or a crazy family.

Today it is widely accepted that many personality traits are direct genetic hand-me-downs from our parents. For this reason, shy parents usually have shy children, and passionate parents tend to have babies who are little chili peppers.

> Andrea was the spirited baby of Zoran, a former race-car driver, and Yelena, a mile-a-minute research psychiatrist. A real handful from the moment she was born, by two months of age Andrea shrieked her complaints almost twenty-four hours a day. As Zoran noted, "She's as tough as nails, but what else would you expect? Two Dobermans just don't give birth to a cocker spaniel!"

Let's take a closer look at temperament and see why, even though it may contribute to colic, it's not the main cause.

Temperament: The Sea Your Child Sails On

> People are wrong when they think that quiet babies are good and fussy babies are bad. The truth is that some gracious and softhearted babies fuss a lot because they can't handle the turbulence of the world around them.
>
> Renée, mother of Marie-Claire, Esmé, and Didier

Your baby is like a boat and her temperament the sea she sails on. If her boat is stable (a good self-calming ability), and the sea is smooth (she has a calm temperament), she will sail through infancy. However, if the boat is

unstable (a poor self-calming ability), or the sea is rocky (she has a challenging temperament), she's in danger of getting tossed about. Once children get older and their self-calming ability becomes stable, the turbulence of their passions is no longer such an overpowering experience. But for young babies, a very intense temperament may be more than they can handle.

Luckily, most babies are mild-tempered and easy to calm, like sweet little lambs. But challenging babies are more like a mix of skittish cat and bucking bronco. These excessively sensitive and/or intense babies engage in a daily struggle to keep their balance during their first months of life.

Easy-Tempered Babies—"Mary Had a Little Lamb . . ."

Mild and mellow from the first moments of life, rather than scream at birth, an easy baby might shyly fuss, as if to say, "Please Mummy, it's a teensy bit too bright in here!"

Sabrina was one such undemanding baby:

> Sabrina's dark lashes framed eyes the color of the sky. She was
> extremely alert, watching the world with the peaceful gaze of an
> old Zen master. Sabrina slept beautifully and hardly ever cried.
> Even when she was hungry, she rarely made a noise louder than
> a whimper to get her parents' attention.

Easy-tempered babies have terrific state control and are great self-calmers. They are easygoing little "surfer dudes" who have no trouble taking all the craziness of the world in stride.

However, babies who are very sensitive or intense—or, Heaven help you, both—and who have poor self-calming skills may not be able to keep from screaming as the world's strange mixture of action and stillness toss them around like boats in a storm.

Infants with a Challenging Temperament—Little Babies with Big Personalities

> Lizzy and her twin sister Jennifer were like two peas in a pod, both super-sensitive to noise and sudden movements. When unhappy, their faces flushed and cries flew out of their mouths with deafening force.
>
> However, while Jenny was usually able to quiet her own crying, Lizzy's screams pulled her like a team of wild horses. Once she got rolling, she had no ability to rein herself in!
>
> Lizzy's mother, Cheryl, tried to regain control of her frenzied daughter with pacifiers, wrapping, and constant holding, but nothing helped. "For the first three months, I walked around every day not knowing when the 'train wreck' would occur."

Babies like Lizzy are tough. During the first few months of life, their personalities can be too big for them to handle. That's why parents often dub these babies with funny names to remind themselves not to take life too seriously. For example, Amanda's parents nicknamed her "Demanda," Natalie Rose's parents called her "Fussy Gassy Gussy," and Lachlan's parents referred to him as "General Fuss-ter."

Two types of temperament can be particularly challenging for new parents: sensitive and intense.

Sensitive Babies: Perceptive Infants Who Can Be as Fragile as Crystal

Of course, we all know that some people are much more sensitive than others. One person can sleep with the TV on while another is annoyed by any little sound. Some newborns also show signs of being extra sensitive, such as jumping when the telephone rings, grimacing at the taste of lanolin on your nipple, or turning her head to the smell of your breast.

Sensitive babies are wide-eyed and super-alert; their reactions to the world are as transparent and pure as crystal. But like crystal, sensitive infants are often fragile and require extra care. They are *so* open to everything around them they can easily become overloaded. That's why these babies have such a hard time settling themselves when they're left to cry it out. In other words, they can *go* bonkers from *being* bonkers!

If your newborn has a sensitive temperament, she may occasionally look away from you during her feeding or playtime. This is called "gaze aversion." Gaze aversion occurs when you get a little too close to your baby's eyes. Imagine a ten-foot face suddenly coming right in front of *your* nose. You, too, might need to look away or pull back a bit and check it out from a more comfortable distance! Don't mistake this for a sign that she doesn't like you or want to look at you. Just move back a foot or two and allow her to have slightly more space between her eyes and your face.

Intense Babies: A Cross Between Passionate . . . and Explosive

Throughout your baby's normal waking cycles, he's bound to experience tiny flashes of frustration, annoyance, and discomfort. Calm babies handle these with hardly a fuss, but intense babies handle these *intensely*. It's as if the "sparks" of everyday distress fall onto the "dynamite" of their volatile temperament, and "*Kapow!*" they explode. When babies lose control like that, they may get so carried away that they can't stop screaming even when they're given exactly what they want.

This intense crying was what Jackie experienced when she tried to feed her hungry—and passionate—baby. Two-month-old Jeffrey often began his feedings like this:

> "He would let out a shriek that sounded like, 'Feed me or I'm gonna die!' I would leap off the sofa, take out my breast, and insert it into his cavernous mouth. However, rather than gratefully taking it, he would often shake his head from side to side and wail around my dripping boob as if he were blind and didn't even know it was there. At times I worried that he thought my breast was a hand trying to silence him rather than my loving attempt to come to his rescue.
>
> "Fortunately, I had already figured out that Jeffrey couldn't stop himself from reacting that way. So, despite his protests, I

*kept offering him my breast until he realized what I was trying
to do. Eventually, he would latch on and start suckling. And
then, lo and behold, he'd eat as if I hadn't fed him for months."*

Jackie was smart. She realized Jeffrey wasn't intentionally ignoring her gift of food; he was just a little bitty baby trying to deal with his great big personality. Like a rookie cowboy on a rodeo bull, he was trying so hard to hold on that he didn't notice she was right there next to him, ready to help.

Does a Baby's Temperament Last a Lifetime?

As babies grow up, they don't get less intense or sensitive, but they do develop other skills to help themselves control their temperaments and better cope with the world. By three months they begin to smile, coo, roll, grab,

What's Your Baby's Temperament?

Even on the first days of your baby's life, you can get glimpses of his budding temperament. The answers to these questions may help you determine if your child's temperament is more placid or passionate:

1. Do bright lights, wet diapers, or cold air make your baby lightly whimper or full-out scream?
2. When you lay him down on his back, do his arms usually rest serenely at his sides or flail about?
3. Does he startle easily at loud noises and sudden movements?
4. When he's hungry, does he slowly get fussier and fussier or does he accelerate immediately into strong wailing?
5. When he's eating, is he like a little wine taster (calmly taking sips) or an all-you-can-eater (slurping the milk down with speedy precision)?
6. Once he works himself into a vigorous cry, how hard is it for you to get his attention? How long does it take to get him to settle back down?

These hints can't perfectly predict your child's lifelong temperament, but they *can* help you begin the exciting journey of getting to know and respect his uniqueness.

and chew. And shortly thereafter they add the extraordinarily effective self-calming techniques of laughter, mouthing objects, and moving about.

With time infants develop enough control over their immature bodies to allow them to direct the same zest that used to spill out into their shrieks into giggles and belly laughs. Passionate infants often turn into kids who are the biggest laughers and most talkative members of the family. ("Hey, Mom, look! *Look!* It's incredible!") And sensitive infants often grow into compassionate and perceptive children. ("No, Mom, it's not purple. It's *lavender.*")

So if you have a challenging baby, don't lose heart. These kids often become the sweetest and most enthusiastic children on the block!

Is Temperament the True Cause of Colic? Probably Not.

Is a baby's temperament the key factor that pushes him into inconsolable crying? No. This reasonable theory fails because it doesn't explain three of the universal colic clues:

- *Colicky crying usually starts at two weeks, peaks at six weeks, and ends by three to four months of age.* Since temperament is present at birth and lasts a lifetime, colic caused by a challenging temperament should begin at birth and persist—or even worsen—after the fourth month of life. It doesn't.

Goodness of Fit—What happens when two cocker spaniels give birth to a Doberman?

Since temperament is largely an inherited trait, a baby's personality almost always reflects his parents'. However, just as brown-eyed parents may wind up with a blue-eyed child, mellow parents may unexpectedly give birth to a T. rex baby who makes them run for the hills!

Parents sometimes have difficulty handling a baby whose temperament differs dramatically from their own. They may hold their sensitive baby too roughly or their intense baby too gently. These parents need to learn their baby's unique temperament and nurture him exactly the way that suits him the best.

- *Preemies are no more likely to have colic than full-term babies. (And it starts about two weeks past their due date.)* One would expect an immature preemie with a sensitive and/or intense personality to be *more* prone to colic than a mature full-term baby. Similarly, one would expect his colic to begin right away, not weeks to months later.

- *There are many cultures around the world where babies never get colic.* Temperament can't be the cause of colic because in many cultures colic is nonexistent among their most intense and passionate infants.

So if one million U.S. babies aren't crying because of gas, acid reflux, maternal anxiety, brain immaturity, or inborn fussiness, what *is* the true cause of colic? As you will see in the next chapter, the only theory that fully explains the mystery of colic is . . . the missing fourth trimester.

5

The True Cause of Colic:
The Missing
Fourth Trimester

Main Points:

- The First Three Trimesters: Your baby's happy life in the womb
- The Great Eviction: Why babies are so immature at birth
- Why your baby wants (and needs) a fourth trimester
- A "Womb with a View": A parent's experience of the fourth trimester
- The Great American Myth: Young babies can be spoiled
- The connection between the fourth trimester and other colic theories
- Ten reasons why the missing fourth trimester is the true cause of colic

Once upon a time, in a faraway land, four blind wise men were asked to describe the true nature of an elephant. Each took a turn touching the beast. One by one, they spoke.

"This animal is long and curved like a spear," said the first blind man after grabbing a tusk. The next, clutching the giant's leg, raised his voice. "I disagree! This animal is thick and up-right—like a tree." As they began to argue, the next man

touched the ear and compared it to a giant leaf. Finally, the last man, wrapped up in the elephant's trunk, declared triumphantly that they were all wrong—the animal was like a big, fat snake.

What Is the Fourth Trimester and How Did It Become Missing?

In this story, each man described a *part* of the elephant. Yet, he was so sure his view was the whole truth, he didn't consider the possibility that there was another explanation that could account for all the different observations.

Similarly, wise men and women trying to solve the mystery of colic have focused on single bits of truth. Some heard grunting and thought gas was the culprit. Others saw a grimace and thought it was pain. Still others noticed that cuddling helped and assumed the infants were spoiled.

In recent years, colic has been blamed on pain, anxiety, immaturity, and temperament. Yet, while each is a piece of the puzzle, colic can only be understood by viewing all the pieces together. Only then does it become clear that the popular colic theories are linked by one previously overlooked concept: the missing fourth trimester.

Your baby's nine months—or three trimesters—inside you is a time of unbelievably complex development. Nevertheless, it takes most babies *an additional* three months to "wake up" and become active partners in the relationship. This time between birth and the end of your baby's third month is what I call your baby's fourth trimester.

Now let's see what a baby's life is like before they're born, why they must come into the world before they're fully mature, and the ways great parents soothe their babies by imitating the womb for the first three months of their baby's life.

The First Three Trimesters: Your Fetus's Happy Life in Your Womb

Did you think your baby was ready to be born after your nine months of pregnancy? God knows *you* were ready! But in many ways, your baby wasn't. Newborns can't smile, coo, or even suck their fingers. At birth, they're really still fetuses and for the next three months they want little more than to be carried, cuddled, and made to feel like they're still within the womb.

However, in order to mimic the sensations he enjoyed so much in your uterus, you need to know what it was like in there. Let's backtrack to the time when your fetus was still in the womb and see life through his eyes. Imagine you can look inside your pregnant uterus. What do you see? Just inside the muscular walls, silky membranes waft in a pool of tropical amniotic waters. Over there is your pulsating placenta; like a twenty-four-hour diner, it serves your fetus a constant feast of food and oxygen.

At the center, in the place of honor, is your precious baby. He's protected from hunger, germs, cold winds, mean animals, and rambunctious siblings by the velvet-soft walls of your womb. He looks part-astronaut–part-merman as he floats weightlessly in the golden fluid. Over these nine months, your fetus develops at lightning speed. His brain adds two hundred fifty thousand nerve cells a minute, and his body grows one billion times in weight and infinitely in complexity.

Let's zoom in on your baby's last month of life inside you. It's getting really tight in there. Like a little yoga expert, your fetus is nestled in, folded and secure. However, contrary to popular myth his cozy room is neither quiet nor still. It's jiggly (imagine your baby bouncing around when you hustle down the stairs) and loud (the blood whooshes through your arteries, creating a rhythmic din noisier than a vacuum cleaner).

Amazingly, all this commotion doesn't upset him. Rather, he finds it soothing. That's why unborn babies stay calm during the day but become restless in the still of the night. It's an ideal life in there—so why do babies pack up and pop out after just nine months, when they're still so immature?

The Great Eviction: Speculations on Why Our Babies Can't Stay in the Womb for a Fourth Trimester

Upon thee I was cast out from the womb.

Psalms 22:10

During the past century, archaeologists have pieced together a clearer picture of how humans evolved over the past five million years. They have studied such issues as why we switched from knuckle-walking to running upright and when we began using language and tools. However, what has not been fully appreciated until now is that over millions of years evolutionary changes gradually forced our ancestral mothers to deliver babies who were more and more immature. I believe that eventually, prehistoric human mothers had to *evict* their newborns three months early because their brains got so big!

In the very distant past, our ancestors likely had tiny-headed babies who didn't need to be evicted early from the womb. However, a few million years ago, our babies began going down a new branch of the evolutionary tree—the branch of supersmart people with big-brained babies. Pregnant mothers began stuffing new talents into their unborn babies' brains, filling them up like Christmas stockings. Eventually, their heads must have gotten so large that they began to get stuck during birth.

Perhaps that would have ended the evolution of our big brains, but four adaptations occurred that allowed our babies' brains to continue growing:

1. Our fetuses began to develop no-frills brains, containing only the most basic reflexes and skills needed to survive after birth (like sucking, pooping, and keeping the heart beating).

2. An ultrasleek head design slowly evolved to keep the big brain from getting wedged in the birth canal. On the outside it had slippery skin, squishable ears, and a tiny chin and nose. On the inside it had a compressible brain and a soft skull that could elongate and form itself into a narrower, easier to deliver cone shape.

3. Their big heads began to rotate as they exited the womb. (You've probably noticed it's easier to get a tight cork out of a bottle if you twist it as you pull it out.)

These three modifications helped tremendously. However, the crowning change that allowed the continued growth of our babies' brains was the fourth change—"eviction."

4. I believe that over hundreds of thousands of years, big-brained babies were less likely to get stuck in the birth canal—and more

likely to survive—if they were born a little prematurely. In other words, if they were evicted.

Today, mothers give birth to their babies about three months before they're fully mature in order to guarantee a safe delivery.

However, as any mother can tell you, even with all these adaptations, giving birth is still a very tight squeeze. At eleven and a half centimeters across, our fetuses' heads have to compress quite a bit to get pushed through a ten centimeter, fully dilated cervix. No wonder midwives call the cervix at delivery the "ring of fire"!

Childbirth has always been a hazardous business occasionally putting both children and mothers in mortal peril. That's why, through the ages,

Imagine giving birth to a baby half the height or weight of an adult. Of course, a three-foot-long, eighty-pound newborn would be ridiculous. Now imagine giving birth to a baby with a head half the size of an adult's. That sounds even more absurd, but the fact is that such a head would be *small* for a new baby. At birth, our babies' noggins are almost two-thirds as big around as an adult head. (Ouch!)

many societies have honored childbirth as a heroic act. The Aztecs believed women who died giving birth entered the highest level of heaven, alongside courageous warriors who lost their lives in battle.

Early eviction lessened that risk and was made possible by the ability of prehistoric parents to protect their immature babies. Thanks to their upright posture and highly developed manual dexterity, early humans could walk while carrying their infants to keep them warm and cuddled. And our ancestors used their hands for more than holding. They created warm clothing and slinglike carriers that mimicked the security of the womb.

The hard work of imitating the uterus was the price our Stone Age relatives accepted in exchange for having safer early deliveries. However, in recent centuries, many parents have tried to wiggle out of this commitment to their babies.

They still wanted their babies to have big smart brains and be born early, but they didn't want to feed them so frequently or carry them around all day. Some misguided experts even insisted that newborns should be expected to sleep through the night and calm their own crying. Like kangaroos refusing their babies' entrance to the pouch, parents who subscribed to these theories denied what mothers and fathers for hundreds of thousands of years had promised to give their new infants.

Why Your Baby Wants (and Needs) a Fourth Trimester

The baby, assailed by eyes, ears, nose, skin, and intestines at once, feels it all as one great blooming, buzzing confusion.
William James, *The Principles of Psychology,* 1890

When you bring your soft, dimpled newborn home from the hospital, you may think your peaceful nursery is perfectly suited for his cherubic body and temperament, but that's not how your baby sees it. To him, it's a disorienting world—part Las Vegas casino, part dark closet!

His senses are bombarded by new experiences. From outside, he's assaulted by a jumble of lights, colors, and textures. From inside, he's flooded with waves of powerful new feelings like gas, hunger, and thirst. Yet, at the same time, the stillness of the room envelops him like a closet, devoid of the rhythms that were his constant comfort and companion for the past nine months. Imagine how strange the quiet of a hospital room must be to your baby after the loud, quadraphonic shhhh of the womb. No wonder babies look around as if they're thinking, *This just can't be real!*

Most infants can deal with these changes without a hitch. However, some babies can't. They need to be held, rocked, and suckled for large chunks of the day. These sensations duplicate the womb and form the basis of every infant-soothing method ever invented. This fourth-trimester experience calms babies *not* because they're spoiled and *not* because it tricks them into thinking they're back home, but because it triggers a powerful response inside our babies' brains that turns off their crying—the calming reflex.

The fourth trimester is the birthday present babies really hope their parents will give them.

A "Womb with a View": A Parent's Experience of the Fourth Trimester

When the baby comes out, the true umbilical cord is cut forever . . . yet the baby is still, in that second, a fetus . . . just a fetus one second older.

Peter Farb, *Humankind*

What an unforgettable moment the first time you see and touch your new baby. His sweet smell, open gaze, and downy soft skin capture your heart. But newborns can also be intimidating. Their floppy necks, irregular breathing, and tiny tremors make them seem so helpless.

This vulnerability is why I believe that a fourth-trimester period of imitating the womb is exactly what new babies need.

This need was probably obvious to you when your baby's sobs melted away the moment he was placed on your chest. Your ears and his cry will now become a virtual umbilical cord, an attachment, like an invisible bungee cord that stretches to allow you to walk around the house—until a sharp yelp yanks you back to his side.

"When Stuart came out of me, he didn't seem ready to be in the world," said Mary, a mother in my practice. "He required almost constant holding and rocking to keep him content. My husband, Phil, and I joked that he was like a squishy cupcake that needed to go back in the oven for a little more baking."

In effect, what Mary and Phil realized was that Stuart needed a few more months of "womb service." But it's not so easy being a walking uterus! Bewildered new moms often observe that they're still in their pajamas at five P.M. Within days of delivery, you'll discover that it takes all day long to accomplish what your uncomplaining uterus did twenty-four hours a day for the past nine months.

From your baby's point of view, being in your arms for twelve hours a day is a disappointment, if not a rip-off. If he could talk, your infant would probably state with pouty disdain, "Hey, what's the big deal? You used to hold me twenty-four hours a day and feed me every single second!"

Unfortunately, many parents in our culture have been convinced that it's wrong to cuddle their babies so much. They have been misled into believing that their main job is to teach and educate their newborn. They treat their young child more like a brain to train than a spirit they are privileged to nurture. Other cultures consider an infant's needs differently. In Bali, babies are never allowed to sleep alone and they barely leave the arms of an adult for the first hundred and five days! The parents bury the placenta and nourish the burial spot with daily offerings of rice and vegetables. On the hundred and fifth day, a holy ceremony welcomes babies as new members of the human race; up until that point they still belong to the gods. In this ritual, babies receive their first sip of water, and an egg is rubbed on their arms and legs to give them vitality and strength. Only then are their feet finally allowed to touch Mother Earth.

It's no coincidence that in cultures like Bali, where colic is virtually nonexistent, parents give babies much more of a fourth-trimester experience than we do.

The Great American Myth: Young Babies Can Be Spoiled

Hide not thine ear to my cry.
Lamentations 3:56

There are at least two things all parents know for sure:

1. There are a lot of spoiled kids out there.
2. You don't want your child to become one of them.

We all want to raise respectful children, and some experts warn us that being too attentive to our baby's cries will accidentally teach them to be manipulative. Can promptly answering your newborn's cries with holding, rocking, and sucking start a bad habit? Can cuddling your baby backfire on you?

Fortunately, the answers to these two questions are . . . no and no. It's impossible to spoil your baby during the first four months of life. Remember, he experienced a dramatic drop-off in holding time as soon as he was born. One mother told me, "I imagine new babies feel like someone who enters a detox program and has to go cold turkey from snuggling. No wonder they cry!"

Today's mothers and fathers aren't the only ones who have worried about turning their children into whining brats. In the early twentieth century, American parents were told not to mollycoddle their babies for fear of turning them into undisciplined little nuisances. The U.S. Children's Bureau issued a stern warning to a mother not to carry her infant too much, lest he become "a spoiled, fussy baby, and a household tyrant whose continual demands make a slave of a mother."

In 1972, however, Sylvia Bell and Mary Ainsworth of Johns Hopkins University shook those old ideas about spoiling to their very foundations. They found that babies whose mothers responded quickly to their cries during the first months of life *did not* become spoiled. On the contrary, infants whose needs were met rapidly and with tenderness fussed less and were more poised and patient when tested at one year of age! As Ainsworth and Bell proved—and most parents know in their hearts—the more you love and cuddle your little baby, the more confident and resilient he becomes.

Despite this evidence, many new parents still have nagging doubts about whether they're holding their babies too much. Although our natural parental instinct is to calm our baby as quickly as possible, the repeated warning, "Don't spoil your baby," has been drummed into our heads so much it makes us question ourselves.

Now, I admit it's easy to feel manipulated when your baby wakes up and screams every time you gently lower him into the crib. But letting him cry is no more likely to teach him to be independent than leaving him in a dirty diaper is likely to toughen his skin. (It's reassuring to know that traditionally many Native American parents held their babies all day and suckled them all night and still those babies grew up to be brave, respectful, and self-sufficient.)

Don't misunderstand me. I'm not arguing against establishing a flexible feeding/sleeping schedule for your baby. (See the discussion of scheduling in Chapter 15.) Some babies and families find scheduling very helpful. However, trying to mold passionate babies who have irregular sleeping and eating patterns into a fixed schedule usually leads to frustration for everyone.

As the Bible says, "To everything there is a season." I believe disciplining is a very important parental task—but not with young infants. The beginning of the fourth month is the earliest time concerns about accidentally spoiling your baby become an issue. However, before four months, you have a job that is *one hundred times* more important than preventing spoiling; your job is nurturing your baby's confidence in you and the world.

Building our child's faith is one of parenting's greatest privileges and responsibilities. I'm convinced that a rapid and sympathetic response to our baby's cries is the foundation of strong family values, not the undermining of them. When your loving arms cuddle your baby or warm milk satisfies him, you're telling him, "Don't worry. I'll always be there when you need me." This begins your baby's trust in you and becomes the bedrock of his faith in those closest to him.

Please treasure these amazing first months with your sweet, kissable baby. There will be plenty of time later on for training and disciplining, but now is the time for cuddling. Enjoy this time because, as any experienced parent will tell you, it will be over faster than you could imagine.

The Missing Fourth Trimester: The True Basis of Colic

There's no place like home.
Dorothy, *The Wizard of Oz*

After centuries of myths and confusion, I am convinced that the true basis of colic is simply that fussy babies need the sensations of the womb to help stay calm.

You might ask, "If all babies get evicted early and need a fourth trimester, why don't they all get colic?"

The reason is simple: Most babies can handle being born too soon because they have mild temperaments and good self-calming abilities. Thus, despite being exposed to waves of overstimulation and understimulation, they can soothe themselves.

Colicky babies, on the other hand, have big trouble with self-calming. They live through the same experiences as calm babies, but rather than taking them in stride, they overreact dramatically. These infants desperately need the sensations of the womb to help them turn on their calming reflex.

The Colic Elephant: A Blend of the Fourth Trimester and Other Colic Theories

As we've discussed, experts have blamed colic on tummy troubles, anxiety, immaturity, and temperament. But, like the blind men and the elephant, these experts perceived only parts of the problem and overlooked the all-important common link—the missing fourth trimester.

The missing fourth trimester makes babies vulnerable to the unstable qualities of their individual natures (brain immaturity and challenging temperament) and to small daily upsets.

This is how I believe all the colic theories relate to one another:

1. **Brain Immaturity**—This inborn characteristic can greatly increase a baby's need for a fourth trimester. Fussy infants have such poor state control and self-calming ability that even small amounts of over- or understimulation can set off a chain reaction of escalating flailing and loud cries.

2. **Temperament**—A baby whose nature is extremely sensitive and/or intense often overreacts to small disturbances and needs a great deal of help turning on the calming reflex.

3. **Big Tummy Troubles**—Pain from food allergies or acid reflux can occasionally make a baby frantic. But these problems are much more distressing in babies whose self-calming ability is immature or who have challenging temperaments.

4. **Tiny Tummy Troubles**—Constipation and gas can spark discomfort that provokes crying in babies with brain immaturity and/or a challenging temperament.

5. **Maternal Anxiety**—Fussy babies sometimes cry more when their anxious mothers handle them too gently or jump chaotically from one ineffective soothing attempt to another.

Putting the Theory of Fourth Trimester to the Test

There's a reason behind everything in nature.
Aristotle

For a colic theory to be proven correct it must fit all ten colic clues. After long and exhaustive study, I have found the only theory that explains all ten and solves the centuries-old mystery of colic is the concept of the missing fourth trimester:

1. *Colicky crying usually starts at two weeks, peaks at six weeks, and ends by three to four months of age.*

For the first two weeks of life, newborns have little alert time. This helps keep them from getting over- or understimulated and thus delays the onset of colic.

After two weeks, babies start staying alert for longer periods. Mellow babies can easily handle the stimulation this increased alertness exposes them to. However, babies who are poor self-calmers or who have challenging temperaments may begin to get overwhelmed. Thus the crying starts.

By six weeks, these vulnerable babies are very alert and very overstimulated, yet they still have poor state control. They launch into bouts of screaming that can be soothed only by masterful imitations of the womb.

By three to four months, colic disappears. Now babies are skilled at cooing, laughing, sucking their fingers, and other self-calming tricks. They are mature enough to deal with the world without the constant holding, rocking, and shushing of the fourth trimester. At last, they are ready to be born!

2. *Preemies are no more likely to have colic than full-term babies. (And their colic doesn't start until they are about two weeks past their due date.)*

Preemies are good sleepers, even in noisy intensive-care units. Their immature brains have mastered the sleep state, but not the complex state of alertness. This near absence of alert time fools preemies into thinking they're still in the womb. They don't no-tice they're missing the fourth trimester until they're past their due date and become more awake and alert.

3. *Colicky babies have twisted faces and piercing wails. Often, their cries come in waves (like cramps) and stop abruptly.*

Your baby's colicky cries may sound identical to the wails he makes when he's in pain. However, many babies overreact to triv-ial experiences (loud noises, burps, etc.) with pain-like screams. They're like smoke alarms that go off even though only a little piece of toast burned.

The fact that these shrieks can be quieted by car rides or breast-feeding proves these babies aren't in agony. What they're really suffering from is the loss of their fourth trimester.

4. *Their screams frequently begin during or just after a feeding.*

Babies who cry during or right after meals are usually overreacting to their gastro-colic reflex, the intestinal squeezing that occurs when the stomach fills with food. Most babies have no problem with this reflex, but for colicky babies, at the end of the day (and at the end of their patience), this sensation may be the last straw that launches them into hysterics.

That this distress vanishes after three months (while the gastro-colic reflex is still going strong) further supports the notion that this crampy feeling triggers screaming only in babies who need the calming sensations of the fourth trimester.

5. *They often double up, grunt, strain, and seem relieved by passing gas or pooping.*

All babies experience intestinal gas; however, this sensation triggers screaming only in infants with sensitive and/or intense temperaments. Even those babies usually stop crying when rescued by the calming rhythms of the womb.

6. *Colic is often much worse in the evening (the "witching hour").*

Just as some harried moms crumble at the end of their toddlers' birthday parties, some young babies unravel after a full day's roller-coaster ride of activity. Without the fourth trimester to settle them down, these vulnerable infants bubble over each evening like pots of hot pudding.

7. *Colic is as likely to occur with a couple's fifth baby as with their first.*

Each new baby represents a reshuffling of their parents' personal deck of genetic traits. That's why a couple's first four babies may be calm and easy to keep happy, while their fifth may inherit traits like sensitivity or poor state control that make him fall apart unless he's held and rocked all day.

These colicky babies require the sanctuary of the fourth trimester to help them cope until they're mature enough to soothe themselves.

8. *Colicky crying often improves with rocking, holding, shhhhing, and gentle abdominal pressure.*

This clue is compelling proof that the true cause of uncontrollable crying in babies is their need for a few more months in the uterus. That's because each of these calming tricks imitates the womb, and after three months they're no longer required.

9. *Babies are healthy and happy between crying bouts.*

If the only reason babies have colic is because they're born too soon, it's logical to expect immature infants to be healthy and happy until something pushes them over the edge.

10. *In many cultures around the world, babies never get colic.*

The babies of the villagers of Bali, the bushmen of Botswana, and the Manali tribesmen of the Himalayan foothills all share one trait: these babies never suffer from persistent crying. When anthropologists study "colic-free" cultures, they find that the mothers in those societies closely follow the fourth-trimester plan. Women hold their infants almost twenty-four hours a day, feed them frequently, and constantly rock and jiggle them. For several months, these moms give their babies an almost constant imitation of the womb.

Only the missing fourth trimester explains *all* the colic clues. However, if soothing a screaming baby is just a matter of imitating the womb with some wrapping and rocking, why do these approaches so often fail to calm colicky kids? The reason is quite simple: Parents in our culture are rarely taught how to do them correctly.

Thankfully, it's not too late to learn, and in the next part of this book, I will share with you detailed descriptions of the world's most effective methods for calming crying babies.

PART TWO

Learning the Ancient Art
of Soothing a Baby

6

The Woman Who Mistook
Her Baby for a Horse:
Modern Parents
Who Forgot About the
Fourth Trimester

Main Points:

- Unlike newborn horses, our babies are not up and running on the first day of life; they need a fourth trimester to finish getting ready for the world
- The striking differences between four-day-old and four-month-old babies
- Ancient lessons you can learn from some mothers whose children never get colic

That which was done is that which shall be done; and there is no new thing under the sun.

Ecclesiastes 1:9

Picture a crisp December day, gleaming like a jewel. Yesterday your life changed with the birth of a beautiful baby boy. Now, as the nurse wheels his bassinet into your room, your son lifts his fragile head, slowly turns to face you, and flashes a big grin! Then he vaults into your arms and, with a

laugh that makes your heart melt, proclaims, "You're the best mom in the whole world!"

Of course, no one expects their baby to walk and talk right after birth. However, many modern parents are unprepared for how dependent and vulnerable newborns truly are. They expect their babies to be more mature, sort of like baby horses! Within minutes of birth, newborn horses can stand, walk, and even run. A baby horse's survival depends on these crucial abilities to keep away from hungry predators. By comparison, our new babies are still immature little fetuses.

The Surprising Truth: The Differences Between Four-Day-Old and Four-Month-Old Babies

After the first month, I wanted some recognition that my twin girls could distinguish me from the woman down the block. When Audrey was two months old, she peed on me, then suddenly smiled. I know it sounds crazy but I was ecstatic!

Debra, mother of Audrey and Sophia

When I teach prenatal classes I often ask the parents-to-be to describe the differences between four-day-old and four-month-old babies. Those without much baby experience usually answer that a four-month-old is like a newborn, except bigger and more alert.

In fact, there are *gigantic* differences between these two ages. As extraordinary as newborns are, their ability to interact with the world is extremely limited. While a four-day-old can't even coo or turn around to see who's speaking, a four-month-old's delicious smile and glowing eyes reach out like a personal invitation to join her on her amazing life journey.

As noted earlier, baby horses depend on brawn for their survival, so their developed bodies are as big as they can possibly be when they pop out of their mothers' wombs. By contrast, our babies' survival depends on their brains. For that reason, at birth, their heads are as big as they could possibly be and not get stuck. Then amazingly, during the first three months, a baby's brain balloons an additional twenty percent in size. Accompanying that growth is an explosive advance in her brain's speed, organization, and complexity. No wonder parents notice their babies suddenly "wake up" as the fourth trimester draws to a close.

Our ancient relatives realized how immature their babies were at birth. Over the centuries, they discovered that the most effective way of caring for newborns during the early months of infancy was by imitating their previous home—the uterus!

Four-Day-Old Babies	Four-Month-Old Babies

Sensory Abilities

■ Can focus only on objects eight to twelve inches away.	■ Easily focus on large objects across a room.
■ Love looking at light/dark contrasts and designs.	■ Can turn their head to find where a sound comes from.

Social Abilities

■ More attracted to the sound of the human voice than to music or noise. Can recognize their mother's voice from the muffled sounds they heard in the womb.	■ Patiently wait for you to stop talking before they take a turn in the conversation by releasing a symphony of coos, grunts, and giggles.
■ Prefer looking at a person's face rather than an object. May be able to imitate facial expressions like a mom opening her mouth or sticking out her tongue.	■ Enamored with their parents' faces and brighten visibly when they enter the room. Smile and coo to make their parents smile and may become upset when ignored.

Motor Abilities

■ Often get crossed eyes. Can follow only slowly moving objects and have very jerky eye movements.	■ No longer get crossed eyes. Can now follow objects swiftly and smoothly as they move around the room.
■ Hard for them to get their fingers to their mouths and *very* hard for them to keep them there for more than thirty seconds.	■ Much more able to reach out and touch objects. Easily get their fingers to their mouths and keep them there for many minutes.

Physiological Characteristics

■ Hands and feet are blue much of the time.	■ No longer get blue hands and feet unless cold.
■ Bodies occasionally get jolted by hiccups, jittery tremors, and irregular breathing.	■ Rarely hiccup, never tremor, and breathing is smooth and regular.
■ Have little ability to control body movements.	■ Much better at controlling body movements. Can roll over, spin around, and lift head high off the mattress.

Out with the New, In with the Old: Rediscovering the Stone Age Wisdom of Imitating the Fourth Trimester

Do you remember how in *Star Wars* Luke Skywalker achieved victory by using the long forgotten powers of the Force? Well, over the last fifty years, our society has also advanced by returning to ancient wisdom such as getting more exercise, protecting the environment, and eating food grown with less pesticides. Technology is a blessing, but today we are relearning the value of living in harmony with nature; it's just common sense!

That's why there's logic in examining the past to understand ourselves better. Although our clothes and music are contemporary, our biology is clearly prehistoric, and that's especially true for babies.

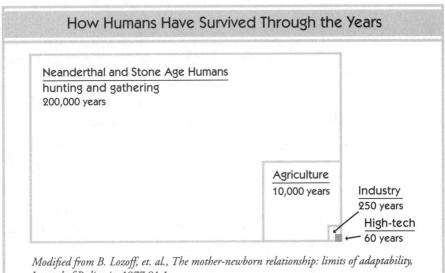

How Humans Have Survived Through the Years

Neanderthal and Stone Age Humans
hunting and gathering
200,000 years

Agriculture
10,000 years

Industry
250 years

High-tech
← 60 years

Modified from B. Lozoff, et. al., The mother-newborn relationship: limits of adaptability, Journal of Pediatrics 1977:91:1.

In the diagram above, we occupy the tiny bottom right corner, the technological age of man. Yet our babies are far from high-tech. In most respects, they haven't changed a hair in the past thirty thousand years! That's why, although most of us would never survive if suddenly sent back to the Stone Age, our infants would feel right at home. Babies expect to be born into a cave family, and they expect us to be as experienced at handling them as our Stone Age cousins were. Unfortunately, most of us are a little rusty—if not completely in the dark—when it comes to those prehistoric parenting tips. What valuable baby-care tricks could you learn if an experienced cave mother lived next door to you?

While we can't go back in time, we can get an idea of some calming techniques cave moms might have used by looking through a virtual "window" to the past, the study of primitive tribes living around the world today.

Please don't be fooled by the word *primitive*. Although it conjures up images of backward people, over the past eighty years research has shown that many so-called primitive peoples possess wisdom of the natural world about which we are ignorant. Some know the medicinal power of rare plants, some know how to find water in the desert—*and some even know how to prevent colic!*

Past Perfect: Lessons from the !Kung San

For hundreds if not thousands of years, the !Kung San (or African bushmen) have lived in isolation on the plains of the Kalahari Desert. Over the past forty years, however, the !Kung have graciously allowed scientists to observe their lives, including how they care for babies.

I've read reports of their newborn care with great interest because !Kung infants hardly ever cry. It's not that they never cry—it's that they never CRY! (And I know you understand that distinction.) While !Kung infants get upset as often as our babies do, their parents are so skilled at soothing them that the average fussy bout lasts only sixteen seconds, and more than ninety percent of their crying jags end in under a minute.

What's their secret? What ancient wisdom do the !Kung know that our culture has forgotten? I believe three facts account for much of this tribe's stunning success:

- !Kung mothers hold their babies almost twenty-four hours a day.
- !Kung mothers breast-feed their babies around the clock.
- !Kung parents usually respond to their babies' cries within ten seconds.

!Kung mothers carry their babies all day long in a leather sling and sleep next to them at night. This closeness makes it easy to soothe any fussiness the instant it starts.

In addition to holding and cuddling, the !Kung calm their babies by giving them quick little feedings on the breast—up to one hundred times a day! We in the West might think such snacking would spoil a baby, but that's not the case. Despite the lavish and immediate attention paid to their crying, !Kung children grow up to be happy, independent, and self-sufficient.

Now, don't worry. I'm not suggesting we adopt all the !Kung ways; they clearly don't fit our busy lives. However, I am suggesting that we study these highly successful parents to learn which of their solutions could be easily adopted by Western moms and dads.

I believe the biggest secret the !Kung know is that all their baby soothing methods share a common thread: They imitate the uterus and provide babies the comfort of the fourth trimester.

Compared to our infants, !Kung babies may be deprived of many material possessions, but compared to the !Kung, our babies are deprived of an important "maternal" possession—long hours of being in our arms. While !Kung mothers are with their infants almost nonstop, studies in the United States show that we leave our young babies alone for up to sixteen hours a day. I'm afraid that for many newborns, this abrupt transfer from cozy womb to empty room ends up making them terribly upset.

For the first few months of life, we need to treat our babies the way our ancient ancestors treated theirs thousands of years ago, with the reassuring rhythms of the fourth trimester. In other words, we should no longer mistake our newborns for little horses. Rather, we should treat them like little kangaroos! Kangaroos "know" their babies need a few more months of TLC before they're ready to get hoppin', so they welcome them into the pouch the moment they're born. Likewise, we need to offer our sweet newborns "pouches" of prolonged holding, rocking, shushing, and warmth. If you do this you'll be amazed. Once you master the skill of imitating the womb, you'll be able to do *exactly* what !Kung moms do: settle your baby's cries in minutes!

Science and the Fourth Trimester: Research Points the Way . . . Back

Imitating the womb to calm colic isn't the only ancient wisdom that has been ignored by our culture. Over the past fifty years, researchers have carefully proved the benefits of another prehistoric skill, breast-feeding, which was rescued from the brink.

Breast-Feeding Makes a Comeback

Within days of your baby's birth, your breast milk appears, as if by magic. It's exactly what the doctor, and your baby, ordered. This sweet, nutritious, easy-to-digest food gives your newborn an almost constant flow of nourishment, just like she had inside the womb.

Early in the 1900s, after millions of years of being developed to perfection, mother's milk was suddenly abandoned in many parts of the world. It was nudged aside by mass-produced artificial formula that was promoted as equally healthful and more hygienic than mother's milk. Many women were convinced that scientists knew better than nature. They fed their babies formula, mistakenly believing that the product of a chemist was better than the old-fashioned product of their own breasts.

Mothers asked their doctors for medicine to dry up their breast milk and to recommend their favorite commercial formula. By the 1950s, breast-feeding became so rare in America that the women who tried it were considered radical or eccentric.

Moms who still wanted to breast-feed often failed because they had no personal experience and little professional guidance. As unbelievable as it sounds, within two generations our culture almost lost this basic human ability that had sustained our species for millions of years! Fortunately, many committed women (and men) were appalled by this lack of support. Through their great efforts, groups like La Leche League were launched and specialists were trained to help new mothers rediscover this wonderful skill.

In recent years, public interest in breast-feeding has dramatically rebounded, spurred by an avalanche of research revealing the shortcomings of formula and the benefits of breast milk. Scientific studies show that breast milk helps build babies' brains, boosts their immunity, protects them against diabetes, and lowers a woman's risk of breast and ovarian cancer. Today, breast milk is so universally accepted as the preferred food for babies that even formula companies recommend women use their product only if they can't breast-feed.

I'm thankful we have excellent artificial formulas to feed babies who are unable to feed at their mother's breast. However, all medical groups agree, if you can do it, "breast is best" for feeding your baby.

7

Your Baby's *Off* Switch
for Crying: The Calming
Reflex and the 5 "S's"

Main Points:

- What reflexes are, and the many built-in behaviors and skills all babies are born with
- The Calming Reflex: Your baby's *Off* switch for crying
- The 5 "S's": How to turn on your baby's calming reflex
- Vigor: The essential tip for calming your little cave baby
- Three reasons your baby may take time to respond to the 5 "S's"

Most people who have taken care of a fussy infant wonder at some point: "Wouldn't it be great if babies came with a secret button to turn off their crying?"

Now don't laugh, it's not such a wild idea. Since babies wail as loud as car alarms, shouldn't there also be a way to turn their "alarm" off?

Well, the good news is, there is! I call this *Off* switch the calming reflex, and, as you will soon learn, it works almost as quickly as the car-alarm reset button on your key chain. But first, let's review what reflexes are and how they work.

Reflexes: Incredible Things Your Baby Knows How to Do Automatically

Reflexes are your body's way of reacting automatically, such as blinking before something hits you in the eye or shooting out your arms when you're knocked off balance. Like a good buddy, reflexes reassure the brain: "Don't even think about it. I'll handle everything."

All reflexes have the following characteristics:

- *They are reliable.* Every time the doctor hits your knee to test your reflex, your foot jumps out. It can be done five hundred times in a row and always works.
- *They are automatic.* Reflexes work even when you're asleep.
- *They require a very specific triggering action.* The knee reflex is automatic and reliable *only* when it's done in exactly the right way. It won't work if your knee is hit too softly or an inch too high or low.

Could you imagine having to teach your baby how to suck or poop? Thankfully you don't have to, because these and more than seventy other automatic reflexes are packed away in your newborn's compact brain.

Most of these reflexes help your baby during the first months after birth. The rest are either fetal reflexes (useful only during his life inside you), leftover reflexes (valuable to our ancestors millions of years ago, but now just passed from generation to generation, like our intestinal appendix), or mystery reflexes (whose purposes are unknown).

Here's a list of some common reflexes you'll probably see your baby performing:

1. **Keeping-safe reflexes:** These protective reflexes help prevent accidental injury. (Most are so important they continue to work in adults.)

    Crying—Crying, the "mother" of all baby safety reflexes, can be triggered by any sudden distress and is extraordinarily effective at getting your attention.

    Sneezing—Your newborn's sneeze usually isn't a sign of a cold; rather, it's a response to irritating dust and mucous his body is trying to rid from the nose.

2. **Getting-a-meal reflexes:** Even though no food ever passed your fetus's lips, from the moment of birth he was ready to receive and enjoy your milk.

   Rooting—When you touch your baby's cheek or lips, his face will turn toward the touch and his mouth will open and then shut. This reflex helps your baby locate and grasp your nipple, even in the dark. But don't worry if you stroke your baby's cheek and he doesn't respond. This is a smart reflex: It's not there until he's hungry. That's why the rooting reflex is a great way for you to tell if your baby is crying because he wants to eat. If you touch his mouth and he doesn't root, he probably is not crying for food.

   Sucking—Your baby practiced this complex reflex even before birth. Many parents have ultrasound photos of their little cuties sucking their thumbs, weeks before delivery.

3. **Fetal and leftover reflexes:** These reflexes either help our fetuses before they are born or were useful only to our distant animal ancestors.

   Step—Holding your baby upright, let the sole of one foot press onto a flat surface. In a few seconds, that leg will straighten and the other will bend. This reflex helps babies move around a little during the last months of pregnancy, thus helping to prevent pressure sores and getting the fetus into position for delivery.

   Grasping—If you press your finger into the base of your baby's toes or fingers, he will grab on tightly, even when he's sleeping. This reflex is critically important for newborn apes! It helps them cling to their mother's fur while she's moving through the jungle. (Be careful. It works on dads with hairy chests too!)

   The Moro reflex—This extremely important leftover reflex protected our ancient relatives carrying their babies through the trees. It's the "I'm falling" reflex activated the second your baby gets startled (by a jolt, loud noise, or a dream).

The Moro reflex makes your baby's arms shoot out and around, as if he's trying to grab hold of you. This venerable response probably kept countless baby monkeys from falling out of their mother's arms. (Adults who fall asleep in a chair and whose heads suddenly drop back may also experience this reflex.)

As your baby matures his newborn reflexes will gradually get packed away and forgotten, like tattered old teddy bears. However, at the beginning of life, these invaluable responses are some of the best baby gifts a mother could ever hope for.

There is one more built-in, newborn response that parents in my practice think is the most wonderful reflex of all: the calming reflex.

The Calming Reflex: Nature's Automatic Shut-off Switch for a Baby's Crying

I believe once our ancestors began living in villages and cities, they forgot that, since the Stone Age, babies were almost constantly jiggled and wiggled as their moms walked up and down the mountains. Sadly, many babies deprived of these comforting movements began to startle and cry at every disturbance. I'm afraid that in order to explain that crying, modern parents began to mistakenly think that babies were so fragile they could only tolerate *quiet* sounds and *gentle* motion.

This new attitude undermined their confidence in triggering the calming reflex, because as you are about to learn it *can be activated only by vigorous actions*—especially in very fussy babies. Gradually, this ancient calming tool was forgotten.

As you will recall, reflexes require specific triggers. The triggers for your baby's calming reflex are the sensations he felt in the uterus. It is my belief that this precious reflex came about *not* as a way of soothing upset infants but rather as a way of soothing upset *fetuses!*

This vital response saved countless numbers of mothers and unborn babies by keeping fetuses entranced so that they wouldn't thrash around and kink their umbilical cords or get wedged into a position that made delivery impossible. How brilliant of Mother Nature to design this critical, lifesaving response to be automatically activated by the sensations fetuses are naturally surrounded by.

Not only are the rhythms of the uterus profoundly calming to babies, they're also comforting to adults. Think of how you're affected by hearing the ocean, rocking in a hammock, and cuddling in a warm bed. However, while we merely enjoy these sensations, our babies *need* them—and fussy babies need them desperately.

So if you've tried feeding, burping, and diaper changing and your baby is still yelling himself hoarse, it's time to try soothing him this "old" new way.

The Top Ten Ways You Can Imitate the Uterus
1. Holding
2. Dancing
3. Rocking
4. Wrapping
5. White noise or singing
6. Car rides
7. Walks outside
8. Feeding
9. Pacifiers
10. Swings

This list includes just a few of the dozens of ways clever parents have invented to calm their infants. But what you know now is something that no mom or dad throughout history realized, that these tricks relax newborns by switching on the ancient reflex that kept them in a protective, lifesaving trance when they were fetuses.

The most popular baby calming methods can be grouped into five basic categories: *S*waddling, *S*ide/*S*tomach position, *S*hhhhing sounds, *S*winging, and *S*ucking. I call these the 5 "*S*'s"; they are the qualities of the uterus that help activate the calming reflex. However, like all reflexes, even these great techniques only switch on the calming reflex if they're done correctly.

The 5 "S's": Five Steps to Activate Your Baby's Calming Reflex

There should be a law requiring that the 5 S's be stamped onto every infant ID band in the hospital. For our frantic baby, they worked in seconds!

Nancy, mother of two-month-old Natalie

In the early 1900s, baby experts taught new parents to do the following when their infant cried: 1) feed them, 2) burp them, 3) change the diaper, and 4) check for an open safety pin. Authorities proclaimed that when these didn't work, babies had colic and there was nothing else a parent could do. Today, most doctors give similar recommendations.

But for parents of a frantic newborn, the nothing-you-can-do-but-wait advice is intolerable. *Few impulses are as powerful as a mother's desire to calm her crying baby. This instinct is as ancient as parenting itself.* Yet, the frustrating reality is while parents instinctively *want* to calm their babies, knowing *how* to do it is anything but instinctive. It's a skill. Luckily, it's a skill that is fairly easy to learn.

Peter, a high-powered attorney, is the father of Emily and Ted. When his kids were born, Pete and his wife, Judy, had very little baby experience. So, after the birth of each child, I sat down and reviewed the concepts of the fourth trimester and the 5 "S's." Several years later, Peter wrote:

> *It has been more than ten years since I was taught the 5 "S's" as a way to quiet my crying babies. Even today, I like to share them with clients who bring their infants into my office. It's great fun to see the amazed looks when a large, lumbering male like me happily collects their distraught baby and calms the delicate creature in seconds—with a vigorous swaddle, side, swing, shush, and suck. These simple techniques give any parent a true sense of accomplishment!*

The 5 "S's" are the only tools you'll need to soothe your fussy infant.

1. *Swaddling: A Feeling of Pure "Wrap"ture*
   Tight swaddling is the cornerstone of calming, the essential first

step in soothing your fussy baby and keeping him soothed. That's why traditional cultures from Turkey to Tulsa (the Native Americans, that is) use swaddling to keep their babies happy.

Wrapping makes your baby feel magically returned to the womb and satisfies his longing for the continuous touching and tight fit of your uterus. This "S" doesn't actually trigger the calming reflex but it keeps your baby from flailing and helps him pay attention to the other "S's," which *do* activate the reflex.

Many irritable babies resist wrapping. However, it's a mistake to think this resistance means that your baby needs his hands free. Nothing could be further from the truth! Fussy young babies lack the coordination to control their arm flailing, so if their arms are unwrapped they may make themselves even more upset.

Here's how one grandmother learned the ancient tradition of swaddling and passed it along:

> My youngest sister was born when I was nearly ten years old. I remember my mother teaching me how to swaddle her snugly in a warm blanket. That year, mothering and bundling began for me, and they have continued, without interruption, into my sixtieth year!
>
> When my grandchildren began to arrive, I faithfully taught my kids to wrap their babies very tightly in receiving blankets. My passion for swaddling often led to some good-humored discussion: "Watch out for Bubby and her bundling!" Yet somehow it always seemed to help.
>
>
>
> The babies in our family, although beautiful, talented, and brilliant, share a fussy, high-maintenance profile, if only for the first two or three months. But swaddling has always been a big help. I can't tell you how many times I've seen it change their faces from a scowl to serenity.
>
> Barbara, "Bubby" of Olivia, Thomas,
> Michael, Molly, and Sawyer

2. Side/Stomach: Your Baby's Feel-Good Position

Swaddling stops your baby's uncontrolled arm and leg acrobatics that can lead into frenzied crying. In a similar fashion, the side/

stomach position stops an equally upsetting but invisible type of stimulation—the panicky feeling of falling!

Being dropped was such a serious threat to our ancient relatives that their babies developed a special alarm—the Moro reflex—that went off the moment they felt they were falling out of their mother's arms.

Most babies are content to be on their backs if they're in a good mood. However, when your baby is crying, putting him on his back may make him feel like he's in a free fall. That in turn can set off his Moro, which starts him thrashing and screaming.

The side or stomach positions soothe your screaming newborn by instantly shutting off the Moro. That's why these are the perfect feel-good positions for fussy babies. When it comes to putting your small one to sleep, however, the back is the safest position for all babies. Unless your doctor instructs you otherwise, *no baby should ever be put to sleep on his stomach.* (More on this in Chapter 9.)

3. Shhhhing: Your Baby's Favorite Soothing Sound

Believe it or not, a loud, harsh shushing sound is music to your baby's ears. Shhhhing comforts him by mimicking the whooshing noise of blood flowing through your arteries. This rough humming surrounded your baby every moment during his nine months inside you. That's why it is an essential part of the fourth trimester.

Many new parents mistakenly believe their babies prefer the gentle tinkling sounds of a brook or the distant hush of the wind. It seems counterintuitive that our tender infants would like such a loud noise; certainly we wouldn't. Yet babies love it! That's why many books recommend the use of roaring appliances to settle screaming infants.

I have never met a cranky baby who got overstimulated by the racket from these devices. On the contrary, the louder babies cry, the louder the shhhhing has to be in order to calm them.

 In a rush to get out of the house, Marjan put off feeding her hungry baby for a few minutes while she went into the bathroom and finished getting ready to leave. Two-week-old Bebe didn't care for this plan, and she wailed impatiently for food. However, after a few minutes Bebe suddenly quieted. Marjan panicked, was her tiny baby okay? When Marjan opened the

bathroom door, she was relieved to see that her daughter was fine. Then she realized that Bebe had stilled the very instant she turned on the hair dryer.

Marjan shared this exciting discovery with her parents, but they were not supportive. They warned her it was dangerous to use the hair dryer to calm an infant: "It's so loud it will make her go crazy!"

Despite their concerns, Marjan used her new "trick" with 100% success whenever her baby was crying (but only when her family was not around).

4. Swinging: Rock-a-Bye Baby

Lying on a soft, motionless bed may appeal to you, but to your baby—fresh out of the womb—it's disorienting and unnatural. Newborns are like sailors who come to dry land after nine months at sea; the sudden stillness can drive them bananas. That's why rhythmic, monotonous, jiggly movement—what I call swinging—is one of the most common methods parents have always used to calm their babies. Swinging usually must be vigorous at first to get your baby to stop screaming, and then it can be reduced to a gentler motion to *keep* him calm.

In ancient times and in today's traditional cultures, babies are constantly jiggled and bounced. Many third-world parents use cradles or hammocks to keep their babies content, and they "wear" their infants in slings to give the soothing feeling of motion with every step and breath. Even in our culture, many tired parents use bouncy seats, car rides, and walks around the block to try to help their unhappy babies find some peace.

> *Mark, Emma, and their two kids were visiting Los Angeles from London. While I was examining four-year-old Rose, little Mary, their two-month-old baby, startled out of a deep sleep and immediately began to wail. Without missing a beat, Mark scooped her up so she sat securely in his arms. He began swinging her from side to side as if she were a circus performer and he the trapeze. Within twenty seconds, her eyes glazed over, her body melted into his chest, and we were able to finish our conversation as if Mary had never cried at all.*

5. Sucking: The Icing on the Cake

Once your cranky baby starts to settle down from the swaddle, side position, shushing, and swinging, he's ready for the fifth glorious "S": sucking. Sucking is the icing on the cake of calming. It takes a baby who is beginning to quiet and lulls him into a deep and profound state of tranquillity.

Obviously, it's hard for your baby to scream with a pacifier in his mouth, but that's not why sucking is so soothing. Sucking has its effect deep within your baby's nervous system. It triggers his calming reflex and releases natural chemicals within his brain, which leads in minutes to a rich and satisfying level of relaxation.

Some parents offer their infants bottles and pacifiers to suck on, but the all-time number-one sucking toy in the world is a mother's nipple. As was previously mentioned, mothers in some cultures help keep their babies calm by offering them the breast up to one hundred times a day.

> *Hannah thought her first son, Felix, was almost addicted to the pacifier. "He insisted on using it for years. So when my second child was born, I vowed to try not to use it. But once again it became an invaluable calming tool. Harmon was so miserable without it, and so content with it, that I couldn't bring myself to deny him that simple pleasure."*

In summary, the first two "S's"—swaddling and side/stomach—start the calming process by muffling your baby's flailing movements, shutting off the Moro reflex and getting him to pay attention to what you're doing as you begin to activate the calming reflex. The third and fourth "S's"—shhhhing and swinging—break into the crying cycle by powerfully triggering the calming reflex and soothing your baby's nervous system. The fifth "S"—sucking—keeps the calming reflex turned on and allows your baby to guide himself to a profound level of relaxation.

The 5 "S's" are fantastic tools, but as with any tools, your skill in using them will increase with practice. Since the calming reflex works only when triggered in precisely the right way, you'll find that mastering these ancient techniques is one of the first important tasks of parenthood.

Interestingly, not only do parents get better with practice, so do babies. Many parents notice that after a few weeks of swaddling their babies straighten their arms and begin to calm the instant they're placed on the blanket. It's as if they're saying, "Hey, I remember this! I really like it!"

You might read about the 5 "S's" and think, "So what's new? Those soothing techniques have been known for centuries." And you would be partly right. The methods themselves are not new; however, what *is* new are two essential concepts for making the old techniques really effective—vigor and combining. In Chapter 13, you will learn how to perfectly combine the 5 "S's" in the "Cuddle" Cure, but now I would like to share with you one of the least understood and most important elements of calming a screaming baby . . . the need for *vigor.*

Vigor: The Essential Tip for Calming Your Frantic Little Cave Baby

Many of our ideas about what babies need are based on a misunderstanding about their fragility. Of course, babies *are* quite fragile in many ways. They choke very easily and have weak immune systems. For this reason, being told to do *anything* vigorously may seem as counterintuitive to you as being told that adding a slimy, raw egg to a cake will make it delicious . . . yet, it's every bit as true!

That's because, in many other ways, your newborn is a tough little "cave" baby. He can snooze at the noisiest parties and scream at the top of his lungs much longer than you or I could. Parents are often amazed at how forcefully nurses handle babies when they bathe and burp them. Even breast-feeding may feel pushy when you first learn how. Yet experienced moms know they *must* be assertive when latching their baby on the breast or else they'll end up with sore nipples and a frustrated baby.

One mom in my practice, a psychologist, realized how impossible it was to gently guide her baby from screaming to serenity:

> *"Because of my professional training, I'm very good at remaining calm and reasonable even in the face of frantic and angry outbursts. I expected that this mild demeanor would also help me guide my one-month-old, Helene, out of her primitive*

*screaming fits. What a joke! This little brawler needed me to take
control like police subduing a rowdy mob."*

Parents often mistakenly believe that their job is to lead their unhappy baby into calmness by responding to his wails with soft whispers and gentle rocking. While that's a very reasonable, civilized approach, it rarely calms an infant in the middle of a meltdown.

> *Jessica tried to calm her frantic six-week-old by wrapping
> him up, turning on a tape recording of the vacuum, and putting
> him in the swing. But it backfired. Like a little Houdini,
> Jonathan freed himself from the swaddle in minutes and wailed
> longer and louder than ever. I suggested that Jessica try tighten-
> ing the wrapping and turning on the real vacuum, not a tape.
> Jonathan's screaming bouts shortened from hours to minutes!*

Most first-time parents don't feel instantly comfortable with their fussy baby's need for vigor. Let's face it, as a parent you're given so much contradictory advice. One minute, you're warned to handle your baby gently and the next you're told to deposit your shrieking child into a buzzing bouncy seat beside a roaring vacuum cleaner. Yet experienced baby "wranglers" know the more frantically a baby is crying the tighter his swaddling, the louder the shushing, and the more jiggly the swinging must be, *or else they simply won't work.*

The fastest way to succeed in stopping your baby's cycle of crying is to *meet his level of intensity.* Only after your screaming baby pauses for a few moments can you gradually slow your motion, soften your shushing, and guide him down from his frenzy to a soft landing.

The best colic-calmers say that soothing an infant is like dancing with him—*but they always let the baby lead!* These talented people pay close attention to the vigor of their infant's crying and mirror it with the vigor of their 5 "S's." If crying is frantic, the rocking and shushing are as spirited as a jitterbug. As cries turn into sobs, the response shifts to the fluid pace of a waltz. And once the baby slips into serenity, their actions slide into the gentle to-and-fro of a slow dance. Of course, any return to screaming is immediately met with renewed vigor and a bouncy tempo.

Three Reasons Your Baby May Have a Delayed Response to the 5 "S's"

You'll be able to soothe your baby quickly once you become skillful at using the 5 "S's." However, the first few times you use these methods you may notice something peculiar: Your baby may ignore you or even cry louder.

This is normal, so please don't worry. His brain may be having a little trouble getting your new message:

Augie was dozing angelically when I arrived at his hospital room to examine him. However, the moment I unwrapped him and the cool air touched his skin, he began to howl. I quieted him with some intense rocking and shushing, but as soon as I stopped and began probing his soft, marshmallow belly, he began to cry again. Were my hands too cold? Did I hurt him? No, he just hadn't fully recovered from his prior upset, and my touch rekindled his protests.

Augie bellowed and flailed, then suddenly he became stone silent. I looked down to see him staring out into space as if he were trying to ignore me. The calm was only momentary, however. In seconds, his frantic cry cycled through him once more.

I snared his hands and held them to his chest. Then I leaned over his struggling body, rocked him, and simultaneously made a harsh shhhh sound in his ear. Within seconds, Augie was again completely at ease.

Five seconds later, however, his cry surfaced one last time, like an exhausted boxer trying to get up off the mat. After just a few more seconds of vigorous shushing and rocking, Augie finally gave in and his little body relaxed for good.

As you can see, even if your "S's" are perfect, you may have to patiently wait a few minutes for your crying baby to fully respond. Three particular traits of an infant's nervous system can fool you into thinking the 5 "S's" aren't working:

1. Baby brains have a hard time shifting gears.

If *you* think your baby is screaming loudly, you should hear what's going on inside *his* head! Chaos so distracts and overloads your newborn's immature brain that he has a difficult time escaping his frenzy to pay attention to you. It's like when your good buddy is in a fight. You try to pull him out of it, but he struggles against you to keep slugging away. It's not until later, when he finally calms down, that he admits, "Thanks, you're a real friend. I just couldn't stop myself."

So expect your baby to resist the 5 "S's" until he calms down enough to realize that your shushing and jiggling are *exactly* what he needs from you.

2. Baby brains are very s-l-o-w.

When your baby is four months old, his eyes will quickly track you as you move around the room, but for now his brain is a little too undeveloped to do that. During these early months of life, it takes a couple of seconds for messages from his eyes ("I just saw mom move!") to travel to the part of his brain that gives out the commands ("Okay, so follow her!").

This dragged-out response time is even more pronounced in colicky babies. All the tumult going on inside their heads overwhelms their brains, making their processing time even slower.

3. Baby brains get into cycles of crying.

When your crying newborn does start responding to the 5 "S's," he may only settle for a minute before he bursts into crying all over again. That's because your baby's distress from crying is still cycling through his nervous system like a strong aftershock following his just ended "baby earthquake."

Your baby may need you to continue the 5 "S's" for five to ten minutes—or more—after he calms down. That's how long it may take for his upset to finish cycling through him and for the calming reflex to finally guide him into sleep.

These cycles can be confusing. They make it seem as if your baby has experienced a jolt of pain, but that's rarely the case. Instead, what's occurring is like what happens when you catch a fish. The fish struggles, gives up for a few moments, then suddenly fights again. With persistence you'll find that the 5 "S's" help your baby's cycles of crying gradually diminish and melt into a blissful peace.

> *Calming baby Frances reminded Suzanne of her job as a teacher. "It's like quieting a classroom of yelling five-year-olds. At first you raise your voice a little to get their attention. Then, as they begin to settle, kids who are still revved up from before have occasional outbursts. Gradually, the excitement cycles down and all the kids become still and focused."*

The next six chapters will teach you exactly how to switch your baby's crying reflex off and his calming reflex on. Once you have mastered these skills, crying will no longer be a cause of frustration. In fact, as odd as it sounds, you may even start appreciating your baby's wails as a great opportunity for you to help him feel loved—and to help you feel like a terrific parent.

8

The 1st "S": Swaddling—A Feeling of Pure "Wrap"ture

Main Points:

- Swaddling is the cornerstone of calming. It gives nurturing touch, stops flailing, and focuses your baby's attention
- Swaddling by itself may not halt crying, rather it prepares babies for the other "S's" that *do* switch crying off
- The reasons our ancestors stopped swaddling centuries ago
- Six unnecessary concerns today's parents have about swaddling
- The perfect baby swaddle: The DUDU wrap

As my office was about to close one evening, Alex's mother called, in tears. Betsy said Alex had been having bouts of pain for more than two weeks. Here's how Betsy described it.

> *"When Alex was six weeks old, she began having terrible gas pains. At night she would wake up screaming almost hourly. I watched my diet, in case something I was eating was giving her gas. But that didn't alleviate her crying at all."*

Betsy asked me for some anti-gas medicine to help Alex with what she assumed were stomach cramps. She was surprised when I focused on how to calm her rather than curing the gas. I taught Betsy about the calming reflex and showed her how to swaddle, shhhh, and swing Alex to help her fall asleep. But, Betsy remained skeptical.

> "I didn't use Dr. Karp's technique the first night. Swaddling Alex tight didn't feel natural. I was afraid she would be uncomfortable or have difficulty breathing. And I still believed the main issue was gas. That night Alex's 'pain' seemed severe, and I decided I would follow Dr. Karp's advice in the morning.
>
> "The next day I swaddled Alex from morning till night, and surprisingly she seemed much more comfortable. At bedtime, even before I had finished wrapping her, Alex fell asleep—and she slept for seven hours. I could hear her stomach rumbling and knew that she was still having gas, but it was no longer waking her up.
>
> "Tight bundling helped Alex become a much better sleeper. By the time she was four months old she slept well without needing any swaddling."

Swaddling: The Cornerstone of Calming

As Betsy discovered with Alex, soothing an irritable infant is one hundred times easier when her hands are snuggled straight at her sides. Why does this work so well? Here are three ways swaddling benefits fussy babies:

1. The Sweet Touch of Swaddling

Skin is the body's largest organ, and touch is the most calming of our senses. Swaddling envelops your baby's body with a continuous soft caress.

Every mother knows how delicious the touch of her baby's soft skin feels against her own, but for your baby, touch is more than a nice sensation—it's as lifesaving as milk! Babies given milk but never held or touched often wither and die. Of course, swaddling isn't as rich an experience for your baby as being cuddled, but it's a good substitute for those times she is not in your arms.

2. Swaddling Keeps Your Baby from Spiraling Out of Control

Not only does swaddling feel cozy, it also keeps your baby from whacking herself and inadvertently getting more upset. (You may have noticed how much calmer your baby is when she is "wrapped" in your arms.) Before birth, your uterus kept your baby's arms from spinning like a windmill. After her "eviction," this restriction disappears. Without the womb walls to prevent flailing, your baby's small upsets can quickly switch on her Moro reflex (the falling reflex) and start her thrashing and crying.

3. Wrapping Helps Your Baby Pay Attention to What You're Doing to Calm Her

When your baby is crying, she experiences a sensation similar to ten radios playing in her head—at the same time. Each jerk and startle shoots another alarm message to her brain, and together those signals make such a racket that your crying infant may hardly notice you're there!

Your little screamer desperately needs you to tell her, "That's it, I'm taking over now." And that's exactly what swaddling does. By

The Great Surprise About Swaddling

The biggest myth parents have about wrapping is that it's supposed to quiet their fussy baby. *Wrong!* Swaddling by itself doesn't turn on the calming reflex.

This point often confuses inexperienced parents. In fact, many new moms and dads lose patience with bundling because initially it makes their babies scream louder not less!

So why is swaddling the first step of calming? Because it prepares your baby for the soothing steps you will do next that *will* trigger her calming reflex.

Think of it this way: What's the first thing a mother does when her hungry toddler clamors for food? Set the table to serve the meal. Yet doing that often makes her scream louder, as if she's yelling, "Hey, just dump the spaghetti on the table!" Of course, *you* know she needs utensils and a plate before she can enjoy her delicious meal, so you buzz through your preparations despite her protests.

In essence, swaddling "sets the table" for the feast of calming you're about to serve. It's the critical step of preparation before the actual shhhhing and jiggling begin. So don't worry if your baby struggles more right after you've wrapped her snugly. Once you begin "feeding" her the other 4 "S's," you'll satisfy her needs completely.

restraining your baby's movements, you turn off most of the distracting "radio stations" so she can tune in and focus on all the wonderful things you're doing to soothe her. Wrapping also prevents new twitches from igniting the crying all over again.

Once upon a Time: How Parents Have Used Swaddling in Other Times and Cultures

I banish from you all tears, birthmarks, flaws, and the troubles of bed-wetting. Love your paternal and maternal uncles. Do not betray your origins. Be intelligent, learned, and discreet. Respect yourself, be brave.

Ritual instructions spoken when
swaddling a baby by the Berber people of Algeria,
Béatrice Fontanel and Claire d'Harcourt, *Babies Celebrated*

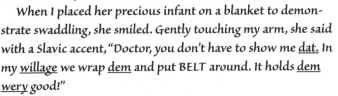

After Elena emigrated from Russia to Los Angeles, she gave birth to a healthy baby girl named Olga. As I examined Olga, I described to her proud mother all of her daughter's wonderful abilities. Elena concentrated intensely as I spoke, struggling to understand my words.

When I placed her precious infant on a blanket to demonstrate swaddling, she smiled. Gently touching my arm, she said with a Slavic accent, "Doctor, you don't have to show me <u>dat</u>. In my <u>willage</u> we wrap <u>dem</u> and put BELT around. It holds <u>dem</u> <u>wery</u> good!"

For tens of thousands of years, mothers living in cool climates have swaddled their babies. While those in very hot climates hardly ever swaddle, they do hold their infants in their arms or in slings almost twenty-four hours a day. Parents all over the globe wrap their infants because:

- *It's safe*—Babies are less likely to suddenly wiggle out of their parent's arms.
- *It's easy*—Babies can be strapped on a parent's back or slung on their hips.

Great Swaddling Moments in History

- History has recorded that Alexander the Great, Julius Caesar, and Jesus were all swaddled as babies.
- In Tibet, babies have always been swaddled tightly in blankets. Traditionally, the wrapping was secured with rope and the baby was tied to the side of a yak to be carried as the family hiked through the valleys.
- On the high plains of Algeria, babies were swaddled to protect them from drafts and evil spirits.
- During the Middle Ages, European parents kept their babies immobilized in a tight, bulky swaddle for the first four to nine months.
- The American Academy of Pediatrics insignia features a swaddled fifteenth-century Italian baby.
- Many Native American tribes carried their papoose—young baby—tightly packaged and slung onto their backs. (The 2000 U.S. one-dollar coin displays an image of the Native American guide Sacajawea with her tiny baby snugly bundled on her back.)

- *It's calming*—Babies get less upset because they can't flail about.

These parents envelop their babies in blankets and then usually secure the wrapping with strings and belts. And now, our nation has also rediscovered that babies like being wrapped as snug as a bug in a rug. In most U.S. hospitals, new moms are taught how to swaddle their babies, and I've even seen some nurses use masking tape to keep the blanket from unraveling.

Swaddling Gets Unraveled: How Our Ancestors Did the *Wrong* Thing for All the *Right* Reasons

Even in the Middle Ages, the top fashion ideas originated in Paris. However, about three hundred years ago, these trendsetters goofed when they declared, "*Le swaddling* is passé."

Before the 1700s, all Europeans wrapped their babies. Swaddling made babies easy to carry and kept them warm and quiet. Parents also believed wrapping prevented their infants from accidentally plucking out their own eyes or dislocating their arms.

Then two revolutionary trends became popular: science and democracy. As wonderful as these movements were, they led to two unfortunate misunderstandings that contributed to the abandonment of swaddling:

Science makes mistake #1: In the 1700s scientists proved that unwrapped infants *never* plucked out their eyes or dislocated their arms. From these observations they wrongly assumed that swaddling was a waste of time.

Democracy makes mistake #2: In the years leading up to the Declaration of Independence, our founding fathers (and mothers) wanted their children to live in freedom, but this attitude led them to reject swaddling as a form of "baby prison."

Within one hundred years, the combined pressures of science and democracy convinced most parents in the Western world to stop swaddling. While these great thinkers were right that unwrapped babies didn't hurt themselves and that adults would feel enslaved by such tight bindings, they were absolutely wrong to recommend parents stop bundling their infants. They didn't realize that swaddling had continued throughout the centuries because it truly helped babies stay happier. As parents stopped wrapping their newborns, the unexpected happened: The number of babies suffering from uncontrollable crying dramatically *increased!*

In their eagerness to stop this tidal wave of colic, scientists made yet another colossal mistake. They concluded that babies were crying because of pain, and encouraged parents to give their shrieking infants the two most effective anesthetics of the time—gin and opium. Of course, as soon as the serious side effects of those colic treatments were realized, they fell out of favor.

A Parent's Hesitations—Six Unnecessary Wrapping Worries

In the U.S. today, many parents and grandparents still hesitate to swaddle their babies. They worry that tight wrapping may deprive their babies of some unwritten constitutional right. But I'm afraid they are confusing the right to *bear* arms with the right to *flail* arms.

Through the years, I have asked many parents to tell me their secret prejudices against swaddling. Here are their six most common concerns:

1. *Swaddling seems primitive and old-fashioned.*

Well, it is. But what's wrong with primitive and old-fashioned? Eating and sex are both primitive and old-fashioned, and who wants to abandon them? Besides, swaddling may be a prehistoric practice, but it really works.

2. *Babies might be uncomfortable with their arms tightly down at their sides.*

Many new parents think their crying babies want their arms up. If that was why these infants cried, calming them would be a snap: Just never wrap them! Of course, as you've probably noticed, releasing your baby's arms usually only makes her scream even more.

It is true that your baby's arms have tightened into the bent-arm position by the end of your pregnancy. And, as a result, if you place them at her sides, they tend to *boing* right back up, like curly hair pulled straight then released. However, the arms-down position is not at all uncomfortable, which is why babies sleep extra-long when they're bundled that way.

3. Wrapping may make a baby feel trapped.

Personally, I would hate to be swaddled. Without revealing too much about my married life, let me say that the first thing my wife and I do when we get into bed is untuck the blanket and give our feet some breathing room.

Of course, most of us would hate living in a womb. However, it's a mistake to think our babies want the same things we do. She's not struggling against the wrapping because she hates it. She looks like she wants her hands free, but the opposite is true. Newborns love being confined, and when they're frantic and out of control they need your help to restrain their frantic arms and legs.

4. Babies will get spoiled or dependent on swaddling.

Fortunately, this worry is totally unfounded. Holding your baby twelve hours a day is not an overindulgence; it's a fifty percent cutback from what she got in your womb! Once your baby is four months old she'll be able to push up, roll over, and grab, and she no longer will need to be wrapped. Until then, swaddling can be a great comfort.

5. Wrapping frustrates an infant's attempts to suck her fingers.

It was easy for your baby to suck her fingers before she was born: The walls of your uterus kept her hands right next to her face. After birth, however, it's much harder for her to get her fingers in that position. Even though she tries, they often jerk away as if yanked on by some practical joker. (Pacifiers were invented exactly because babies have such a hard time keeping their hands in their mouths.)

Please, don't misunderstand me, it's fine to let your infant have her hands out so she can suck on her fingers—*as long as she's happy.* Unfortunately, most babies aren't able to keep their hands there, especially when upset. So rather than calming a baby, loose hands usually fly by their owner's mouth, frustrating her and increasing her screams!

It will take three to four months for your baby to coordinate her lips, tongue, shoulder, and arm—all at the same time—to keep her fingers in her mouth. However, once your baby is able to manage all that, swaddling becomes unnecessary (although it may still help her sleep longer).

6. Tight bundling might interfere with a baby's ability to learn about the world.

Of course, your baby does need her hands unwrapped sometimes so she can get some practice using them. However, when she's crying your job isn't teaching, it's calming. In fact, even when your infant is calm, bundling may actually *help* her learn about the world, because she can pay attention better when her arms aren't constantly in motion.

It's Time for Swaddling to Make a Comeback

For centuries, parents have been hesitant about swaddling their babies. Critics have claimed swaddling was just a fad—and some continue to do so:

> About ten years ago, I visited a nursery for newborns in northern Italy. I shared with the nursery director the concept of the missing fourth trimester and my belief that the time had come for a worldwide "renaissance of wrapping."
>
> The director listened politely, but his face wore an amazed and amused expression. After I finished my impassioned speech, he patted my shoulder in a grandfatherly way and said discreetly, "We haven't done that in Italy for generations. We believe that babies must have their hands free to encourage their muscle development."
>
> At that moment, his secretary summoned him to take a phone call. No sooner had he left the room than a nurse shyly came up to me and whispered, "You know, Il Directore likes to keep the babies unwrapped, but as soon as he leaves for the day, we always bundle them all back up again!" She winked at me, adding, "They really are happier that way."

Y ou probably already know that the number-one way to calm your fussy baby is to pick her up and hold her tightly in your arms. That's exactly what swaddling does, except it has the extra benefit of giving you a few minutes to cook a meal or go to the bathroom!

Swaddling is easy to do, but it does require precise technique and some practice. Many books recommend wrapping, but they rarely teach how to do it, which is problematic because incorrect swaddling can make your baby's crying worse.

Here's everything you need to know to become the happiest (and best) swaddler on the block. Don't worry if it feels weird at first; after five to ten tries swaddling will become as automatic for you as changing a diaper.

There are as many ways to swaddle babies as there are to fold napkins for a dinner party. But one method that a wonderful midwife taught me many years ago is clearly the best. I call it the DUDU wrap (pronounced "doo doo," standing for Down-Up-Down-Up).

Getting Started

You'll need a large *square* blanket. These are easier to use than rectangular blankets because their symmetry allows for an even, balanced wrap. Blanket fabric is your choice. Some like flannel, while others prefer stretchy, waffle-type fabrics. (You may find it's easiest to learn to wrap if you first practice it on a doll or when your baby is calm.)

1) Place the blanket on your bed and position it like a diamond, with a point at the top.

2) Fold the top corner down so the top point touches the center of the blanket.

3) Place your baby on the blanket so her neck lies on the top edge.

4) Hold your baby's right arm down straight at her side. If she resists, be patient. The arm will straighten after a moment or two of gentle pressure.

You now have your baby in the starting position for the DUDU wrap. An easy way to remember what to do next is to sing this little song as you do it:

DOWN . . . tuck . . . snug
UP . . . tuck . . . snug
DOWN . . . a smidge . . . hold
UP . . . across . . . snug

1) DOWN   Just as swaddling is the cornerstone of calming, this first DOWN is the cornerstone of swaddling. This must be done well or the wrap will unravel.

As you hold your baby's right arm straight against her side, grab the blanket three to four inches from her right shoulder and pull it *very* tightly down and across her body. (It should look like half of a V-neck sweater.)

Tuck—*Keeping the blanket taut, finish pulling it all the way down and **tuck** it under her left buttock and lower back. This anchors the wrap.*

Snug—*Hold the blanket against her left hip (with your left hand), grab the blanket right next to her left shoulder and tug it very, very snug. This will remove any slack around your baby's right arm and stretch the fabric tight.*

After this first "DOWN . . . tuck . . . snug," her right arm should be held so securely against her side that she can't bend it up, even if you let go of the blanket. (More on the critical importance of straight arms on page 118.)

Please don't be surprised or lose confidence if your baby suddenly cries louder when you pull the blanket tight. You're not hurting her! Her cry means she's still out of control and unaware that she's just seconds away from happiness.

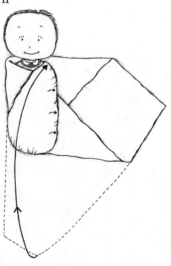

2) UP   Now straighten her left arm against her side and bring the bottom corner straight up to cover her arm. The bottom blanket corner should reach just over her left shoulder. It's okay if her legs are bent (that's how they were in the womb), but be sure her arms are straight. If her arms are bent, she'll wiggle out of the wrap as fast as you can say, "Oops, she did it again!" And she'll cry even more.

Tuck—*Hold her covered left arm against her body, and tuck the blanket edge under it.*

Snug—*While your left hand holds her left arm down, use your right hand to grab the blanket three inches from her left shoulder and snug it (stretch it as much as possible). This again removes any slack from around her arms.*

3) **DOWN**   Still holding the blanket very taut, three inches from her left shoulder, pull the blanket *down* a smidge.

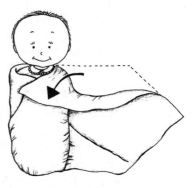

A smidge—*This DOWN should bring only a tiny bit of fabric over her shoulder to her upper chest, like the second half of the V-neck sweater. (Don't bring this fold all the way down to your baby's feet. Remember, it's just a smidge.)*

Hold—*Hold that tiny smidge of blanket against her breastbone with your left hand, like you are holding down a ribbon while making a bow.*

4) **UP**   Keeping that smidge in place, grab the last free blanket corner with your right hand and pull it straight out to your right. This will remove every last bit of stretch and slack from the wrap. Then, without releasing the tension, lift that corner in one smooth motion, up and across her body.

Across—*Bring it **tightly** across her waist and then all around her body like a belt. The belt should go right over her forearms, holding them down against her sides.*

Snug—*Finish the DUDU wrap by snugging the belt **tightly** to remove any slack. If the wrap is tight (and your blanket is big enough), the end of the belt will reach around her body and back to the front, where you can tuck it into the beginning of the belt. This last tight snug and tuck is crucial to keep the whole swaddle from popping open.*

The ancient tradition of bundling babies isn't a fad. It's the *end* of a fad—an anti-swaddling fad! Televisions and computers may become forgotten novelties a thousand years from today, but swaddling is as old as the trees and it's time for it to become part of our babies' lives once again.

Ironing Out the Wrinkles: Fixing the Most Common Swaddling Mistakes

Swaddling is simple, but watch for these common mistakes:

- *Wrapping too loosely*

  The key to wrapping is to keep it snug . . . snug . . . snug. Make sure you pull the blanket tight, removing any slack with every step of the DUDU wrap.

  Denise discovered the tightness of the wrap was the secret ingredient for her six-week-old son. "Our running joke was we swaddled Augie so tightly we were scared his eyes would pop out! But swaddling helped him enormously, and tight was exactly the way he needed it to be!"

- *Swaddling a baby with bent arms*

  Even with tight swaddling, it's easy for your crying baby to wiggle her hands out if she was wrapped with her arms bent. While it's true that new babies are comforted by having their bodies flexed into the fetal position, and preemies do best with bent arms at least until they reach their due date, babies swaddled with their arms down still have lots of flexion in their legs, fingers, and neck to keep them happy.

  Swaddling helped Ted and Shele's two-month-old daughter, Dylan, sleep through the night. To keep her arms straight, Ted tucked Dylan's hands under the waistband of her tiny sweatpants before wrapping her. He said, "I have to do this because every time she gets her arms bent, she pops them out and gets even madder."

- *Letting the blanket touch your baby's cheek*

  If your baby is hungry and the blanket touches her cheek, it may fool her into thinking it's your breast, accidentally setting off the powerful rooting reflex and making her cry out of confusion and frustration. To keep the blanket off the face, make it look more like a V-neck sweater.

■ *Allowing the finished swaddle to pop back open*

Another basic rule of wrapping is: "Whoever gets loose loses!" It's no use wrapping your baby tightly if she can pop out in seconds. That's why experienced parents in other cultures swaddle their infants and then secure the wrap by tightly tying it with ribbons, strings, or belts.

> *Ken and Kristie said, "Whenever Henry sneaks out of his blanket, he cries as if to say, 'What have you done for me lately?' We've found that securing the wrap with duct tape gives us an extra forty-five minutes of sleep between feedings!"*

Dads—The Swaddlers Supreme

I was surprised! I thought my baby girl, Valerie, wouldn't like to be wrapped, but once swaddled, she calmed within seconds. I even taught a guy in the barbershop how to do it.

Pedro, father of Valerie

If women are from Venus and men are from Mars, then mothers are from Cuddleland and fathers are from Jiggleland! That is to say, men usually handle children much more vigorously than women do. We throw our older kids on the bed, have pillow fights, and hoist them into the air above our heads—but what about tiny babies? How do men handle them?

At first, we are often more intimidated by infants than our wives are; babies seem so tiny and fragile. When we *do* carry our little ones around, we often hot-potato them back to our wives the moment they cry.

Swaddling, however, is a great way for dads to build confidence. Fathers often have a natural talent for doing the tight wrapping. In my experience, their strength, vigor, and dexterity make them swaddlers supreme!

· Mark said, "I can wrap Eli pretty easily. But my wife, Fran, has a hard time swaddling him. I think she's too timid to do it tightly enough."

The Whys About the "S's":
Questions Parents Ask About Swaddling

1. *When should I start wrapping my baby?*

    Babies can be swaddled as soon as they're born. It makes them feel cozy and warm, like they're "back home."

2. *Are there babies who don't need to be swaddled?*

    Many calm babies do well with no swaddling at all. But the fussier your baby is, the more she'll need it. Tight bundling is so successful at soothing infants that some even have to be *un*swaddled in order to wake them up for their feedings.

3. *Can swaddling help a baby sleep?*

    Yes! Even easy babies who don't need wrapping to keep calm often sleep more when swaddled. Bundling keeps them from startling themselves awake. But make sure the wrapping is tight. It's not safe to put babies in bed with loose blankets.

    When Wendy and Brent swaddled Brandon, their two-month-old increased his night sleeping from a four-hour stretch to five to seven hours!

4. *If a baby has never been swaddled, when is it too late to start?*

    You can start wrapping your baby at any time during her first three months. But be patient. You may have to practice a few times before she gets used to it. Try swaddling when she's already sleepy and in her most receptive frame of mind.

5. *When is a baby too old for swaddling?*

    The age for weaning off swaddling varies from baby to baby. Many parents think they should stop after a few weeks or when their baby resists wrapping. But that's actually when bundling becomes the *most* valuable.

    To decide if your infant no longer needs to be wrapped, try this: After she reaches two to three months of age, swaddle her with one arm out. If she gets fussier, she's telling you to continue wrapping for a few more weeks. However, if she stays happy without the swaddling, she doesn't need it anymore.

With few exceptions, babies are ready to be weaned off wrapping by three to four months of age, although some sleep better wrapped—even up to one year of age. (For more on using swaddling to prolong sleep, see Chapter 15.)

> Twins Ari and Grace benefited from swaddling until they were eight months old. Unwrapped they would wake every three hours, but bundled they slept for a glorious ten hours.

6. How many hours a day should a baby be wrapped?

All babies need some time to stretch, be bathed, and get a massage. But you'll probably notice your baby is calmer if she's swaddled twelve to twenty hours a day to start with. (Remember, as a fetus, she was snuggled twenty-four hours a day.) After one to two months, you can reduce the wrap time according to how calm she is without it.

7. How can I tell if I'm swaddling my baby too tightly?

In traditional cultures, parents swaddle their babies tightly because loose wraps invariably pop back open. Although some Americans worry about snug swaddling, I've never heard of it being done too tightly. On the other hand, I've worked with hundreds of parents whose bundling failed because it was done too loosely. That's because no matter how snugly you do it initially, your baby's wiggling will loosen the blanket a little.

However, for your peace of mind, here's an easy way for you to make sure your wrapping is not too tight: Slide your hand between the blanket and your baby's chest. It should feel as snug as sneaking your hand between your pregnant belly and your pant's elastic waistband—at the end of your ninth month.

8. How can I tell if my baby is overheated or overwrapped?

Hillary thought her new son, Rob, needed the room temperature to be the same tropical 98.6°F he loved inside her body! But, she was taking the idea of the fourth trimester a bit too far. In 1994, doctors at UCLA tested babies to see if they could get overheated by heavy bundling. They put thirty-six babies (two to fourteen weeks old) in a room heated to about 74°F and wrapped them in terry coveralls, a cap, a receiving blanket, *and* a thermal blanket. Unexpectedly, their study showed the babies' skin got warmer but their rectal temperatures barely increased.

Preemies often need incubators to keep them toasty, but full-term babies just need a little clothing, a blanket, and a 65–70°F room. If the temperature in your home is warmer than that, just skip some clothing and wrap your baby in only her diaper in a light cotton blanket. (Parents living in warm climates often put cornstarch powder on their babies' skin to absorb sweat and prevent rashes.)

It's easy to check if your baby is overheated—feel her ears and fingers. If they're hot, red, and sweaty, she's overwrapped. However, if they're only slightly warm and she's not sweaty, her temperature is probably perfect.

9. How can I tell when my baby needs to be swaddled and when she needs to eat?

Your baby will give you several hints when she's hungry:

- When you touch her lips, her mouth will open like a baby bird waiting for food from the mother bird.

- She'll only suck on a pacifier for a minute or two before getting frustrated with it.

- If given the breast or bottle, she'll suck and swallow vigorously.

Please don't worry that swaddling might make your baby forget to eat. It may help calm a baby who's mildly hungry, but it won't satisfy one who's famished.

10. My baby often seems jumpy and nervous. Will swaddling help this?

Some babies can sleep through a hurricane, yet others startle every time the phone rings. These babies aren't nervous; they're just sensitive. Swaddling helps by muffling their startle reactions and keeping them from upsetting themselves.

11. Is there any risk to putting my baby to sleep wrapped in a blanket?

As mentioned earlier, doctors recommend that babies not sleep with loose bedding, such as pillows, soft toys, etc. Only use a blanket that is securely wrapped around your baby.

12. Shouldn't we be teaching our children to be free and not bound up?

Freedom is wonderful, but as we all know, with freedom comes responsibility. If a baby can calm herself, she has earned the right to be unwrapped. However, many newborns can't handle the great big world. They still need a few more months of cozy swaddling to keep from thrashing about uncontrollably.

13. *What happens if my baby gets an itch when her arms are swaddled?*
    Luckily, this is never a problem. Young babies don't get clear messages from their bodies, so they don't get an itchy feeling. Babies also have short attention spans. Unlike adults who go wild when they can't reach an itch, infants never give it a second "thought." (Besides, they couldn't really control their bodies well enough to scratch themselves even if they did get an itch.)

A Parent's Perspective: Testimonials from the Trenches

Swaddling helps the little one know where she is. Without it she has no sense of where her body ends and the universe begins.
Al, father of Marie-Claire, Esmé, and Didier

The vast majority of new babies stay calmer and sleep longer when they are swaddled. Here are some of their stories:

The day after Marie-Claire was born, she was crying. Not one of those newborn squeals that makes you go, "Ahhhh," but rather a really powerful bellow. I was shocked that a one-day-old could make such a sound!

Just then Dr. Karp came into our room. He casually walked over to the bassinet, picked our baby up, and wrapped her like a burrito. Then he put her on his lap with her feet toward his belly and her head at his knees and bending his face toward her ears, he made a loud "shhhh" noise. The swaddling and white noise worked together so well that she stopped crying almost instantly.

My husband and I were astonished. It was unlike anything we had ever witnessed. So we learned how to swaddle our baby tight, tight, tight in a receiving blanket, and she was the happiest, most content baby on the planet!

After she was three months old, people would often look askance when we wrapped her, as if we were resorting to barbaric measures. When curious onlookers asked, "Why have you wrapped your baby like that?" we'd proudly answer, "Because it makes her happy." And, as if on cue, Marie-Claire would smile ear-to-ear, and even the most skeptical person would be won over!

Renée, Al, Marie-Claire, Esmé, and Didier

Sophia had problems nursing when she was born. Our nurse practitioner advised me to use a special device to supplement her feedings. So, I taped this tiny tube to my breast and inserted it into her mouth, along with my nipple.

About that time, when she was three weeks old, she started becoming very fussy. During feedings, she would scream and flail, often accidentally knocking out both my nipple and the tube.

Despite my frustration, I stuck it out until the night before her two-month checkup. That night she was worse than ever. Sophia was thrashing, yanking on the tube, and mangling my nipple. I swore I would never feed her that way again, even if it meant I could no longer breast-feed.

The next day I told Dr. Karp about my struggles feeding Sophia, and he said four words that changed everything: "Don't forget the swaddling." We had swaddled Sophia initially but stopped after a few weeks because she fought it so much. However, Dr. Karp encouraged us to give it another go.

That afternoon, I tightly swaddled her and tried her on the breast (without the feeding tube). The most extraordinary thing happened: She breast-fed calmly and with focus. It was as though she never had a problem.

Sophia is now three months old, and feeding has been a breeze for the past month. We swaddle her now only if she has a bad day when she can't settle herself, and the cozy wrapping always works like a dream.

Colin, Beth, and Sophia

Starting at about one month of age, Jack began getting fussy each evening between six P.M. and midnight. I could comfort him but only by breast-feeding him nonstop.

Jack needed to be nursed to sleep and vehemently refused the pacifier, as if I were trying to swindle him out of his inheritance.

Then I discovered the greatest thing (besides breast-feeding) for calming him down: swaddling. He's not crazy about it while it's being done, but it settles him down within minutes. At a baby class I showed my friend how tightly we wrap him, and she was shocked when he went from screaming to complete calm right in front of our eyes! I was so proud of myself and of my great little boy.

Kelly, Adam, and Jack

In The Middle of the Night: Switch off

It's the middle of the night and you want to calm your baby! Can't remember exactly what to do? Here's a summary for those times when you want all the "S's" in one place to help you become the "Best Baby Calmer On The Block."

As you do the 5 "S's," remember these important points:

1) Calming your baby is like dancing with her...but you have to follow her lead. Do the 5 "S's" vigorously only lessening the intensity after she begins to settle.

2) The 5 "S's" must be done exactly right for them to work.

The 1st "S" – Swaddling

Don't worry if your baby's first reaction to wrapping is to struggle against it. Swaddling may not instantly calm her fussies but it will restrain her uncontrolled flailing so she can pay attention to the next "S" that will turn-on her calming reflex and guide her into sweet serenity!

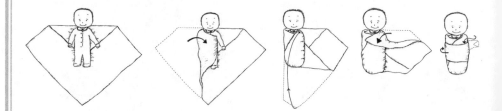

The 2nd "S" – Side/Stomach

The more upset your baby is, the unhappier she will be on her back. Rolling your infant onto her side or stomach will make her much more serene. Just this simple trick can sometimes activate a baby's calming reflex...within seconds.

The 3rd "S" – Shhhh

Shushing crying babies magically makes them feel at peace and back home, but you've got to do it about as loud as your baby's crying and close to her ear...or she won't even notice it. Use this super-effective "S" to keep her calm throughout her fussy period by using a radio tuned to loud static, a tape recording of your hair dryer, or a white noise machine.

The 4th "S" – Swinging

Like vigorous shushing, energetic jiggling can turn your baby from screams to sweet serenity in minutes...or less. As you support your baby's head and neck, wiggle her head with fast, tiny movements, sort of like you're shivering. Once she's entranced you can move her swaddled into a swing for continual, hypnotic motion. (Make sure the strap is between your baby's wrapped legs, the swing is fully reclined, and it's set on the fastest speed.)

The 5th "S" – Sucking

This last "S" usually works best after you have already led your little one into calmness with the other "S's." Offering her your breast, finger, or a pacifier will be the icing on the cake of soothing. You can teach your baby to keep the pacifier in her mouth by using "reverse psychology"—the moment she begins to suck on the pacifier, gently tug on it as if you're going to take it out. She'll suck it in harder and soon she'll learn to keep it in her mouth even when she's cooing.

9

The 2nd "S": Side (or Stomach)—Your Baby's Feel-Good Position

Main Points:

- How the side and stomach positions can calm your baby by switching his calming reflex on and his Moro (falling) reflex off
- Important information about SIDS and your baby's sleeping position
- The reverse-breast-feeding hold and other great ways to cuddle your baby and soothe his crying

Dugger's eyes opened wide when he saw how I handled his baby girl, Bobbie. The moment Bobbie cried, I placed her cheek in my palm and rolled her small body onto my sleeve, resting her chest and stomach against my forearm—Bobbie calmed in mid-scream! Then I jiggled her up and down like I was the most nervous person on the planet and she was asleep within two minutes.

Dugger later told me, "Football was my favorite sport when I was a boy, and I carried the ball as if it were a treasure. But I never would have felt okay handling Bobbie like that if I hadn't seen you do it first. Now I carry Bobbie like a football every day and I can usually make her fall right asleep."

In real estate, the most important rule is: location, location, location. In baby calming it's position, position, position!

There's no question that fussy newborns are easier to calm when they're lying on their side or stomach. Many babies are happy to lie on their backs when they're in a good mood, but it's a tough position to calm them in when they get cranky. Other babies feel insecure on their backs even when they're not fussy. These irritable infants often quiet as soon as they're put on their sides or have their tummies draped over their parent's shoulder or forearm.

Why Do the Side and Stomach Positions Make Your Baby Happy?

The side and stomach positions work so well because:

They trigger the calming reflex by imitating your baby's position in the uterus. Before birth, your fetus was never flat on his back. He spent most of his time on his side in the fetal position—head down, spine rounded, knees pressed against his belly. Over millions of years this position became a potent trigger for the calming reflex, keeping fetuses serene so they didn't accidentally move into a bad position or kink their umbilical cords.

Once out of the womb, bending your baby's neck down a bit, touching his stomach, and laying him on his side activate position sensors inside his head that trigger the calming reflex. Specialists in the care of premature infants place them flexed and on their sides as soon as these tiny newborns are healthy enough to be handled. (Even many adults find coiling up into the fetal position comforting.)

"Tummy touching" might also turn on calming as a reflex left over from our ape ancestors. For millions of years it has been crucial for ape babies to stay still when they were tummy-to-tummy, clutching their mama's fur. It's possible that those animals who were soothed by the sensation of tummy touching thrashed less, fell less, and therefore survived and passed their genes along to their own babies.

The side and stomach positions keep your baby from accidentally setting off his Moro (falling) reflex. Cuddling a fussy baby on his back is a little like calming and pinching him at the same time! The holding part feels great, but lying on the back can make some young infants feel insecure. In that position, any twitch or cry can trigger the brain's position sensors and unleash the Moro reflex, making your baby shriek and fling his arms out as if he's being dropped out of a tree.

On the other hand, putting your baby on his side or stomach makes the position sensors in his head send out a message that says, "Don't worry. Everything's fine!" (Once your baby's Moro has been turned on, it may take his brain a minute or two after he's rolled onto his side or stomach for an all-clear message to be recognized and the calming reflex turned on.) Some infants are so sensitive to position that just rolling them from their sides slightly over toward their stomachs calms them, and rolling them a tiny bit from their sides toward their backs makes them panic.

A Position for Life: Helping Babies Avoid SIDS

Babies love to lie on their sides and to be touched on their stomachs. These positions are like cookies and warm milk for them. However, while having your infant in these positions is great during his waking hours, your baby's back is the preferred position in which to put him to sleep.

In 1992, the American Academy of Pediatrics (AAP) recommended that babies never sleep on their stomachs. Research showed that infants who were put down in that position had an increased risk of dying from crib death, or what's known as Sudden Infant Death Syndrome (SIDS). In a giant victory for families, we were able to lower the death rate from SIDS from six thousand babies a year to three thousand five hundred, just by keeping sleeping babies off their stomachs.

In March 2000, the AAP issued its latest advice on protecting babies from SIDS. They stated that SIDS was rare under one month of age, peaking between two and four months. They also noted that babies with the highest risk of SIDS were those who slept on their stomachs, slept on a soft substance, had moms who smoked, were overheated, had no prenatal care, had teenage mothers, or were born prematurely. They went on to state that the back was the preferred sleeping position and that the side position was also acceptable, although it had a slightly higher risk of SIDS (probably due to babies accidentally rolling onto their stomachs during sleep).

To prevent SIDS, the AAP recommends that you don't smoke during pregnancy and eliminate all smoking from your house; don't take alcohol or sedative drugs, especially when you bed-share; never sleep with your baby on a sofa or waterbed; keep soft objects out of his bed (toys, pillows, sheepskins, loose blankets, comforters); and don't let your baby get hot and sweaty to the touch.

Once Upon a Time: How Parents Have Used the Side/Stomach Position in Other Times and Cultures

Among the Inuit (Alaskan natives), a very deep hood is used as a baby bag and serves as an extension of the womb. The newborn lives in a heated climate, completely buried inside the mother's clothing, and curled up like a half-moon.

Béatrice Fontanel and Claire d'Harcourt, *Babies Celebrated*

In most traditional cultures around the world, babies hang out—literally. Their mothers, sisters, aunts, and neighbors carry them in baskets and sheets on their fronts, backs, hips, and shoulders for up to twenty-four hours a day, seven days a week.

Few parents across the globe place their infants on their backs, but when they do, they usually put them on a *curved* surface, not a flat one. The arc of a small blanket suspended from a tree or tripod puts a baby back into the familiar and reassuring rounded fetal position, which allows him to sleep more restfully.

- The Lapp people of Greenland carry their babies curled up in cradles that hang on one side of a reindeer (counterbalanced on the animal's other side by a heavy sack of flour).

- The !Kung San people of the Kalahari Desert carry their infants in leather slings all day long. They keep them in a semi-sitting position, because they believe that posture encourages a baby's development.

- In parts of Indonesia, loving mothers never let their babies stretch out completely; in their culture that is the feared position of the dead. Infants are compactly bundled in a seated position and suspended from the ceiling to sleep like little floating Buddhas. (Even new mothers must sleep sitting up for forty days after the delivery to evade evil spirits who are attracted to people weakened by illness or injury.)

- The Efé tribe of pygmies in Zaire hate putting their babies down—even for a moment. They keep their tiny tots happy by holding them upright or curled up in their arms all day long, and even while they are sleeping. However, since it's such a big effort for one person to do all this carrying, the Efé believe in teamwork. For the first several months, tribal members pass newborns back and forth among up to twenty people, an average of eight times an hour!

Even when women in different cultures take their infants out of their arms, they hang them over their laps or chests, which allows their babies' soft tummies to remain in constant contact with their mother's warm, comforting skin.

Go with the Winning Side: How to Use Position to Help Soothe Your Baby

Here's how you can treat your baby to the calming pleasure of being on his side or stomach. First, wrap your baby in a cozy swaddle, then try one of these positions used by countless experienced parents:

The Reverse-Breast-Feeding Hold

This hold is my favorite for carrying a crying baby while I'm walking or bouncing him into tranquillity. It's easy and comfortable to do, and it supports his head and neck perfectly.

1. Sit down and lay your baby on your lap; have him on his right side with his head on your knees and his feet on your left hip.

SHHHHH

2. Slide your left hand between your knee and his cheek so you support his head (or head and neck) in your palm and outstretched fingers.

3. Roll him onto your left forearm so his stomach rests against your arm and bring him in to your body, lightly pressing his back against your chest.

   In this position, your thumb will be right next to his face and you can even let him take it into his mouth for added pleasure. (Always wash your hands first.)

The Football Hold

Fathers love the football hold. This stomach-down position requires a little extra arm strength, but it's fun and effective. In fact, silencing babies, mid-squawk, with the football hold is one of the greatest baby "magic tricks" of all time.

1. Sit your swaddled baby on your lap, face him to your left, and place your left hand under his chin, supporting it like a chin strap.

2. Gently lean him forward and roll his hips over so his stomach is lying on your left forearm. His head rests in

your palm, his chest and stomach are snugly cushioned against your forearm, and his legs are straddled over your arm, hanging limp.

The Over-the-Shoulder Hold

Hoisting your fussy baby up onto your shoulder can have a powerful, soothing effect. Often, simply lifting your baby into an upright position gets him to open his eyes and perk up.

When your baby is upright you can also let the weight of his body press his stomach against your shoulder to provide him with some extra tummy touching, making this hold doubly comforting. Be sure to swaddle your baby *before* you put him over your shoulder. It will help him stay asleep when you move him off your shoulder to his bassinet.

This is by no means an exhaustive list of calming baby holds. You can also try the cannonball position, where your baby is curled in a ball, knee to chest, across your lap, or the hot-water-bottle position, with your baby draped over a warm hot-water bottle so the heat and pressure are against his stomach. (Remember, don't let him sleep on his stomach.) Have fun discovering the position that makes your baby the happiest.

The Whys About the "S's":
Questions Parents Ask
About the Side/Stomach Position

1. *Where should I put my baby's hands when he's on his side?*

   Your baby's arms should be placed straight along his body. Even with the tightest wrap, there's enough wiggle room to allow your baby to move his bottom arm a little bit forward to get into a comfortable position.

2. *Can a baby's arm ever go to sleep when he's lying on his side?*

   No. Arms only fall asleep when there's firm pressure on the part of the elbow called the funny bone. That's why it happens when you snooze on a hard desk using your arm as a pillow. Since the arms of a swaddled baby move a little bit forward once wrapped, there's never enough pressure on the arm to cause it to fall asleep.

3. *If babies miss the womb sensations, wouldn't it make sense to position them upside-down?*

   Well, that's an interesting thought, but the answer is no. You might think babies who have spent months upside-down would like this position, but the womb is filled with fluid so the fetus actually floats almost weightlessly inside. Once outside of the uterus, the buoyancy is gone, and an upside-down baby would develop uncomfortable pressure as blood pools in his head.

A Parent's Perspective: Testimonials from the Trenches

These fussy babies were "be-side" themselves with joy when their parents put them in these feel-good positions:

Dina was confused. At the hospital, she was told to let Noah sleep on his back, but when her mom came to visit she told her the opposite. "We argued about the best position for my six-week-old baby to sleep in. He had a really hard time settling himself when he was flat on his back. I had to pat him for fifteen to twenty minutes until he finally drifted off, and even then he'd still wake up every three hours.

"My mom said I should let him sleep on his stomach. While he did sleep more soundly in that position, I was terrified of doing anything that might increase his risk of SIDS.

"I asked Dr. Karp his opinion. He showed me how to wrap Noah tightly and put him down to sleep on his back. I was thrilled because it worked as well as my mother's stomach-down position, but was much safer."

Alfre said that when she was growing up she learned an easy way to calm babies, which the women in her family had passed down from generation to generation. It was called the "Big Mama" technique.

The way it worked was to sit down with a pillow on your lap and place the screaming baby stomach-down on top of it. Then you start bouncing the heels of your feet up and down (hard), patting the baby on the bottom (hard), and singing a lullaby right in the baby's ear.

Once the sun went down, two-month-old Ruby began her nightly twist-and-fuss routine. Her parents, Steve and Sarah, worried she was suffering from stomach pain, until they discovered that Ruby would promptly fall asleep if they placed her over their shoulder with her stomach pressing firmly against them as they marched around the backyard, jiggling her body with every step.

Baby Michael's father was the family pro at soothing Michael's screaming. He would sit in the rocker with a pillow on his lap, lay Michael belly-down on top of the pillow, and rock him hard and fast. Within five minutes Michael was always out in lullaby-land.

10

The 3rd "S": Shhhh—Your Baby's Favorite Soothing Sound

Main Points:

- Shhhh triggers your baby's calming reflex
- The whooshing sound your baby heard in your uterus was as loud as a vacuum cleaner
- Shhhhing only soothes screaming babies if it is loud
- Ten machines you can use to make a soothing white noise

My young husband walked our crying baby up and down, making that shshshshshing sound of comfort that parents know only too well.

Eliza Warren, *How I Managed My Children from Infancy to Marriage*, 1865

As I was making my rounds at a local hospital, I saw Carol trying to calm a crying newborn in the nursery. Carol, a wonderful and experienced nurse, had wrapped the baby snugly, placed her on her side, and was softly whispering in her ear, "It's okay. It's okay." She even offered her a pacifier, but nothing helped.

I asked Carol if I could try soothing the baby. She describes what happened next:

"Sophia had been inconsolable for her first two days of life. After Dr. Karp offered to help he bent over Sophia's bassinet, with his face near her ear, and emitted a harsh, continuous 'shooshing' sound for about ten seconds. That was it! Sophia stopped crying within the first few seconds of this magical sound and remained silent for the next two hours."

Of course, one loud shhhh won't keep an infant calm forever, but it was exactly what Sophia needed to get her attention long enough for Carol's other calming methods to work.

Why Does Shhhhing Make Your Baby So Happy?

Did you ever notice how the sound of the wind or the rumble of the ocean makes you feel relaxed and at peace? Shhhhing is so deeply a part of who we are that it's even profoundly calming for adults.

For new babies, loud shhhhing is the "sound of silence," the anti-cry. Shushing may seem a strange way to help a crying baby; however, so is turning on a vacuum cleaner. Yet that's what many baby books suggest! What's so special about that sound?

The answer is, this loud white noise imitates your baby's experience inside the womb and switches on her calming reflex.

When I asked Nancy and Gary to guess what their baby, Natalie, heard inside the womb, Nancy said it was probably something like, "Hey, Gary, get over here!" Nancy was partly right. Fetuses do hear the muttering of voices and other "outside" noise. However, most of their daily entertainment is a continuous, rhythmic symphony of shhhh. Wave upon wave of blood surging through the arteries of your womb makes this harsh, whooshing sound, which is as loud and rough as a gale wind blowing through the trees.

How do we know this is what they hear? In the early 1970s, doctors placed tiny microphones into the wombs of women in labor and found the power of the sound was an incredible eighty to ninety decibels (even louder than a vacuum cleaner)! (You may have heard this womb noise

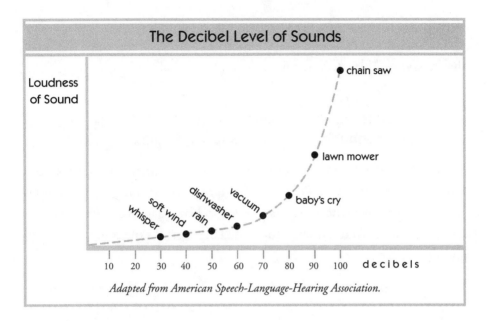

The Decibel Level of Sounds

Loudness of Sound

chain saw

lawn mower

dishwasher

vacuum

baby's cry

soft wind

whisper

rain

| 10 | 20 | 30 | 40 | 50 | 60 | 70 | 80 | 90 | 100 | decibels |

Adapted from American Speech-Language-Hearing Association.

when your doctor or midwife checked your fetus with an abdominal microphone.) To get a good idea of what this sounds like to your baby, try dunking your head under the bathwater while the faucet is turned on—full blast.

Don't worry that your newborn baby might get overwhelmed by such a forceful noise. Although the sound inside the uterus is louder than a vacuum cleaner, *your baby doesn't hear it that loud.* That's because her middle ears are waterlogged with fluid, her ear canals absorb sound and are plugged with waxy vernix, and she has thick, inefficient eardrums.

These sound-damping factors last until a few months after birth. Gradually your baby's hearing will improve as her eardrum changes from being like a piece of thick paper to a tightly stretched piece of cellophane that vibrates with any distant noise. However, for a while, her reduced hearing reduces the intensity of your shhhhing, or vacuum cleaner, to a comforting din.

Imagine your baby's shock at birth when she emerges from that rich uterine world of loud quadraphonic whooshing into the quiet world of whispering and tiptoeing that parents create for their newborns. Sure, *we* may enjoy resting in a still room, but for your baby the silence can be deafening. And her muffled hearing will make your house seem even more stark and empty. New babies experience a type of sensory deprivation, and so it shouldn't surprise us that they cry from excessive quiet. It's as if they're saying, "Please, someone make a little noise!"

Once Upon a Time: How Parents Have Used Shhhhing in Other Times and Cultures

Do you remember when your grade-school librarian shushed you? All humans go "shhhh" (or "ssss") to say "Be quiet" to each other. This sound is one of the very few vocalizations understood by *all* humans, in every corner of the globe. And in many unrelated languages it's the root of the word asking for silence:

"chut" *(Urdu)*   "shuu" *(Vietnamese)*

"chutee" *(Serbian)*   "soos" *(Armenian)*

"chuu-chuu" *(Kahnada of So. India)*   "teeshina *(Slovenian)*

"hush," "silence" *(English)*   "toosst" *(Swedish)*

"hushket" *(Arabic)*   "chupraho" *(Hindi)*

"sheket" *(Hebrew)*   "shuh-shuh" *(Chinese)*

"stille" *(German)*

Even the Japanese use shhhh as the root of their request for quiet: "shizukani" (although as a lover of Japanese food I might have guessed it would be "shu-shi").

As strange as it may seem, I believe that the calming effect of shhhh is something that babies taught *us*. If it were not for the immediate reaction cave babies had to shushing, parents would never have noticed its tremendous value. I'm sure that once a Stone Age mom learned this great trick, she couldn't wait to share it with her friends. And through the centuries, the discovery and teaching of this technique was probably repeated in every village and tribe around the world.

Unfortunately, most of us today haven't had much experience watching women with their babies. That's one of the reasons why so many parents and grandparents have forgotten this age-old, effective technique.

The Story of Shhhh: The Calming Sound That Babies Taught . . . Us

How did mothers from the Alaskan tundra to the swamps of Albania discover that this strange sound soothes screaming babies? No one is absolutely sure, but my guess is that it happened something like this:

About fifty thousand years ago, two Stone Age mothers were eating lunch together when one woman's baby started to shriek. Her mom immediately leaned over her "cave" baby's cradle and tried to calm her by squawking in her ear—the way she had seen a mother pterodactyl sucessfully calm her young. But the baby continued to cry.

When the poor child had just about wailed to the point of "Neanderthal-mania," her mom's friend asked if she could try something she had once seen another mom do to soothe her frantic baby. The "cave" mother handed her wild little "infantasaurus rex" over and watched in amazement as her friend held her tightly and made a harsh, shhhhing sound right in her infant's ear. Like magic, the baby suddenly became calm!

THERE'S GOTTA BE A BETTER WAY...

As a nurse walked by the room of a first-time mother, the door popped open and the father emerged, pushing a bassinet that was practically vibrating from the cries of his red-faced, screaming baby. In an attempt to help the poor little girl, the nurse lovingly leaned her face over the baby and let out a "Shhhh" as loud and harsh as a burst steam pipe!

I'm confident that had she continued her shushing for a few moments longer, the infant would have calmed. But she was stopped in her tracks when the baby's father yanked the bassinet away. Glowering at her, he said, "How dare you tell my daughter to shut up!"

Of course, this caring nurse was not telling the baby to shut up. But this father reacted as he did because he didn't understand that the nurse was speaking in a different "language."

In "adult-ese," shhhh is a rude way of telling someone to be quiet or to shut up. However, in this case the nurse was speaking "baby-ese," in which shhhh is a very polite infant greeting. All babies recognize the "word" *shhhh,* and they love it!

Mothers all around the world shush their babies in exactly the same way. Here's how to do it:

1. Place your mouth two to four inches away from your baby's ear.

2. With your lips pursed, start releasing a shhhh sound.

3. Quickly raise the volume of your shhhh until it *matches* the noise level of your baby's crying. Try to sound like the world's most irritated librarian! This is not a gentle or polite shush but a rough, harsh, insistent shhhh. But remember, your shushing will sound much louder to you than it will to your baby because her hearing is quite muffled. And besides, her own screaming gets broadcast at a jolting seventy to eighty decibels (louder than a vacuum cleaner)—and that's blasting right next to her ears!

Some parents feel it's callous and vulgar to shhhh their colicky baby or that it has an angry sound to their ears. However, to a baby's ears, shhhh is a sound of love and welcome.

4. As mentioned earlier, calming your baby is like a dance—but she is leading. You aren't guiding her into quiet, you're following her there. So, don't soften your shhhh until her decreasing cries show you she's ready for it.

When you first try shhhhing, your baby should quiet within a minute or two. And, after you get really good at it, you may find she calms in seconds. However, once your fussy baby settles, she will probably need continuing, moderate white noise to keep her from returning to crying. This shouldn't be a surprise to you. After all, she used to be serenaded by this loud sound 24/7, so needing it for a few hours, or even all night long, is a major compromise on her part.

(It's fun teaching your older children how to shhhh. It makes them more involved in baby care, and they feel so proud when *they* can calm the baby's cries just like daddy and mommy!)

Mary and Sigfried were delighted at how well shushing helped soothe their crying three-week-old baby, Eric:

"We never would have thought Eric could be quieted by such an annoying sound, but we've discovered the louder he cries, the louder our shushing needs to be. And, we can only lessen the intensity of our sound after he starts to quiet down.

"Shushing for two to three minutes can make us pretty dizzy. Yet Eric often seemed to need it for longer periods of time. Finally, after several days of taking turns shushing him, we realized that a sustained hiss from our music synthesizer was a perfect substitute for our flagging lung capacity. This sound works really well all by itself. And it's one hundred percent successful when combined with swaddling and motion."

Making a Shhhh-ound Investment for Your Baby

Continuous intense shhhhing can be hard to do, so parents have invented methods of making white noise to entrance their fussy babies. For example, some Amazonian Indians present new mothers with a baby sling decorated with monkey bones that make a rattling white noise with her every move.

However, if you and your family are out of monkey bones, I suggest you acquire a mechanical sound assistant. Some people feel strange using these, but if you can drive a machine to work every day, why not use one

Testing Out Your Baby's Shhhh Sensitivity

If your baby is fussy but not hungry, try this experiment to test her shhhh sensitivity:

Swaddle your baby and place her over your shoulder. Put your mouth right by her ear and shhhh softly for ten seconds. If she continues to cry, let your shhhh become louder and harsher.

When you have found the right sound she will quiet in seconds, as if suddenly entranced. Practice making the shhhh at different pitches and see what works best with your baby.

After your infant calms, gradually lower the volume of your sound. If she starts to wail again, just crank back up the intensity.

Weird Noises You Can Make at Home (But Don't Let Your Friends Hear You)

For soothing their newborn's cries, Alise says her husband swears by a deep, resonating hum that's a cross between shushing and the vibrations of a bouncy seat.

Tom and Karen discovered their son, Ben, quieted when they moaned. "He gets alert when I make a loud moan, like when I was in labor or like a bunch of Buddhist monks chanting together. Ben likes the sound to be deep and vibratory."

Several noises other than a simple shhhh can help your crying baby come down for a soft landing. Some parents I've worked with make a rhythmic chant like Native Americans doing a rain dance (*Hey . . . ho, ho, ho*); others sound more like foghorns or buzzing bees.

Pediatrician William Sears recommends what he calls the "neck nestle." You snuggle your baby's head into the groove between your chest and jaw, with your voice box pressed against her head, and make deep groaning sounds in the back of your throat.

to help make your baby happy? Here are ten useful shhhh substitutes that can help your baby in the throes of colic:

1. A noisy appliance, like a hair dryer or vacuum cleaner
2. A room fan or a microwave or bathroom exhaust fan
3. Running water
4. A white-noise machine
5. A CD with white-noise sounds
6. A toy bear with a recording of the sounds of the uterus
7. Static on the radio or baby monitor
8. The clothes dryer with sneakers or tennis balls inside (never leave the baby alone on a dryer . . . she can fall off)
9. A dishwasher
10. A car ride

The best way to know exactly the right level of sound your baby needs is to gradually increase the volume and see how she responds.

These final tips will help you use your shhhh-ound investment wisely:

- Harsh whooshing sounds work better than the patter of rain or the sound of a heartbeat.
- Tape-record the sound so you can start by playing it at the volume that works the best and then lower it after your baby is deeply asleep.
- Place the sound one to six feet away from your baby's ears to get the maximum effect with the lowest volume.
- Don't hesitate to use your white-noise sound machine all night if it helps your baby sleep longer and better. (See Chapter 15.)
- If the sound is driving you absolutely nuts, try some earplugs!

The Story of Tessa and the Vacuum Cleaner

Tessa, now five years old, is a "pistol"—smart, funny, and passionate. However, during her first weeks of life, she would get as frantic as a hurricane. Her parents, Eve and Todd, wrapped her, walked her, and even went for car rides, but nothing worked.

One afternoon, Tessa was really wailing but Eve couldn't hold her because she had to get the house ready for company. So she left her baby to cry and began to vacuum. The instant the vacuum was switched on, Tessa became stone silent!

Eve bolted over to check her. Tessa was sleeping sweetly, her body relaxed. She wasn't sleeping despite the ruckus but because of it! Amazingly, the womb experience that Tessa was missing most was "channeled" to her through the sound of Eve's seven-year-old upright vacuum.

From that moment on, whenever Tessa went ballistic, her parents used the vacuum cleaner to soothe her. Eve and Todd began to joke that Tessa was receiving secret messages from the planet Hoover. This calming trick was so predictable that they began inviting their friends over during Tessa's fussy time to watch the show.

Over the next six months, whenever Eve had to take Tessa to work with her, she always brought along a little portable vacuum to help Tessa settle in for a good long nap!

The Whys About the "S's":
Questions Parents Ask About Shhhhing

1. *Which sound will calm my cranky baby the best: a heartbeat, lullaby, or shhhh?*

   When your baby is resting peacefully, all of these can lull her into a deeper level of relaxation. However, if she's really upset, the most effective calming sound is a white noise that imitates the turbulent "shhhh" of your womb.

2. *How many hours a day can I use these sounds? Is all night too much?*

   Many babies sleep better, and longer, when their parents use calming white noise all night long. Even if you use it twelve hours a day, that's a fifty percent cutback from what you gave her in your womb.

   You don't have to worry about making your baby dependent on the sound, because—if you want to know the truth—she already is! She's dependent on it because, for her nine months inside you, she was surrounded by loud shushing every minute of the day.

   > *Jane's six-week-old son, Josh, woke up fussing every two to three hours during the night until she began using white noise. "The first night I used a white-noise machine, Josh calmed down quickly and slept five hours. Then he fed and slept for another three hours!"*

3. *When should I wean my baby off white noise?*

   Most parents who use these soothing sounds to help their babies sleep begin to gradually lower the volume after their babies turn three months old. Some parents, however, find that white noise continues to be a great sleeping aid for many more months. (See the discussion on weaning off the 5 "S's" in Chapter 15.)

4. *Does shushing lose its effectiveness if you do it too much?*

   You would think babies would eventually get bored with this

sound, but they don't. Just like milk, it continues to be comforting for infants for months and months.

5. I worry that white noise is too strong for my baby. Is it possible that, rather than calming her, it overwhelms her?

Please remember three things:

1. Your baby is accustomed to the loud noise of your womb, not the silence of your home.

2. You will always be right if you follow your baby's lead. Only use loud sounds when she is screaming, and gradually lower the intensity once she calms.

3. All new babies have muffled hearing. So the noise that sounds loud to us sounds much quieter to them.

A Parent's Perspective: Testimonials from the Trenches

The different types of shhhhing noises moms and dads come up with are inspired examples of parental ingenuity. Here's how some parents I know used sound to guide their babies to happiness:

Patrick noticed that his son, Chance, was calmed by the sounds of aquarium pumps. So he mounted one on each side of his little boy's crib. The noise and vibration helped Chance settle himself and fall asleep.

When Talia began screaming in the supermarket, I put my face right next to her ear and uttered a rough "shhhh" until she calmed. While this seemed rude to the people watching me, it soothed her in seconds.

Once, when Talia had a mini-meltdown at the local Federal Express office, I quieted her with this same technique. The shushing worked so well that a clerk asked me for a repeat demonstration. She told me her daughter had twins and was searching for an effective tool to relieve their crying.

Sandra, Eric, Talia, and Daniel

We turned on the radio for our fussy daughter, Camille, but instead of putting on soft music we tuned it between stations to get loud hissing static. We discovered Camille didn't like the popping, crackly sound of static on the AM radio—she was an FM static aficionado only! Within a few minutes of tuning in to her favorite "non-station," her face would soften and then she would close her eyes and drift into a peaceful sleep.

Hylda, Hugo, and Camille

Steve and Nancy's six-week-old, Charlie, stayed calm in the car only if they played a tape of the hair dryer while they were driving. After he was four months old he no longer needed the tape to help him tolerate car rides.

Not only did two-month-old William have serious fussy periods, but he slept so lightly that he heard every squeak in the house. His parents, Fern and Robert, discovered that the white noise of their room fan muffled the outside sounds and helped him sleep longer.

Annette calmed her baby, Sean, by calling him "Shhhh-ean." It worked so well, the family joke became that when he was four years old, the little boy thought his name was pronounced "On"!

11

The 4th "S":
Swinging—Moving in
Rhythm with Your
Baby's Needs

Main Points:

- Vigorous jiggly movement can switch on your baby's calming reflex
- The three key points to successful swinging
- Lullabies: What swinging sounds like when it's put to music
- The "Windshield Wiper": A great way to calm your fussy baby when you're tired
- Eight tricks for turning a swing into your baby's best friend

Life was so rich within the womb. Rich in noises and sounds. But mostly there was movement. Continuous movement. When the mother sits, stands, walks, turns—movement, movement, movement.

Frederick Leboyer, *Loving Hands*

Every night, Ellyn and Harold put their son Zachary in his stroller and rolled him repeatedly over an elevated threshold on the floor. Each time, Zack got jolted like a car racing over a

speed bump. Harold sometimes bounced Zach this way one
hundred times in a row to get him to stop crying. And if his
son was still fussing after that—he did it one hundred times
more!

Zachary's brother, Ezra, preferred another type of motion
to snap him out of his yelping. Ellyn and Harold held him while
"bopping" to the Rolling Stones. Ellyn said over four months
they almost wore out their living-room carpeting from dancing
Ezra around for hours each night!

Why Does Swinging Make a Baby So Happy?

When we think of the five senses—touch, hearing, vision, smell,
taste—we often forget we have a powerful sixth sense. No, not ESP; I'm
referring to our ancient and deeply satisfying sense of movement in space.
This wonderful sense is exactly what gets stimulated when you sway side-
to-side to settle your fussing infant (and it also explains why rocking chairs
are such a favorite of grandparents).

Rhythmic movement, or what I call swinging, is a powerful tool for
soothing our babies—and ourselves. Most of us can remember being
lulled by the hypnotic motion of a porch swing, hammock, or train.

Why do these movements cause such profound relaxation? Swinging
motions that mimic the jiggling your baby felt inside you turns on "motion sensors" in his ears, which then activate the calming reflex.

Once Upon a Time: How Parents Have Used
Swinging in Other Times and Cultures

*There was something so natural as well as pleasant in the wavy
motion of the cradle . . . and so like what children had been
used to before they were born.*
Michael Underwood, *Treatise on the Diseases of Children*, 1789

Since the dawn of time, perceptive parents have recognized the wonderful
effect movement has on babies. For our ancestors, soothing their infants

with continuous motion was easy, because they spent all day long walking and working with their infants on their hips.

As every parent knows, it's impossible to keep still while you're holding a baby. You constantly shift your weight, pat your baby's bottom, touch her head, and kiss her ears. Imagine how foreign the stillness of a bassinet must feel to your baby compared to the gentle strokes and movements she's pampered with while she's in your arms.

Of course, all moms have to put their babies down every once in a while. But in many cultures it's dangerous to place a baby on the ground, so a mother will hand her infant to a relative or put her in a homemade moving device, like a cradle.

In *Gynecology*, one of the world's oldest medical books, a 200 A.D. physician named Soranus instructed women on how to keep their babies healthy. Some tips from this "Dr. Spock" of ancient Rome have not stood the test of time, such as warning parents that carrying their son on their shoulders could injure his testicles and turn him into a eunuch! However, some of his advice has proved priceless, like his recommendation to jiggle babies by "balancing the crib upon diagonally opposed rocks" and teetering it back and forth. This idea inspired the invention of the cradle (a crib placed upon rockers instead of rocks), which rewards babies with an equally hypnotic, albeit much less jolting, motion.

In many countries today, babies are still kept in constant motion. Their bodies are bounced and wiggled all day while strapped to the backs of their mothers or sisters or family yak. Thai parents rock their babies in baskets fastened to the ceiling. Eastern European women swing their infants in blankets that they hold like a hammock. Iranian women sit on the floor, with their babies placed in the grooves between their outstretched legs, and pivot their heels side-to-side, swishing their tiny children like metronomes.

In the United States, however, parents have long been warned not to handle their babies too much. In the early 1900s, Dr. Emmett Holt, America's leading pediatrician at that time, wrote in *Care and Feeding of Children*: "Babies less than six months old should never be played with at all. To avoid overstimulation, babies need peaceful and quiet surroundings." He worried parents would jar their babies' fragile nervous systems.

By the 1920s, the question "to rock or not to rock" a baby was no longer open to discussion. Quite frankly, no one dared admit doing it anymore.

Of course, it goes without saying that one has to be gentle with babies. You must always hold and support your baby's head when she's in your arms or when you're moving her from one place to another. But remember your baby was constantly bounced and jiggled inside your uterus as you walked, or hustled up and down stairs. Savvy mothers know that when their baby is fussy, vigorous rocking calms them much faster than slow, gentle movements.

Putting the Moves On:
Using Motion to Calm Your Fussy Baby

Jeannie drove Jordan around to quiet her fiery outbursts and was shocked to discover that her little red-haired "tornado" settled best when her mom hit every pothole she could find.

When Ruby was in the middle of a scream-fest, Jean Marie would pick her four-week-old up, sit on the bed with her feet on the ground, and bounce up and down in quick, jerky little motions like a child on a pogo stick.

Babies love to bounce. Why else do we call our infants bouncing baby girls and boys? Over the centuries, parents have perfected countless innovative ways to jiggle their unhappy tots into tranquillity. Here are the Top Ten:

1. Rocking in a rocking chair
2. Dancing (with quick little moves up and down)
3. Infant swings
4. Rhythmic pats on the back or bottom
5. Hammocks
6. Baby carriers
7. Car rides
8. Vibrating bouncy seats
9. Bouncing on an exercise ball
10. Brisk walks

A Bonus Eleventh Technique—
The Milk Shake

This method may sound odd, but you'll be amazed how well it works:

1. Sit your baby on your lap (facing to your left) and place your left hand under his chin like a chin strap. Lean him forward a little so his chin rests solidly in your hand.

2. Slip your right hand directly underneath his buttocks.

3. Lift him straight up into the air with your right hand; he'll be leaning forward a tiny bit so his head will be cradled in your left hand a few inches in front of his body.

4. Now, with your right hand, bounce him with *fast* (two to three times a second) but *tiny* (one to two inches) up-and-down movements, like you're making a milk shake.

The Milk Shake is also a great way to burp your baby—and build your biceps.

Swinging Rules: The Three Key Points to Successful Motion

Those who find that rhythmic rocking doesn't work are almost certainly rocking too slowly.

Penelope Leach, *Your Baby and Child*

For really fussy babies, the swaddle must be tight, the shhhh must be harsh, and the swinging must be fast and jiggly. Remember, swinging refers to all manner of rhythmic actions, from patting to car rides to bouncing.

The three rules of successful swinging are:

1. Start Out Fast and Jiggly

Calming most frantic infants requires small, trembly movements, like someone with the world's biggest case of shivers. This type of motion switches on the calming reflex and makes your baby think, *Wow . . . that feels really good!*

Some babies also like the free-fall feeling their parents give them when they suddenly dip or bend over. But be careful. If your baby is sensitive, that motion may startle him and set off his Moro reflex, upsetting him even more.

2. The Head Jiggles More Than the Body

Jiggling triggers your baby's calming reflex by switching on motion detectors in his head. So, it is the jiggling of the head (the site of these sensors), *not* the motion of the body, that really turns the reflex on.

As you jiggle your baby, don't cup your hands firmly around his head. It's critical that you allow your hands to be a little open and relaxed so his head makes tiny wiggles, *like Jell-O quivering on a plate.* If you hold his head too snugly, it won't wiggle and you probably won't activate the reflex.

3. Follow Your Baby's Lead

How forceful should your jiggling be? The vigor of your motion should reflect the level of your baby's crying. Gentle movements are fine for relaxed, sleepy infants, but the more agitated your baby is, the faster and more jiggly you need to be. Wait for his cries to lessen before you reduce your pace. Then, the calmer he gets, the slower your swinging can become.

Tamar and Dan realized they had to play "follow the leader" with their baby:

> *The most effective technique we've found to quiet Damian is putting him up on our shoulders and thumping his back quickly and firmly. As he calms, we downshift the intensity of the patting, bit by bit.*
>
> *Vigorous movement also works, either in a rocking chair or dancing from side to side. And, combining rocking and patting is a winning combination for us that never fails to settle him as long as he's not hungry or wet.*

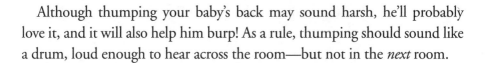

Although thumping your baby's back may sound harsh, he'll probably love it, and it will also help him burp! As a rule, thumping should sound like a drum, loud enough to hear across the room—but not in the *next* room.

Is Jiggling Ever Bad for Babies?

> *Ken and Lisa were hesitant to jiggle baby Emily. Like many other parents, they feared it would make her spit up, get overstimulated, or even harm her. But when they tried it, they were amazed: "We worried it would be too strong for her, but it worked like a charm!"*

Almost any mother with more than three kids has learned that fussy babies settle fastest when they're energetically bounced. And jiggling is certainly much safer for infants than driving them around town with a weary parent behind the wheel. However, for many first-time moms and dads, jiggling may seem counterintuitive and wrong. When I teach new parents my technique, they often ask in a concerned voice, "I know it's been done for millions of years, but are you sure jiggling can't accidentally cause Shaken Baby Syndrome?"

Fortunately, the answer is . . . No! No! No!

Shaken Baby Syndrome: The Big Difference Between a Jiggle and a Shake

The act of shaking leading to Shaken Baby Syndrome is so violent that individuals observing it would recognize it as dangerous and likely to kill the child.
American Academy of Pediatrics, Report on
Shaken Baby Syndrome, July 2001

Shaken Baby Syndrome is a horrific type of child abuse that requires a force even greater than falling off a bed or out of your arms. It occurs when a baby's head is whipped back and forth, an extreme movement that has also been referred to as Baby Whiplash Syndrome. Why whiplash? Because it involves the forceful snapping of his head, side to side, like cracking a whip. That aggressive shaking can tear open tiny veins under the skull, causing bleeding and brain damage.

Jiggling, on the other hand, differs from the violent whipping motion that causes Shaken Baby Syndrome in two important and fundamental ways:

1. With jiggling, your motions are fast but *tiny.* Your baby's head does not dramatically flail about. Instead, it moves—at most— one to two inches from side to side.
2. With jiggling, your baby's head always stays in line with his body. There is no whipping action with the body going in one direction and the head moving abruptly in the opposite one.

It is my firm belief that jiggling can actually help prevent Shaken Baby Syndrome. Because it calms babies so quickly and successfully, it can keep parents from reaching the point of desperation that might drive them to a violent response.

Nevertheless, even with all the very best tips and advice, parenting can sometimes make anyone feel frustrated, edgy, and inadequate. That's why it's crucial that you *never shake—or even jiggle—your baby when you're angry!*

Please—if you're at the end of your patience, put your baby down (even if he is crying) and give yourself a break. Don't hesitate to call for help from your spouse, your family, a friend, or a crisis hotline.

Kristi Discovers How to Calm Kyle's Colic with the "Jell-O Head" Jiggle

Kristi and John's son, Kyle, was a big, apple-cheeked baby with a wave of copper hair. He would be fine one night but scream for three hours the next! Kristi called for help after her five-week-old baby had been shrieking at the top of his lungs for hours. I made a house call.

Kristi describes what happened that Sunday night:

"As luck would have it, Kyle finally fell asleep moments before Dr. Karp arrived. I didn't really want Dr. Karp to wake him up or even touch him. Sure enough, when he placed his stethoscope on Kyle's chest, he started shrieking.

"Dr. Karp apologized for waking him, but reassured us that Kyle seemed healthy and his biggest problem was that he was having trouble calming. Then he deftly swaddled and jiggled our frantic baby, and we were stunned that within a minute Dr. Karp had Kyle resting angelically on his lap as if his last explosion had never happened.

"John and I practiced the technique and did okay, but we wimped out and asked Dr. Karp to put Kyle back to sleep before he left. Our boy did great that night, but the next day he was unbelievably fussy. And we just didn't feel comfortable trying the tricks we had learned the night before.

"Finally, my mom came to the rescue. She wrapped Kyle tightly, placed him on her lap (laying him on his side with his head cradled in her hands), shhhhed loudly, and did what I like to call the 'Jell-O head.' She wiggled her knees back and forth, making his head quiver between her loosely cupped hands, like Jell-O on a plate. At first, Kyle resisted her efforts. He strained against the blanket and cried even harder. However, after three or four minutes he quieted, and after fifteen minutes he was fast asleep!

"My mother repeated this miracle many times throughout her stay with us and I began to view _her_ as the expert on Dr. Karp's method. I found that I had a hard time doing the Jell-O-head part, but I kept working at it and eventually began to feel more confident.

"At first it took almost twenty minutes for this trick to settle Kyle into sleep. But soon I got it down to ten minutes, and by the time he was seven weeks old I could take him from shriek to smile in two minutes flat.

"The more I practiced, the more I learned that the crucial steps for Kyle were tight swaddling and the Jell-O head. Gentle rhythms helped him when he was already quiet, but to calm screaming he needed almost an earthquake. Then, after a short time, he would heave a huge sigh and tension seemed to leave his body. I felt like a great mom! By four months of age, Kyle was adorable, happy, and doing fine without swaddling, the swing—or the Jell-O-head jiggle."

Kristi, John, Kyle, and Cassandra

CALMING A BABY WITH THE JELL-O-HEAD JIGGLE

Lullabies: What Swinging Sounds Like When Put to Music

The word *lullaby* means *to sing to sleep,* and the tempo of these tunes is usually one beat per second—approximately the same as a heartbeat. The slow, rhythmic pace of lullabies is perfect for your baby after he has been fed and is drifting into the land of Winken, Blinken, and Nod.

However, these tranquil songs are usually powerless to stop babies in the midst of a crying frenzy. By that point, they're so lost in screams they can't hear you, even though you may be singing their favorite song. Just as adults can be "blind with rage," babies can become "deaf with distress."

Fortunately, you can rescue your baby from crying by switching to a tune with a zippy rhythm of two to three beats per second. These fast songs work especially well after your baby is swaddled. They're the original "Wrap" music! If you're a Beatles fan, try calming your baby with a fast jiggle like "It's Been a Hard Day's Night." As he begins to settle, slow down to "We Can Work It Out" or "All You Need Is Love." And when he's putty in your hands, shift to a slow song like "Golden Slumbers" or the number-one favorite of all new parents, "I'm So Tired."

Lullabies work better and better with repetition, as your baby gradually learns to associate the music with the sweet cuddling you give him every time you sing.

Lullabies Help Parents Too!

Lullabies calm babies—and parents. These songs gently soothe *our* jangled nerves and lull us into a more peaceful state of mind. Lullabies also often contain a dash of black humor to help sleep-deprived parents vent their feelings and laugh a little. Consider, for example, the lyrics of the classic lullaby, "Rock-a-Bye Baby":

> Rock-a-bye baby on the treetop,
> when the wind blows the cradle will rock,
> when the bough breaks the cradle will fall,
> *and down will come baby, cradle and all.*

The rhythms may be for sleepy babies, but the words are definitely for frazzled grown-ups!

The Windshield Wiper and Infant Swings: Two Great Ways to Move Your Baby in the Right Direction

Deborah's two-month-old son, Max, loved being lifted up and down, over and over again, using his mother like a carnival ride.

Genevieve's mom found she had to walk her baby, lap after lap, around the block to keep her happy.

Dancing, bouncing, and carrying your baby all day is hard work, especially when you're exhausted. Is there a way to jiggle your baby that doesn't wear out your back, your carpet, your tires, or your sense of humor?

I suggest these two user-friendly and highly successful calming motions: the Windshield Wiper, which is great for calming frantic babies, and the infant swing, which keeps babies quiet after they've been calmed.

The Windshield Wiper: How to Use Your Lap to Quiet Your Colicky Baby

The Windshield Wiper perfectly combines the 5 "S's" for a very powerful soothing experience. It's my favorite method for switching on a baby's calming reflex.

Don't get discouraged if the movement seems a little complicated the first time you try it. After five to ten practices, you'll see it's one of the easiest ways for pooped parents to soothe upset infants. (It's best to practice the Windshield Wiper with a doll or when your baby is quiet and alert.)

Here's what to do:
1. Swaddle your baby tightly (the 1st "S").
2. Find a comfortable chair to sit in with your feet resting flat on the floor. (Most parents find that sitting forward in the chair works best.)
3. Sit with your knees together and your feet a few inches apart (approximately the same distance as your shoulders).
4. Nestle your baby on his right side in the groove between your legs (the 2nd "S"), allowing his cheek and head to rest in your left hand (on top of your knees). If your baby is long, or your arms are short, pull him closer to you and let his ankles rest on your left hip.
5. Slide your *right* hand under his head so your two hands overlap a bit and his head is cradled in an open, *loose* grasp.
6. Soften your shoulders, take a deep breath, and let your body relax.
7. Roll your baby partly, or totally, onto his stomach. His tummy

should press against your left arm or legs. *Make sure he's not at all rolled toward his back.*

8. Lean forward over his body, and make a rough shhhh right next to his ear (the 3rd "S"). Your shhhh should be as loud as his crying.

9. Now swing (the 4th "S") your knees side-to-side—like a windshield wiper. If he's crying hard, move faster *but* make your moves smaller and smaller. In seconds you'll be making quick, tiny movements—two to three beats per second and one inch from side to side. The louder your little one cries, the faster and smaller your swinging should be. Then, as he calms, gradually slow your motion down. (Remember, his head must jiggle like Jell-O back and forth between your hands to turn on the calming reflex.) Some parents prefer bouncing their baby up and down on their knees, but this often doesn't work as well as swinging.

10. Finally, if your hands are well positioned, your left thumb should be in front of his mouth. Offer him your clean thumb to suck on (the 5th "S"). Don't worry about your thumb being too big to fit; remember how big he can open his mouth when he cries! Or, if

you prefer, your hand is also in position to hold a pacifier for him to suck on.

A Beginner's Version of the Windshield Wiper

Until you master the Windshield Wiper, try this easier version:

1. Swaddle your baby and securely wedge him on his side (as described in Chapter 9) in the bassinet or crib.
2. Grab the bassinet on the side, near his head.
3. Jiggle it quickly, like you're shivering, making his head wiggle like Jell-O.
4. Shhhh loudly or turn on some harsh white noise.

Your baby should calm after twenty to thirty seconds of this method. Then roll him on his back and let him sleep.

Infant Swings: Get Your Fussy Baby into the Swing of Things

Many of you probably live far from your families, and the burden of baby care falls on your shoulders twenty-four hours a day. No wonder you need some help! That's why it was inevitable that the inventors of labor-saving devices like washing machines and garbage disposals would create some baby-calming devices like swings, bouncy seats, and . . . cars. (Of course, cars weren't invented for this reason, but that's how many parents use them.)

Many weary parents find products that vibrate or swing are even better than car rides. When used properly, these devices are more effective, don't cause accidents or pollution, and they let you stay in your PJ's!

Unfortunately, some parents hesitate to use swings because they believe myths like: "It moves too fast." "It can hurt a baby's back." "It makes them vomit." "Babies get dependent on them." "It's meant for older infants."

Betsy found the swing helpful, but she was so afraid it would hurt Hannah that she put two pounds of bananas in it with her just to slow the thing down!

Lisanne felt torn. The swing helped Sasha, but she worried, "I don't want him to become hooked on it."

Of course, the last thing any parent would ever want to do is hurt her child or impair his development. But, don't forget, babies are jiggled and rocked for months in the womb. That's why, far from spoiling Sasha, his eight hours in the swing were a small compensation for his having been evicted from the uterus. Once Sasha reached three months, he was old enough to soothe himself without any help from a swing. Like Sasha, most babies by three to four months of life find the swing isolating and boring. I've never seen a baby who couldn't be easily weaned from the swing by five months of age. (See Chapter 15 on weaning babies from the swing.)

Occasionally, your friends and families may also have worries about infant swings. Some comment disapprovingly: "Babies should be in their mother's arms, not in a machine." Or, "It shouldn't be called a swing, it's really a 'neglectomatic'!"

All this is silly. Thinking you're a better parent because you never use a swing is like thinking you're a better cook because you never use an electric can opener. Remember, throughout time, parents have had kith and kin to lend hands of support. In today's mini-families, a swing can help replace that missing extra pair of hands you need to comfort your baby while you shower, go to the bathroom, or just sit and rest for a moment. Your swing is like the substitute of a helpful next-door neighbor—only it's battery-operated and there are no loud parties.

Eight Tricks for Getting the Most Out of Your Swing

> *Fern boasted, "The swing was magic for our son William. The motion and the noise worked great to get him into a peaceful sleep. It became my third hand."*

Like all baby-calming techniques, there are tricks to using swings that can improve your success with them.

1. **Start swinging early.** Three weeks of age is not too young for a baby to be in the swing; they've been rocking and rolling in your belly for months. (Always consult your doctor before using a swing if you have a sick or premature baby.)

2. **Never put your baby into the swing when he's screaming.** Karp's Law of Swings states: If you put a screaming baby in a swing, what you'll get is a swinging screaming baby!

A little-known fact about swings (and bouncy seats too) is that they're not very good for *making* frantic babies calm. However, once your baby's crying has been temporarily quieted, they're great for *keeping* him calm and lulling him into sleep. So, always settle your baby for several minutes before you put him in the swing.

3. **Keep your baby's arms wrapped.** Swaddling helps swinging babies quiet faster and stay quiet longer. However, you still need to strap him securely into the swing's seat by putting the bar or belt between his wrapped legs.

4. Recline the seat back as much as possible. If the seat is too upright, it can be hard for your baby to support his head. Recline it back as far as it can go or use a swing with a cradle attachment.

5. Do a twenty-second jiggle whenever crying starts up again. After your baby is in the swing, he may start to fuss again. Remember, only *vigorous* motion turns on the calming reflex. So if his crying flares up, grab the back of the swing seat and start jiggling it forward and back an inch, two to three moves a second. Within twenty seconds he should relax again.

6. Use the fastest speed. Unless your baby is soundly asleep, the slow speed will probably be too mild to keep him into a deep state of relaxation. Cranky kids settle best on the fast speed and many sleep best that way all night long. See what works best for your baby.

7. Use loud white noise at the same time. Play a loud white noise one to two feet from your baby's head until he is so deeply asleep you can lower it a bit (to a strong rumble) without waking him up.

8. Practice makes perfect. As with all of the 5 "S's," after a few pleasant experiences in the swing, your baby may start getting happy as soon as you put him in it.

> Sandy could calm Harriet in her lap, but when she moved the baby to the swing, little Harriet roared all over again. Sandy, warned not to overstimulate her already frantic child, would set the swing on the slowest speed. But this was too gentle to keep her little firecracker "zoned."
>
> Sandy changed her approach by wrapping Harriet's arms snugly and turning on the hair dryer to quiet her momentarily. Then she hustled her into the swing and jiggled it by hand for a few seconds. Once her baby looked peaceful, Sandy set the swing at the maximum speed. Immediately, everything came together. Soothing Harriet became a snap, and suddenly the swing worked every time.

The Whys About the "S's":
Questions Parents Ask About Swinging

1. *Are swings ever bad for a baby's legs, hips, or back?*

    No. Inside the womb, your baby was twisted like a pretzel. His supple body is incredibly flexible, which is why he can be placed in a swing without any concern for his legs, hips, or back.

2. *I sometimes worry my baby's neck is too doubled over in the swing. Is that possible?*

    In the swing, your baby should be reclined back as much as possible. His neck should not be doubled over. That could make it hard to breathe especially if he is premature or sick.

3. *Should I avoid rocking my baby vigorously right after he has eaten?*

    Believe it or not, jiggling doesn't make babies spit up more. In fact, keeping him from crying may even make your baby less likely to throw up. Bouncing can also loosen a gas bubble and help your baby burp.

4. *Can a baby get dizzy or nauseous from the swing or the Windshield Wiper?*

    No. Jiggling motion does not set off the nausea center of the brain. Dizziness and nausea are triggered by big *wide* movements like driving down a curvy mountain road. Swinging makes fussy babies feel more comfortable, not less.

5. *If I put my baby in the swing too much, will it lose its effectiveness?*

    Some babies love to suck, some need white noise to stay calm, and others are only happy when they're swinging all day. Luckily, what babies love, they love all the time! That's why they never tire of milk, cuddling, or swings.

6. *What should I do if my baby cries more when I rock him fast?*

Your infant may keep yelling for a few minutes after you begin jiggling him, since it can take a little time for him to realize you're doing something he likes. If, however, your baby continues crying despite vigorous jiggling, check your technique. Make sure your moves are fast and tiny, you're using loud white noise, he's tightly wrapped, and, when he's in your lap or arms, that he's on his side or stomach.

A Parent's Perspective: Odes to Swings and Other Things

Everyone knows that people can be moved to tears, but many parents are learning that their babies can also be moved to happiness. Here are a few babies who calmed once their parents got a little mojo happening:

When baby Noah began to cry, David tried burping him by hoisting Noah onto his shoulder and lightly patting his back. Despite David's loving attempts to get a burp out, Noah continued to wail.

Perhaps out of frustration or from some ancient instinct, David started patting Noah harder. He thumped him like a tom-tom drum, with a cupped hand, at about two pats per second.

Almost instantly, Noah quieted. His body melted into his dad's arms and a few minutes later he fell asleep. "I was surprised to see how firmly he liked to be patted. But he relaxed so fast and so deeply that I knew it was right."

When Margie and Barbara's son, Michael, was six weeks old, he screamed so loudly at night that their downstairs neighbor would often bang on the ceiling.

Margie tried to placate him with gentle rocking and soothing songs, but nothing worked until she discovered what she called the "Native war dance." She clutched Michael to her chest, his stomach pressed against her and her arms around him like a straitjacket, and shouted, "HA-ja ja ja, HA-ja ja ja." With each loud "HA" she doubled over and bent at the knees, making Michael feel as if he'd fallen through a trapdoor. With each "ja" she thumped him on the back and ratcheted her body partway back up. By the third "ja" she was standing straight again, ready for the next "HA."

Margie said that at three A.M., the vigor of the rhythm and the loudness of the chant were essential. Usually, within ten minutes or so Michael was snoozing again.

12

The 5th "S": Sucking—
The Icing on the Cake

Main Points:

- Sucking calms babies by satisfying their hunger and by turning on their calming reflex
- Three ways to help your baby succeed with pacifiers
- How to sidestep six common pacifier problems

Suck, and be satisfied.
Isaiah 66:11

If mixing all the "S's" together is like baking a cake, then sucking is the icing on the cake. This last sweet nudge allows babies to settle down, let go, and fall asleep.

A baby's survival outside the womb depends on her ability to suck. Like an actor rehearsing for a starring role, your baby began practicing sucking on her fingers long before birth. (Ultrasound photos of fetuses show them sucking on their hands as early as three months before their due date.) It was easy for your fetus to suck her fingers, because the soft walls of your womb kept her hands conveniently right in front of her mouth. Likewise, once she reaches four months of age and has enough muscle control to park her thumb in her mouth anytime she wants, it will again become a breeze for her to suck her fingers.

However, during your baby's fourth trimester she'll spend very little time sucking her fingers. It's not that she doesn't want to—she'd probably slurp on them twenty-four hours a day if she could. But for a newborn, getting a finger into the mouth and keeping it there is almost a Herculean feat. Even when your baby concentrates hard, drooling in anticipation of her success, her poor coordination usually causes her hands to fly right by their target, like cookies narrowly missing a hungry toddler's mouth!

Why is sucking such a sweet experience for babies? What does it do that gives them so much pleasure?

Why Does Sucking Make Babies So Happy?

Sucking makes babies feel extraordinarily good for two reasons:

1. It satisfies their hunger—of course. Who doesn't love to eat? Well, new babies love it so much that they pack away a milky meal eight to twelve times a day! For babies, all this eating means hours of pleasure from sucking, sucking, sucking.

Some people say that babies eat like "little pigs," but even piggies have a hard time holding a candle to a baby. Every day, young infants "snort down" about three ounces of milk for every pound of their body weight. That's equivalent to an adult drinking five gallons of whole milk a day, seven days a week. No wonder they need to eat so often.

2. It turns on their calming reflex. Babies suck to eat, but sucking is yet one more way prehistoric fetuses used to turn on their protective calming reflex and improve their chances of survival.

Sucking for food is called eating, and sucking for soothing is called non-nutritive sucking. If your baby is hungry she'll probably only suck a pacifier for a minute before crying, as if to complain, "Hey, I ordered milk—not rubber!" However, if she just wants some comfort, she'll happily suck on the pacifier for a good long while.

Can a Young Baby Suck Too Much?

Some authors warn parents not to let their babies suck "too much," cautioning that sucking is habit-forming. (I wonder if, given the option, these experts would reach into your womb and pull your baby's thumb right out of her mouth!) Fortunately, it's impossible for young babies to suck too much. Sucking isn't candy or an addiction; it's a highly sophisticated, self-calming tool. It's an integral part of the fourth trimester and one of your baby's first steps toward self-reliance.

The same deep calm that's activated in your baby's brain by sucking can also be switched on in the brains of older kids and adults by other "sucking" experiences, such as lollipop licking, cigarette smoking, and nail biting. (No wonder psychologists compare cigar smoking to thumb sucking!)

Many studies have shown that non-nutritive sucking is healthy for babies. It's like vitamin S! It lessens stress (blood pressure, heart rate, etc.) and can stimulate the release of natural pain-relieving chemicals in a baby's brain that decrease suffering from shots, blood tests, or circumcisions. Scientists have also found that premature babies who suck pacifiers grow faster, and full-term babies who are "paci" suckers have a lower risk of SIDS.

Once Upon a Time: How Parents Have Used Sucking in Other Times and Cultures

Have you ever noticed how nicely your baby falls asleep while sucking? Most babies just soften like melted butter. Of course, mothers throughout time have traditionally satisfied their infants' need to suck the old-fashioned way, with the breast. Mother's milk is the center of an infant's world—which is why some people even refer to breast-feeding moms as Earth Mothers.

But, rather than Earth Mother, I think a breast-feeding mom should be called Galactic Goddess! That's because the ancient Greeks invented the words *galaxy* and *galactic* out of their word *gala,* meaning *milk.* Legend said that the stars in the heavens came from milk spraying out of the breasts of the goddess Juno, which is also why we call our galaxy the Milky Way.

For mothers from tribes like the Efé of Zaire and the !Kung San of Botswana, sucking is usually the first solution they try to calm their babies. At the least little squawk, these moms plunk their babies onto the boob thirty, forty, one hundred times a day!

In past centuries, it was common in some cultures to put sugar inside a rag for babies to suck on. Sometimes this "sugar teat" was dunked in brandy if a baby was particularly fussy. My friend Celia, raised in Russia in the 1920s, remembers that her neighbors, unable to afford sugar, instead offered colicky babies a small piece of chewed-up bread wrapped in a thin cloth.

As rubber nipples for bottles became popular in the early 1900s, so did rubber pacifiers for sucking on. The English called these "dummies," choosing this name not because a baby looked dumb with a pacifier in the mouth, but because these little rubber teats silenced cries so well.

Helping Your Baby "Suck"ceed with Pacifiers

For most babies, sucking their thumb is like picking up ice with chopsticks—it slips away despite the best efforts. That's why they usually need a little sucking assistance.

You can satisfy your baby's sucking needs one of two ways:

1. *You* as a pacifier
2. *Use* a pacifier

For thousands of years, mothers have offered their breasts to their babies as pacifiers. That arrangement may be fine for some moms, but it's a burden for others. Luckily, parents today have a very effective alternative—pacifiers.

As with other aspects of baby calming, there are certain tricks to using pacifiers well. These tips increase your baby's chances for pacifier "suck"cess:

- *Try different nipples*—In my experience, no pacifier shape is superior to another. Some babies like orthodontic pacifiers, with their long stems and tips that are flattened on one side. Others prefer nubbier pacifiers with short stems. Ultimately, the perfect pacifier shape for your baby is the one she likes the best.

- *Don't try the hard sell*—You can try putting the pacifier in your baby's mouth when she's crying, but don't force it if she refuses. You'll be most successful if you calm her first with the other "S's" and then offer the pacifier.

- *Use reverse psychology to keep the pacifier from falling out*—This is the best trick I've ever seen for teaching a baby to keep the pacifier in her mouth. When your baby is calm, offer her the pacifier. The moment she starts to suck, tug it lightly as if you were starting to take it out of her mouth (but don't tug so hard that it actually comes out).

  Your baby will respond by resisting your tug and automatically sucking on the pacifier a little harder. Wait a moment and then give a little pull again. Repeat this process ten to twenty times, whenever you give your newborn the pacifier. Her natural tendency to resist you will train her mouth to keep a firm grip on the pacifier. Many two- to three-month-old infants can be trained to keep the pacifier in their mouths even while smiling—and crying.

  This reverse psychology technique is based on a simple principle of human nature: We all believe that what is in our mouth belongs to us! That's why trying to pull your nipple out of your baby's mouth is like prying a toy from the arms of a two-year-old; the harder you pull, the more she resists, and thus develops the coordination and strength to keep hold of it.

Pacifier Pitfalls

Some parents and grandparents worry that pacifier use may teach a baby bad habits. But truthfully, a pacifier is just a tool to help calm your baby until she can do it herself. There are, however, six potential pacifier problems you'll want to steer clear of:

1. **Nipple confusion**—Before nursing is well-established, some breast-feeding babies get confused when they're given rubber nipples to suck on. A baby sucking on a rubber nipple often uses a lazy, biting

motion, which requires much less effort and coordination than sucking on the breast. Unfortunately, this also sometimes teaches a baby
an improper way to use her mouth muscles.

You may offer your baby a pacifier on Day 1, but be prepared to
stop using it for a while if your baby is having any trouble breast-
feeding. I recommend you not offer your baby a bottle until she's two
weeks old and the feeding is going really well. Then a bottle every
day is fine. Most moms fill the bottle with breast milk, water, glucose
water, or non-caffeinated peppermint or chamomile tea.

Don't wait one to two months before introducing the bottle. Parents who do this are often rudely surprised by their baby's emphatic
rejection of the synthetic nipple.

2. Chemical contamination—Buy clear silicone pacifiers instead of
yellow rubber ones. The yellow rubber gets sticky and deteriorates after
a while and may release tiny amounts of unwanted chemical residue.

3. Keep sweets away—Don't dip a pacifier into syrup to make your
baby suck on it more eagerly. Sweeteners like honey and maple or
corn syrup run a risk of giving your baby botulism (a disease causing
temporary paralysis, and even death).

4. Keep it clean—When you buy a pacifier, wash it well with soap
and hot water. Rinse it when it falls on the floor—and several times a
day even if it doesn't. Don't suck your baby's pacifier to clean it in your
mouth, since your saliva may spread colds, herpes, or other illness.

5. No strings attached—Never hang a pacifier around your baby's
neck. Strings or ribbons may get caught around her fingers, cutting
off the circulation, or wrap around the throat and choke her.

6. Enough is enough—Once a baby reaches four to five months of
age, I usually get rid of pacifiers. By that time, your infant can suck
on her own fingers and do many other things to calm herself. Stopping the pacifier after six months is more difficult, because by then
your baby has already started to develop a close emotional relationship with her "paci," much like a teddy bear or security blanket.

The Whys About the "S's":
Questions Parents Ask About Sucking

1. *How can I tell if my baby needs milk or just wants to suck?*
   These signs indicate your baby is crying for food:

   - When you touch her face, she turns her head and opens her mouth in search of the nipple.
   - A pacifier may initially calm her, but within minutes she'll start fussing again.
   - When you offer her milk she takes it eagerly and afterwards becomes sweet and calm.

2. *Does sucking on a pacifier shorten breast-feeding?*
   Since how a baby sucks on a pacifier differs from how she sucks on a breast, wait a week or two, until breast-feeding is going well, before introducing the pacifier. At that point, pacifiers can occasionally make breast-feeding *more* successful by lessening a baby's crying and helping her mom get a break from nonstop sucking.

3. *Can pacifiers cause ear infections?*
   A few studies have reported that babies using pacifiers get more ear infections. This probably happens because sucking hard on a pacifier disturbs the pressure in the ears (the same way pressure changes on airplane flights can give kids ear infections). Fortunately, young infants can't suck a pacifier hard enough to cause much pressure to build up. So you don't have to worry about this for the first four months.

4. *Can pacifiers protect babies from SIDS?*
   Scientific studies consistently report a lower incidence of SIDS among infants who use pacifiers. However, since it's not clear how they might protect babies, the American Academy of Pediatrics

cautions parents not to conclude from these studies that pacifiers actually prevent SIDS.

5. *Can my baby become addicted to the pacifier if she always sleeps with one?*

No! This is one old wives' tale you can put to bed. When Hannah was five months old, it took her mother a mere three days to wean her pacifier use down from all night and several hours a day to just two minutes a day.

However, as mentioned, a baby over five to six months may begin to develop an emotional attachment to her binkie. Although you can still wean her from the pacifier after that age, it's often more traumatic.

6. *If sucking is so important, should I wrap my baby with her hands out so she can get to them?*

Calm babies may do fine with their hands unwrapped, but fussy babies have a hard time sucking their fingers without accidentally whacking themselves in the face. For these kids, having their hands free is a frustrating tease. It's much easier on agitated babies to swaddle them and give them pacifiers, because they can control their bodies and suck better when their arms are not flailing and disturbing them.

7. *Will frequent feeding spoil my baby or make her tummy more colicky?*

Many parents, like Valerie and David, are warned that "overfeeding" can give their baby tummy pain:

> *"Our baby, Christina, was screaming and would calm only on my breast. My husband said I was making her colicky by feeding her every time she cried. My friends warned me I would spoil her by feeding her so often. What should I do?"*

When Valerie asked me this, I told her, first, thank goodness she had a method that worked to calm her baby. Second, it's impossible to spoil a fetus—and all babies are "fetuses" for the first three months. Third, she needed to call her doctor to make sure her baby was getting enough milk.

However, those three points notwithstanding, it sounded to me as if Valerie was making one important error. Do you know the saying, "When the only tool you have is a hammer . . . everything looks like a nail"? Well, it sounded like the only "tool" Valerie had for calming Christina was her breast.

I don't worry about young babies picking up bad habits or that too much milk will upset their tummies, but I did think Valerie was ignoring some other excellent calming tools. So I recommended she and David learn the other 4 "S's."

Dads are especially eager to master other calming tricks, because they often feel left out when the only method that calms their baby is a milky breast. Once fathers learn how to quickly soothe their babies, they feel much more confident caring for them.

8. *If I let my baby suckle on my breasts all night, I sleep well and it feels very cozy. Is there anything harmful in doing this?*

Spending the night with your baby at your side is how most people have slept throughout the ages. I think one of the most blessed feelings a woman can have is the sweet sleep that she shares with her nursing child. When you are together like that, it's natural that she may want to nibble a little on and off. However, it's your choice. You can go along with your baby's wishes or keep your shirt on and try to pacify her another way. There's no right or wrong about this—the decision is yours. (See Chapter 15 for a discussion of the pros and cons about co-sleeping.)

However, if you're sleeping with your baby, please be aware of the following:

- Keep pillows and blankets away, avoid waterbeds, and make sure she can't fall off or get stuck under the headboard or against the wall. (Swaddling will help keep her from scooting into dangerous places.)

- Make sure you're getting enough rest. You're no good to your baby if you get sick or become a menace when you are driving.
- Once your baby's teeth begin to come in, be aware that feedings lasting more than a half hour may cause tooth decay.

9. *There are a lot of thumb suckers in my family. Will giving my baby a pacifier prevent her from sucking her thumb later . . . or encourage it?*

Some babies are just incredibly driven to suck. Their strong desire is not a sign of being overly immature, dependent, or insecure (or of your being too lax as a parent). In my experience, the vast majority of cases of prolonged thumb and pacifier sucking is simply an inherited trait, no different from eye color or dimples. Or, to put it another way, it's one thing you really *can* blame on your parents!

There is little doubt that pacifiers prevent thumb sucking; it's just too hard to get both into the mouth at the same time. But in my experience it doesn't affect the length of time a baby demands to suck on something (finger or paci).

A Parent's Perspective: Testimonials from the Trenches

Some babies are interested in sucking only when they want to eat. For other babies sucking is like a massage, tranquilizer, and hot bath all rolled into one!

Here are stories of some babies who were "suckers for sucking":

Annie and Michael were especially worried when their little boy screamed; Rylan's heart problem made extreme exertion dangerous. So Ann carried him around the apartment for hours, until her back was in such pain that she couldn't stand it any longer.

She resisted giving Rylan a pacifier because she "didn't want to start teaching him bad habits that he would have trouble stopping later on." Finally, however, driven to desperation, Ann reluctantly gave it a try and "Bingo! Giving Rylan the pacifier was a godsend! We still had to entertain him, but the binkie let me walk away and take a break, especially when he was in his vibrating seat."

Stanley began to struggle with his feedings when he was seven weeks old. He had always begun his meals with gusto, but now after ten minutes he was pulling away and licking at the nipple as if he had forgotten how to eat. Seconds later he would arch back and wail as if he wanted to jump out of his mother's arms. But that wasn't what he wanted either, because as soon as Stanley was put down, he cried even harder.

Stanley's parents, Maria and Bill, tried rocking and wrapping him, but when he was really agitated he could free his hands in seconds. Maria, confused and frustrated, wondered if her milk had turned bad or dried up.

Fortunately, the problem was much less complicated than that. Maria had plenty of milk—in fact, too much. When Stanley tried extra suckling for fun at the end of his feeding, Maria's breasts continued releasing a stream of milk into his throat. Stanley had to pull away to avoid choking, but he was in a pickle because he still wanted to suck.

Once Maria and Bill began offering the pacifier at the end of his feedings, he became an angel again.

Steven and Kelly said their one-month-old bruiser, Ian, loved sucking on his paci. But if it fell out of his mouth he started to scream. Kelly lamented, "It works great, but we feel like we're becoming his pacifier slaves. My mom joked that we should just tape it in his mouth. I knew that even kidding about that was terrible, but we were going out of our minds."

When Steven and Kelly called, I taught them about "reverse psychology." One week later Kelly called back, amazed at how quickly the paci problem was solved. Within a week Ian's mouth muscles were so well trained he could hold the pacifier for one to two hours without dropping it.

Kelly said, "It's weird. I thought the best way to keep Ian's pacifier in his mouth was to keep pushing it back in. But what worked was to do exactly the opposite!"

Some babies will suck on anything you put in their mouths, but some are like miniature gourmets. Take Liam, who as a two-month-old refused to suck on anything—not pacifiers, not his fingers, not even a bottle, with <u>one</u> exception: He loved to suck on his mother's second finger!

13

The Cuddle Cure:
Combining the 5 "S's"
into a Perfect Recipe
for Your Baby's Bliss

Main Points:

- Some babies can be calmed with just one "S" but most need several "S's" to settle well
- The Cuddle Cure is the powerful combination of all 5 "S's" at the same time
- Two essential steps for perfecting the Cuddle Cure:

  Precision—A review of the most important points of each of the "S's"

  Practice—Why you must practice to excel at the Cuddle

As you know by now, the most successful baby-calming techniques handed down for centuries are based on the 5 "S's." However, if you haven't yet been successful at soothing your baby in minutes using the 5 "S's," don't lose heart. You can still learn how to guide your unhappy baby from tears to baby bliss using these methods.

To make no mistake is not in the power of man; but from their errors and mistakes the wise and good learn wisdom for the future.

Plutarch

Any one of the 5 "S's" can have a comforting effect on mildly fussy babies. However, for real explosive, colicky kids, a little swaddling or shushing may not make a dent. Here are reasons why your "S's" might not have succeeded in calming your crying baby:

1. She's having a little problem—Your baby may be hungry or struggling with a poop. Fortunately, these problems are usually obvious and easy to resolve without the "S's."

2. She's having a big problem—Approximately ten to fifteen percent of colicky babies have a medical explanation for their irritability, such as food intolerance or stomach acid reflux. (See Appendix A to review the medical causes of colic and Chapter 14 to review the treatment for many of those problems.)

3. The "S's" are being done one at a time—The more powerfully a baby is wailing the more she will need the help of several "S's" simultaneously.

4. The "S's" aren't being done correctly—As with any reflex, if it's not triggered in exactly the right way it just won't happen.

This chapter focuses on perfectly combining the 5 "S's" into the Cuddle Cure and reviews the common mistakes parents make as they begin to learn the "S's."

If One Is Good, Two Are Better:
Calming Babies with Multiple "S's"

Nina and Dimitri were dismayed that their champion cryer, Lexi, got more enraged when they tried to calm her with the sounds of

the hair dryer or the infant swing. However, when they used the
hair dryer and swing <u>together,</u> they worked like a charm.

Someone once said, "There's a sucker born every minute." Well, when it comes to babies that's especially true. In fact, thousands of suckers, swingers, and even shhhhers come into the world every day! Just as babies have different hair color and temperament, each infant differs slightly in the way he needs to be calmed. Some settle best with rocking, others quiet instantly with white noise, and some surrender as soon as they're put on their stomachs. These easy babies require the help of only one of the "S's" to make them feel calm and serene.

Cranky infants, however, need more help. They often require two, three, or four of the "S's" done together to cease their cycle of screaming. And the fussiest, most colicky babies demand all 5 "S's" simultaneously.

Getting Acquainted: An Experiment in Soothing Your Baby

To find your baby's favorite calming technique, place him on his back when he's a little bit fussy. One by one, add another "S" and see how many it takes to settle him down.

1. Shhhh him softly. If that doesn't work, do it louder, right in his ear.
2. Swaddle his arms to keep them from flailing. Do that while shhhhing.
3. Place your wrapped baby on his side or stomach and shush him again.
4. Now add a quick, jiggly motion.
5. Finally, on top of all of these, offer a pacifier or your finger to suck on.

By this time, most fussy babies will usually be calmed.

The Cuddle Cure: Combining All 5 "S's" into a Recipe for Baby Bliss

On a plane from New York to Los Angeles, I watched an elderly
woman calm a baby with such precise, elegant moves that I
imagined I was witnessing an ancient ballet.
*   In mid-flight, this infant suddenly erupted into crying. After*

a few piercing wails, the frail grandmother picked up her frantic traveling companion and began a symphony of responses. She nestled the little girl's stomach against her shoulder, made a continuous shhhh sound in the baby's ear, rhythmically thumped her bottom, and swayed her torso side to side like a snake working its way uphill.

In less than a minute her tiny bundle was sound asleep.

It's tempting to believe that someone who's good at calming babies has "the gift," but that's not the case. Soothing young infants has nothing to do with special talents. It has everything to do with understanding why babies cry and learning and practicing the skills to soothe them.

Most parents automatically rock and embrace their crying babies, but sometimes that's not enough. The Cuddle Cure combines all 5 "S's" into a technique so powerful it turns on the calming reflex in even the fussiest babies.

Mothers in many cultures around the world use variations of the Cuddle. In Tanzania, some women soothe crying babies by cuddling them while they pretend to grind corn! They vigorously bend and straighten and hum rough, grinding noises until the baby settles.

If the Cuddle is like an ancient cake recipe, with the ingredients being the 5 "S's," most baby books are unfortunately like incomplete cookbooks. They list the 5 "S's" but don't mention exactly how to do them or how to mix them together.

Without instructions on how to mix the ingredients for a cake, you're more likely to end up with warm goop than a wonderful dessert. And, without instructions detailing how to do each "S" and how to mix them together, it's easy for parents to end up with a *more* fussy baby rather than a perfectly calmed one!

And, once the Cuddle has helped you stop your baby's screams, that's not the end of it. The Cuddle is also a valuable tool for keeping your baby calm *after* you soothe his crying.

After your little one falls asleep in your arms, you may not be able to put him down and walk away. He may be very relaxed, but he's not in a coma. Deep within their brains, snoozing babies are still aware of the world around them. That's why abruptly stopping the hypnotic rhythms of the Cuddle may make a baby explode back into tears even from what appears to be a sound sleep.

Fortunately, the Cuddle is perfect for keeping your baby calm after you've quelled his cries. Your colicky baby may stay happy for hours as long as he feels like he's still safely packaged in the womb (swaddled, swinging, and with loud white noise playing close by). If your baby suddenly starts thrashing again, simply picking up the tempo should help regain his attention so you can lead him back to serenity.

How to Be the Best Cuddler on the Block

Although the Cuddle works better than anything else for calming colic, it may not feel natural at first. Many new parents find it's like riding a bicycle; it initially seems complicated and intimidating. Some parents give up after a few tries, thinking, *This may work for some kids but our baby hates it.*

I certainly understand this frustration. It's excruciating to try to quiet your baby's shrieking when everything you do seems to make it worse. But, like riding a bicycle, once you get the hang of doing the Cuddle it's really a lot of fun. Soon you'll feel like you've been doing it your entire life.

And if the Cuddle isn't working perfectly, it's probably just because you need a little technique tuneup. The most common reason this ancient method fails is because it's not being done properly. In fact, incorrect swaddling, swinging, and shushing may even make your crying baby *more* upset! So, like the song says, "If you're gonna do it, do it right, right."

Let's recap the important pointers to get each of your "S's" in gear:

Swaddling

Parents often abandon swaddling because their babies strain against it. They misinterpret this struggling to mean, "Let me out. I hate this. It's unfair!" But please don't give up on this crucial first step. To be successful with wrapping, you must:

- Keep your baby's arms straight down at his sides.
- With each fold of the swaddle, tuck and snug the blanket as tightly as possible.
- After swaddling, don't allow the blanket to loosen and pop back open.

Remember, *swaddling is not meant to calm your baby!* Its purpose is to stop his flailing and to help him pay attention to the other "S's," which *will* soothe him.

Side/Stomach Position

Lying on the back is fine when your baby is calm. But if he's sensitive, being rolled toward the back may upset the position sensors in his head and trigger a "red alert," making his crying even worse.

- When your baby is on his side, keep him rolled at least a bit toward his stomach. Some babies are so sensitive they will have difficulty getting calm if they're rolled even slightly toward their backs.

- Make sure your baby is not hungry. If he's eager to eat, holding him in a way that touches his cheek may trigger his rooting reflex and make him think you're offering food. You can imagine how this could confuse and frustrate a famished baby.

Shhhhing

The shhhh sound is easy to make, and most parents find it natural to do—softly. Therein lies the problem: Most parents shhhh too quietly and too far from their baby's ear.

- Crank up the volume of your shhhh until it's a bit louder than your baby's screams. Remember, the sounds in the womb are louder than a vacuum cleaner and your infant's ears naturally muffle sound for the first few months.

- If you're using a machine to make white noise, place it one to two feet from your baby's head so it's loud enough to trigger the calming reflex.

Swinging

Gentle swinging may keep a quiet baby content, but it's much too mild for screaming babies. The most important tips for successful swinging are:

- Move your fussy baby in quick, teensy, shiverlike wiggles. Slow, wide moves may keep a baby asleep, but they're not vigorous enough to calm a crying infant.

- Support your baby's head and neck, but hold his head a little loosely so it can jiggle a little like Jell-O in your hands.

> *Jake's father, Jimmy, told me he tried the Cuddle, but it wouldn't work. I reviewed each step of his technique and discovered he was doing almost everything right, except his swinging was too wide. Rather than sliding his knees an inch from side to side, he was going twelve inches with each move. These wide swings didn't get Jake's head jiggling enough. Once he made the motion fast and short, the swinging calmed Jake almost every time.*

Sucking

Sucking is usually the easiest "S" to get right. But if your baby rejects the pacifier, here's how to change his mind:

- Calm him first. Most babies can't take a pacifier while they're screaming.

- Try different brands. Some babies prefer a particular pacifier shape.

- Use reverse psychology. Gently tug on the pacifier as soon as he begins to suck it. He'll resist you, and the more you play this game, the sooner you'll train his mouth to keep a good long grip on the binkie.

Becoming a Cuddle Expert: Practice Makes Perfect

If at first you don't succeed—you're running about average.
M. H. Alderson

Remember, this technique has worked for millions of years, so even if it doesn't work perfectly the first few times you try it, you'll definitely get the hang of it if you keep practicing. (In the beginning, it's best to practice this technique with a doll or when you and your baby are calm. It's harder to learn when you're exhausted and your little angel is making noises that could shatter glass.)

Parents aren't the only ones who improve with practice. As you get better, your baby is getting better too. Bit by bit, he'll learn to recognize what you're doing—and that he likes it.

Patience is especially important if you're starting these techniques when your baby is already six to eight weeks old. It may take several tries for you to learn them and then several more tries for your baby to unlearn his prior experiences and begin to get used to the 5 "S's." However, if you persevere you can still be one hundred percent successful!

14

Other Colic Remedies:
From Massage and
Feeding Problem Cures
to Old Wives' Tales

Main Points:

- Three ancient colic cures proven to be true paths: massage, fresh air, and extra warmth
- Effective remedies for four medical causes of infant crying: allergies, constipation, feeding problems, reflux
- A look at four unproved colic treatments

Put cotton in your ears and gin in your stomach!

19th-century colic advice

Through the centuries, experts continually thought up colic treatments to fix whatever they believed to be causing their baby's unhappiness. These false assumptions led them to champion many different types of therapies that have proven to be total dead ends: alcohol, sugar water, sedation, anti-cramp medicine, and burp drops. There are, however, besides the 5 "S's" a few other ways of helping crying babies that are true paths.

When you want a break from the 5 "S's," here are three time-honored tricks for colicky babies that work well: massage, walks outside, and a little extra warming.

Massage: The Miracle of Touch

Massage is love which is one unique breath, breathing in two.
Frederick Leboyer, *Loving Hands*

Massage is a very ancient treatment for colic. Its extraordinarily soothing effects are based upon our oldest and most profound sense—touch.

Touch and the Fourth Trimester

There's an old saying, "A *child* is fed with milk and praise," and I would say a *baby* is fed with milk and caresses. Your baby's loving caresses began inside your womb, where she enjoyed a feast of velvety cuddling twenty-four hours a day. Once born, your baby still loves to be touched and stroked. Your skin-to-skin embrace of her is the touch equivalent of calming, hypnotic movement or sound.

Cuddling Builds Brains

A recent study from McGill University asked, "Does extra cuddling make animals smarter?" The researchers looked at two groups of little rat pups. The first group had very "loving" mothers who licked and stroked their babies a lot. The second group received much less affection from their moms.

When the rats became old enough to be taught mazes and puzzles, scientists noticed that the cuddled animals were extrasmart. They had developed an abundance of connections in a part of the brain crucially important in rats (and people) for learning.

The moral of the story is clear: Cuddling your baby feels good, and it may even boost her IQ!

Touch is not only a wonderful reminder of a baby's time as a fetus; like milk, it's an essential "nutrient" for her growth. In fact, in some ways it's even more beneficial than milk. While stuffing your baby with extra milk won't make her any healthier, the more tickles and hugs she gets, the stronger and happier she'll become.

In 1986, a brilliant baby-watcher named Tiffany Field confirmed the benefits of touching in a study on the effects of massage on premature babies. She had nurses massage a group of preemies for fifteen minutes, three times a day, for ten days. The results were astounding. Massaged babies gained forty-seven percent more weight than expected and were able to go home almost a full week earlier than babies who didn't get massaged. In an equally stunning follow-up study, when the massaged babies were examined one year later, their IQ's were higher than the babies' who were handled routinely. Dr. Field also discovered that when healthy full-term babies were massaged for fifteen minutes a day, they cried less, were more alert and socially engaged, gained weight faster, and had lower levels of stress hormones.

Infant Massage: Rubbing Your Baby the Right Way

Beautiful, big-eyed Mica was so sensitive and vigilant that she often had difficulty shutting out the world, even when she was exhausted. When Mica was one month old, I recommended that her parents, Lori and Michael, try using massage to help their daughter wind down:

> At first Mica seemed leery of this type of touching. She accepted some foot massage, but that was as far as I could get before she became unhappy. I stuck with it, though, and after a week, Mica began to enjoy the touching. She even became excited when she heard me rub massage oil into my hands. I was delighted! Massage time soon became our special bonding time. Mica would deeply relax and sometimes fall asleep. I loved doing this for our daughter. And best of all, it helped her become calmer in general and to get over her evening fussies.
>
> Lori, Michael, and Mica

Here are the five steps for giving your baby a perfect massage:

1. Prepare for pleasure—About an hour after your baby has eaten, remove your jewelry, warm the room, dim the lights, take the phone off the hook and, if you like, you may turn on some soft music. Have some slightly heated vegetable oil (almond oil is great) within easy reach, and some wipes and diapers too, just in case.

2. Bring yourself to the moment—Sit comfortably with your naked baby right next to you or on your bare, outstretched legs. Place a towel around her body to keep her warm. Now take five slow, deep breaths to allow yourself to be fully present for this wonderful experience. Massage is not a mechanical routine, it's an exchange of love in one fleeting and tender moment of time.

The first few times you massage your baby, you may notice that you're "in your head," thinking about how to do the massage. Don't worry: Once you become more familiar with the routine, your attention will naturally begin to focus on your fingertips, your baby's soft skin, and your loving heart.

3. Speak to your baby with your hands—Rub some oil between your hands and start by touching your baby's feet. Always try to keep one hand in contact with her skin and softly talk to her about what you are doing and what your hopes are for her life to come or sing a lullaby. Uncover one limb at a time and massage it with a touch that is fluid but *firm.* Let your massage strokes move slowly along her body, in synchronicity with your calm breathing.

Use smooth, repetitious strokes over her feet, legs, stomach, chest, arms, hands, back, face, and ears, gently rotating, pulling, stretching, and squeezing. Twist her arms and legs as if you were lightly wringing a wet sponge. Feel free to experiment with using your fingers and different parts of your hands, wrists, and forearms.

4. Reward your baby's tummy—Thank your baby's tummy for doing such a good job. Bicycle her legs and then firmly push both knees to the belly and hold them there for ten to twenty seconds to give a nice, satisfying stretch. Then massage the tummy in firm, clockwise, circular strokes, starting at her right lower belly, up and across the top of her tummy, and ending at the lower left side. (This sometimes helps babies release gas or poop.)

5. **Follow your baby's signals**—If your baby begins to get restless, it's a sign to change your pace or end the massage. Wipe the excess oil from her body, letting a bit remain to nourish her skin. Bathe her with soap and warm water later that day or the next morning.

Giving your baby a massage is also wonderful for moms and dads because it can lower your stress and boost your self-esteem.

If you would like to learn more about the technique of baby massage, an excellent resource is Vimala McClure's *Infant Massage*.

Walks Outside:
Calming Some Babies Is Just a Stroll in the Park

If our babies could talk, they would probably bug us, "Why can't we live outside like all the other Stone Age families?" Our ancient relatives lived outside, and perhaps that's one reason why some of our little cave babies get deadly bored sitting at home. For them, nothing is more fun than hearing the wind in the trees, feeling the air on their faces, and watching the continually moving shadows.

Some parents ask me how calming by being outside fits with the idea of the fourth trimester. For babies, a walk outside is a parade of calming out-of-focus images and jiggly, soothing rhythms. I believe they are lulled by this hypnotic flow of gentle sensations, like a constant, multisensory white noise.

So, when your baby is crying, try giving her a breath of fresh air. Going for a walk will also help lift your spirits and fill you with a sense of peace.

Warming Your Baby Up to the Idea of Calming Down

In the uterus, infants are constantly in "hot water"! That may be why so many babies love warm things. To help you soothe your baby when she's fussing, try these "hot tips":

- *A warm bath*

  Every time their six-week-old son, Jack, was fussy, Kim and John calmed him by submersing him in warm water. "Jack always gets super relaxed when he is put into a hot bath. He goes into a Zen-like state and is mellow and ready for bed afterward."

- *A warm blanket*

  When her niece, Erica, was very fussy one day, Barbara heated the baby blanket in the clothes dryer for a few minutes, <u>thoroughly checked it for hot spots,</u> and then bundled Erica in it. Erica calmed so quickly that from then on, whenever she became fussy she got swaddled in warm wraps. (Barbara was always very careful to avoid overheating or burning her.)

- *A warm hat*

  Covering your baby's head makes her feel cozy and comfortable. Newborns lose twenty-five percent of their body heat through their heads, so a baby with an exposed head is like an adult walking around on a chilly night in underwear.

- *A warm hot-water bottle*

  Dr. Spock loved to tell parents to lay their colicky babies tummy-down on a warm hot-water bottle. He thought it helped relieve stomach pain, the way warmth can help menstrual cramps, but more likely it works by putting soothing pressure on your baby's stomach and turning on the calming reflex.

- *Warm socks*

    As with a blanket, you can warm up your baby's socks to make her feel extra toasty. Just check for hot spots before putting them on.

Four Modern True Path Colic Cures: A Doctor's Bag of Tricks

Although medical problems are not commonly the cause of colic, I estimate that ten to fifteen percent of extremely fussy babies cry because of one of four tummy troubles: food allergy, constipation, feeding problems, or stomach acid reflux.

Children who suffer from these treatable conditions may get some relief from the 5 "S's" and the grandmother's tips discussed earlier; however, what many of these infants truly need is a medical solution for their particular difficulty.

Here are a few hints on how to soothe these unhappy infants.

Preventing Food Allergies: Getting Tummies Back on Track

It's believed that approximately ten percent of colicky babies cry due to food sensitivities. Unfortunately, doctors have no accurate test to check babies for this problem. To discover if your child has a food allergy, you must play Sherlock Holmes and eliminate foods from your diet or switch your baby's formula to see what happens. (Always consult your doctor before doing so.) It usually only takes two to four days to see if the crying gets better.

If your baby improves when you eliminate foods from your diet, she may have a food allergy. However, sometimes this improvement is just a coincidence. To be sure your child truly has to avoid those foods, I advise you to wait for the fussiness to be gone for two weeks and then to eat a spoonful of the suspected food, or feed your baby a half ounce of the suspected formula. Try this over four to five days; if there's an allergy the crying will return.

Most babies with food allergies are allergic to only one or two foods, with the most common, by far, being cow's milk and dairy products.

Calcium Rules

If you're breast-feeding and you stop eating dairy products because your baby is sensitive to them, rest assured there are many other ways to get adequate calcium in your diet. Besides calcium supplements, you can also get calcium from green vegetables (broccoli, leafy vegetables), sesame-seed butter, dark molasses, fortified orange juice or soy milk, corn tortillas, etc.

Eliminating dairy foods from your diet is not a risk to your child. However, if you stop dairy products for more than a few weeks, speak to your doctor to make sure you're meeting *your* body's calcium needs.

That's why doctors often recommend bottle-fed babies switch from cow's milk formula to soy. Many babies improve by doing this, but as I noted earlier, at least ten percent of milk-allergic babies are soy-allergic too. These babies require a special, hypoallergenic formula; ask your doctor about these.

Constipation: Interesting Ideas on a Dry Subject

Like grandma always said, "It's important to stay regular," and that's especially true for babies! Fortunately, breast-fed babies are almost never constipated. They may skip a few days between poops, but even then the consistency is pasty to loose. Bottle-fed babies, on the other hand, do get constipated, but several commonsense approaches can usually help rectify the problem:

- *Change the formula*—Sometimes changing your baby's formula can help resolve her constipation. Some infants have softer stools when they drink concentrated formula versus powder (or vice versa); others do better with cow's milk formula versus soy; and, rarely, some may improve with a switch to a low-iron formula.
- *Dilute the mix*—Your baby's poops may improve when you add one ounce of water or half an ounce of adult prune juice (organic is best), once or twice a day, directly to the formula. (Never give babies under one year of age honey or corn syrup as a laxative.)
- *Open the door*—One last way to relieve constipation is to get your baby to relax her anus. Infants who strain to poop often accidentally tighten their anus. Like adults who can't pat their heads and rub their tummies at the same time, many babies have trouble tightening their stomach muscles and relaxing their rectums simultaneously.

  Try getting your baby's anus to "loosen up" by bicycling her legs and massaging her bottom. If this fails, insert a Vaseline-greased thermometer or Q-tip one inch into the anus. Babies usually respond by trying to push it out, and they often push the poop out at the same time.

A Poop Advisory: Sometimes Constipation Signals a More Serious Problem

Healthy babies may skip a day or two between poops. However, less frequent BM's may signal a more worrisome problem. If your baby goes more than two or three days without a stool, you should check in with your doctor. He may want to evaluate her for three rare, serious, but curable diseases that can masquerade as constipation:

1. *Hypothyroidism*—This easily treated condition is caused by an underactive thyroid gland and may slow mental development if allowed to continue untreated.

2. *Hirschsprung's disease*—This rare intestinal blockage happens when the rectal muscles can't relax to let the poop out. Surgery can correct it.

3. *Infantile botulism*—This very rare disease temporarily paralyzes babies. It's brought on by botulism spores that live in the ground and in liquidy sweets like honey or corn syrup (which should never be given to babies).

Feeding Problems—Babies Who Cry from Too Much (or Too Little) of a Good Thing

Fortunately, 99.9 percent of the time, your baby and your milk are perfect together. However, getting too little or too much milk may trigger severe crying.

"Got Milk?"—Babies Who Cry Because They Don't Get Enough Milk

It's usually easy to tell if a bottle-fed baby is getting her fair share of milk: Count the number of ounces she eats. With breast-feeders, however, it's trickier. If you are nursing, answer the following questions to figure out if your baby is crying because she's not getting enough milk:

Are your breasts making enough milk? If your breasts feel heavy when you wake up, if they occasionally leak, and if you can hear your baby gulping when she's feeding, it's likely that your breasts are making plenty of milk.

Is your baby happy to suck on your finger or pacifier? Just because your fussy baby wants to suck doesn't mean she's hungry. Offer her your finger to suck on. If she sucks happily for a few minutes, she probably wants recreation, not nutrition.

Does your baby become serene after a feeding? Well-fed babies are usually blissful, calm, and relaxed after a feeding.

Is your baby peeing enough? During the first few days of life, infants don't urinate very often, but once your milk comes in, your baby should pee five to eight times a day.

Is your baby gaining weight normally? Many moms and grandmoms are always worried that theirs is the only skinny baby in town while all the other infants are little sumo wrestlers! To know if your baby is gaining enough weight, you need to put her on a scale. For the most accurate weighing, check her on the scale at your doctor's office. Remember, babies lose eight to twelve ounces over the first few days of life, but thereafter they gain four to seven ounces per week.

If you answered no to any of these questions, you should call your baby's doctor to discuss her feedings because it is possible her cries are a sign of hunger.

Rebuilding Your Milk Supply

If extra milk calms your baby's crying and you want to rebuild your milk supply, you probably can. Speak to your doctor, a lactation consultant, or a La Leche League leader for advice. You can try some of these remedies too:

1. **Diagnose the Problem**
   - Sometimes poor feeding is caused by a "mommy problem." You may be trying to put your baby on the breast incorrectly. Or you may have flat nipples, a thyroid problem, fatigue, pain, poor nutrition, and—rarely—insufficient breast tissue. If your nipples are cracked or sore, let a little of your milk dry on them after each feeding. Breast milk contains special factors that speed the healing of irritated skin.
   - Poor feeding may also be caused by a "baby problem." Some babies have a hard time getting the hang of nursing.

Some are weak, some are "lazy," some suck their tongue instead of your nipple, a few are tongue-tied, and others are just plain confused and try to bite instead of suckle.

Regardless of the cause, if you are having a nursing problem, get help as soon as possible.

2. **Increase Your Supply.** Once you know your breasts are fine and your baby is sucking well, the next step is increasing your milk supply. Here's how:

- Eat well and get as much rest as you can.
- Empty your breasts frequently. Nurse your baby every two to three hours (during your waking hours). Some lactation consultants recommend that moms use only one breast per feeding; however, especially when you want to build up your milk supply, I think it's best to switch breasts frequently (move her from one breast to the other every seven to ten minutes until she stops wanting to suck).

  If you are not too tired or overwhelmed, you may build up your milk supply further by pumping or expressing milk once or twice a day. I recommend pumping for five to ten minutes *before* the first feeding of the morning, or whenever your breasts feel the fullest. Don't worry about depriving your baby of milk. You'll remove some foremilk, but that still leaves the rich hindmilk for her to enjoy. After a few days you should notice your supply increasing.
- Use imagery while you're nursing or pumping to increase milk production. Get comfortable and imagine your favorite safe, relaxing place and visualize your breasts making lots of milk. One mother I know imagined lying in the sun on a tropical island, with rivers of milk flowing out of her breasts to the ocean, turning the seas white—it worked!
- Try some fenugreek tea or a product called Mother's Milk tea made of fennel, anise, mint, and fenugreek to stimulate your breasts' milk glands.
- Ask your doctor about prescription medications that help in-

crease your milk supply or the letting down of the milk you already have. Also ask if you need your thyroid checked.

3. **Supplement Your Baby's Breast Milk with Some Formula.** You could also help your hungry baby by giving her pumped milk or formula. These can be given to her in a bottle or with a device called a Supplemental Nursing System (SNS). The SNS is a bag of milk connected to a soft, strawlike tube, which allows the baby to drink from the bag and the breast simultaneously. This method helps a woman rebuild her milk supply without teaching her baby the wrong way to suckle, a problem that may occur when nursing babies are given too many bottles.

"My D Cup Runneth Over!"—Babies Who Cry Because There Is Too Much Milk

Some babies love milk so much, they overeat. These kids guzzle down four to eight ounces each feeding and then vomit it all up because, as the saying goes, "their eyes were bigger than their stomachs." Other babies, however, guzzle not out of gluttony but out of self-protection. Their mom's milk is pouring out of her breast so quickly that they're trying not to choke.

Flooding can also occur in bottle-fed babies. Rubber nipples that are too soft or have holes that are too big can make a baby with a strong suck feel like she's drinking from a running faucet.

If you think your milk flow may be too much for your baby to handle, look for these signs:

- Does your milk quickly drip out of one breast when your baby is sucking on the other?
- Does she gulp and guzzle loudly?
- Does she struggle, cough, or pull away as soon as the milk starts to flow into her mouth?

If you answer yes to these questions, try expressing one to two ounces from your breasts immediately before the next feeding. Also, during the feed, hold your nipple between your second and third fingers, like a cigarette, and press against the breast to slow the flow of milk and see if the meal goes better.

Stomach Acid Reflux: Calming the Cry by Soothing the Burn

Bitter crying during or just after a feeding may indicate insufficient or excessive milk flow, a strange taste in your milk, a strong gastro-colic reflex in your baby (see Chapter 4), or that your baby is one of about three percent of colicky babies who suffers from stomach acid reflux.

If you suspect acid reflux as the cause of your baby's misery you should review the telltale signs of reflux mentioned in Chapter 4. Of course, if you think your baby may be suffering from this problem, you should consult your baby's doctor.

Through the years, several remedies have been recommended to alleviate reflux. A few are dead ends, but many are true paths to success.

Dead-End Stomach Acid Treatments

- *Position*—Parents of refluxing babies have long been told to keep their baby sitting up in a swing or infant seat after eating so gravity can help keep the milk in the stomach. However, studies show this position does not lessen the frequency or severity of reflux (although some parents still swear by it).
- *Rice-cereal-thickened feeds*—Some doctors recommend thickening a feeding with rice cereal to "weigh" the milk down and keep it in the stomach. But studies have also failed to show that this causes any real improvement in reflux.

True-Path Stomach Acid Treatments

- *Position*—Although sitting up may not help, two positions *have* been proved effective for lessening reflux: lying on the stomach or lying on the *left* side.

  Both positions are great while your baby is awake. The left-side position is also fine for sleep, as long as your baby is swaddled and wedged to keep her from rolling onto her stomach. The back is the preferred position for all babies to sleep in; however, some doctors recommend the side position for babies with severe reflux and nighttime vomiting. Ask your child's doctor for her opinion.

- *Burping*—Burp your baby every five to ten minutes during a feeding. Otherwise a big burp at meal's end may accidentally bring up the burning, acidic contents from your baby's stomach.
- *Feeding tips*—Make sure your infant isn't overeating. Try feeding a little less and see if the spitting stops and the crying improves. You can continue giving her shorter feeds as long as she's gaining four to seven ounces per week and she's satisfied for a few hours after a feeding.
- *Eliminate cow's milk products*—For some babies, reflux indicates a milk allergy. Discuss this possibility with your doctor to decide if the elimination of cow's milk is warranted.
- *Antacids*—Your doctor may suggest over-the-counter antacids or prescription acid-reducing medicines like famotidine (Pepcid), ranitidine (Zantac), omeprazole (Prilosec), and lansoperazole (Prevacid) in the hope of lessening her "heartburn" pain. (Never give your baby antacids without consulting a physician.)
- *Stomach-emptying aids*—During the 1990s doctors discovered that certain medicines caused the stomach to quickly empty its acidic contents into the intestines as well as "shut the door" at the top of the stomach so acid couldn't squirt up toward the mouth. Medicines such as metoclopramide (Reglan) and erythromycin are now occasionally used for babies with stomach acid reflux who continue to scream despite all the other approaches.

Herbal Teas, Homeopathics, Chiropractic, and Osteopathy: Dead Ends or True Paths?

Herbal Teas: A Cuppa Comfort?

Through the ages, herbal teas that aid digestion have been recommended for unhappy babies. Traditionally, mothers brewed either chamomile, peppermint, fennel, or dill for their babies' upset tummies.

The ancient "roots" of this practice are reflected in the names chosen for these herbs. In Spanish, the word for peppermint is *yerba buena,* meaning the *good grass;* in Serbian it's *nana,* meaning *grandmother.* Dill has settled stomachs in ancient Egypt, Greece, and in Viking times. Its English name derives from the Old Norse word *dilla,* meaning *to soothe or calm.*

Chamomile is said to have calming properties; peppermint eases intestinal spasms; dill helps soothe gas; and fennel dilates the intestinal blood vessels, facilitating digestion and producing a warming effect.

As much as I love herbal teas, I'm sorry to say that little proof exists that they offer any real benefit for colicky babies. However, they do no harm, so if you would like to give some to your baby, here's how:

To make dill or fennel tea, steep two teaspoons of mashed seeds in a cup of boiling water for ten minutes. A teaspoon of this may be given to a fussy baby several times a day. If your baby refuses the tea, you may sweeten it by adding a little baby apple juice or sugar (do not use honey or corn syrup).

Additionally, dill can be given in the form of a tonic called "gripe water," a popular folk remedy for colicky babies in Great Britain and the Commonwealth countries (although its effectiveness has never been proved).

Homeopathy, Chiropractic, Osteopathy: Are They Worth a Try?

Homeopathy is a philosophy of healing that teaches "like cures like." In other words, the body can be made to heal itself by giving a tiny dose of something that would actually *cause* the very same problem if given in a large dose. For example, a homeopath might recommend minuscule amounts of poison ivy extract to stop an itchy rash.

Do homeopathic remedies work? Some parents swear by them; however, hard evidence is difficult to find. Hopefully, this will change over the next five to ten years as the National Institutes of Health gets results from studies they are conducting on the subject.

There are four main recommended homeopathic remedies for colic: chamomila, colocynthis, magnesium phosphorica, and pulsatilla. These may be given singly or in combination; however, in general the correct homeopathic remedy is chosen according to the specific characteristics of a patient's symptoms—in this case, a baby's fussiness.

As with Western medicine, it's best to use homeopathics in consultation with an experienced practitioner.

The same uncertainty that surrounds homeopathy surrounds the claims that chiropractic or osteopathy can help calm crying babies. While there are some studies reported by these practitioners about the treatment of colic through the manipulation of the spine or skull bones, I have seen several colicky babies whose frustrated parents sought out chiropractic or osteopathic help with little or no success.

15

The Magical 6th "S":
Sweet Dreams!

Main Points:

- What a baby's normal sleep pattern should be
- How to use the 5 "S's" to help your baby sleep longer and better
- Weaning your sleeping baby off the 5 "S's"
- The truth about putting your baby on a schedule
- A few more helpful sleep hints, from extra feedings to darkened rooms
- Co-sleeping: The natural way to sleep (but it's not for everyone)

At Allison's two-month checkup, her mother told me Ally slept only for three-hour stretches at night. Shaya confided that getting up so often was wearing her down and making it hard for her to be patient with her other two young children.

I asked Shaya if she was still swaddling Ally at night. She wasn't. "I stopped about a month ago because the nights have been so warm and she always gets out of it!" I suggested she dress Ally in just a diaper, wrap her tightly in a larger blanket that could be securely tucked around her, and play some loud white noise in her room. The next week Shaya reported the good news. Allison, now tightly swaddled, was sleeping for an eight-hour stretch every night, without interruption.

Ahhh . . . sleep!

For most new parents, a good night's sleep is the pot of gold at the end of the rainbow, shimmering in your sleep-deprived mind like a mirage. Newborns sleep in such short dribs and drabs that we should never brag we're "sleeping like a baby." It makes much more sense to say we're sleeping like a bear, or a ditch digger, or, better yet, like a new parent.

Why don't babies sleep more? Your baby actually sleeps quite a bit; however, nature could have been a teensy bit more considerate about helping your baby choose when to enjoy his sweet dreams. Most newborns distribute their snooze time pretty evenly throughout the night (and day).

Mothers around the world usually take the erratic timing of these sleep periods in stride. Many years ago, Dr. T. Berry Brazelton reported that babies in rural Mexico also had evening fussy periods, just like our babies. However, their mothers were amused rather than upset by this, joking that since adults gab all day long, nighttime was a baby's turn to talk.

Anthropologists observing the !Kung San of southern Africa found their babies woke as often as every fifteen minutes. Their moms responded by pulling them to the breast for a little snack. Usually, they would fall back asleep in seconds.

In the U.S., most parents prefer to let their newborn sleep in a bassinet by their bed. For the first few months of life, your baby will likely request the pleasure of your company for a meal every two to four hours throughout the night. Bottle-fed babies often sleep a bit longer, because formula turns into big curds that sit in the stomach longer than the easily digested, tinier curds of breast milk.

I'm sure it's hard to believe right now, but your baby's early-morning feedings may turn into some of your sweetest memories. Those beautiful moments—when all noise and commotion are stilled—may make you feel like you're floating in a cloud suspended in time. Gretchen, mother of three, said, "Our two-month-old, Julian, will be our last baby, and as crazy as it sounds, I look forward to nursing him in the middle of the night! It's the only time when we can really be alone, and I get to enjoy my delicious little boy in peace and quiet."

Baby Sleep: Your Infant's Normal Patterns

All babies have sleeping and waking cycles. If you're like most new parents, your goal is to get your baby to do his longest sleeping at night and be most awake during the day.

But, exactly how long should your baby sleep? On average, babies snooze fourteen to eighteen hours in a twenty-four-hour period. That might sound like a lot but it's broken up into little snippets, slipped between short stretches of wakefulness. In effect, it's like being given a thousand dollars—*in pennies!*

As you can see in the sleep pattern graph, during your baby's first weeks of life two-thirds of each day will be spent asleep (gray areas). The average infant takes naps lasting two to three hours alternating with hour-long awake-breaks (white areas) for feeding, fussing, and some alert time. Initially, your baby's longest stretch of sleep will probably be about four hours.

By three months, your baby will still sleep fourteen to eighteen hours a day, but the awake time (white areas) will join into longer periods of wakefulness, and sleeping (gray areas) may extend for up to six to eight hours.

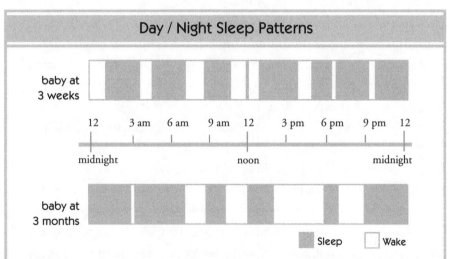

Modified from A. H. Parmelee Jr., Sleep patterns in infancy: A study of one infant from birth to eight months of age, Acta Pediatrica 1961:50:160.

During these initial months, your baby's brain gets better and better at dividing the twenty-four hours of the day into three main activities:

- *Awake time*—to eat and learn about the world
- *Active (REM) sleep*—to dream and "file away" the day's lessons
- *Quiet sleep*—to rest and recover from all the day's efforts

Both babies and adults have two different types of sleep (and I don't mean too little and none). Quiet sleep makes up fifty percent of your baby's slumber. It's when he's out like a log, his breathing easy and regular, his face still and angelic. During quiet sleep your baby's muscles are actually a little tensed; he's not floppy like a rag doll.

The other fifty percent of your baby's snoozing consists of active sleep. This sleep is characterized by sudden bursts of brain activity called REM (Rapid Eye Movement), and it occurs between periods of quiet sleep. REM sleep is when your baby's dreams are spun and his deep memory centers organize all his new experiences of the day. In active sleep, your baby has irregular breathing, sudden twitches, limp dangling limbs that feel like overcooked spaghetti, and, most spectacularly, he makes tiny heart-melting smiles. Contrary to myth, these grins are not caused by gas; rather, your baby is practicing what will soon become his most charming and powerful social tool—his smile.

Adults enjoy a full two hours of REM when we sleep. By comparison, your new baby revels in almost eight hours of REM every day. Why do babies have so much more REM than we do? No one knows for sure, but one theory posits that they need much more time to review the day because so many experiences are new to them. It's as if their brains are saying, "Wow! So much new stuff today, and I want to remember *everything!*" By comparison, most of an adult's day is so routine that our brains fast-forward through this period of review, as if to say, "I can skip all that. I know it already."

Sleeping obviously is not a time of alertness, but it's not "coma" time either. You are aware of many things around you while you snooze. For example, you probably have no trouble hearing the phone ring in the middle of the night and even when you sleep on the edge of the bed you rarely fall out of it.

Babies, too, receive a constant flow of information from the world around them while they slumber. That's why your baby may experience their still bed and the extreme quiet of your home as disturbing understimulation.

The waves of quiet and active sleep that your infant moves through take place within larger cycles of deep and light sleep. These repeat, like the tides, over and over again, all night long. Your baby cycles between deep and light sleep about every sixty minutes. Infants with good state control and mellow temperaments can often stay asleep during their lightest sleep, and even if they wake up, they usually fall right back to sleep. However, babies with poor self-calming abilities and challenging temperaments often have trouble staying asleep when they enter their light-sleep periods. During this phase of sleep, they may be so close to wakefulness that the added stimulation of hunger, gas, noise, or startle may be enough to rouse them to alertness or even agitated crying.

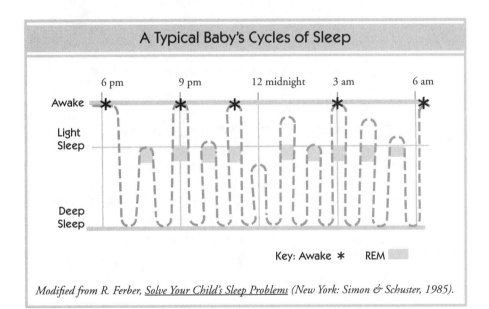

A Typical Baby's Cycles of Sleep

Key: Awake ✳   REM

Modified from R. Ferber, Solve Your Child's Sleep Problems (New York: Simon & Schuster, 1985).

Rest Easy: Helping Your Baby Stay Asleep with the 5 "S's"

When it comes to sleeping, you and your baby are a team, and you will both have to be flexible to make it work. However, as every mother knows, for the first four to six months, you will be the team member who bends the most. You will rearrange your priorities, put off chores, and try to sleep in synch with your baby's schedule.

But don't despair. There are five specific ways you can nudge your baby into a better sleeping schedule during these early months: the 5 "S's." These womb sensations will keep your infant's calming reflex turned on and, when they're used at night, they may even keep him soothed until daybreak.

1. Swaddle—

Tight wrapping prevents your baby's accidental whacks and disturbing startles. Just by swaddling your baby, you may increase his sleeping periods from three to four or even six hours at a stretch. Remember, his blanket must stay tight for it to work all through the night.

Karen's son, Connor, was three months old (and seventeen pounds!), but he still had trouble sleeping more than three hours at a stretch:

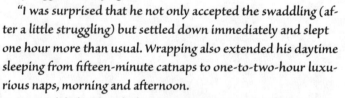

> "When I put Connor down after nursing, he would struggle and squirm for over half an hour until he finally settled down to sleep. He hadn't been swaddled since he was a newborn, but Dr. Karp suggested I try again.
>
> "I was surprised that he not only accepted the swaddling (after a little struggling) but settled down immediately and slept one hour more than usual. Wrapping also extended his daytime sleeping from fifteen-minute catnaps to one-to-two-hour luxurious naps, morning and afternoon.
>
> "I was delighted with this improvement, until a friend came by the next week and showed me that I was still swaddling Connor too loosely. She taught me how to do it tighter and he began sleeping eight hours straight at night!"

2. Side—

The back is clearly the safest sleep position for your baby. The side should ONLY be used if your baby is a terrible sleeper and even then you MUST make sure that he's tightly swaddled and wedged into position by placing receiving blankets (tightly rolled and taped) securely at his waist and lower back to keep him from accidentally scooting onto his stomach. Please consult with your physician if you have further questions.

3. Shhhh—

Most babies sleep better when a harsh, continuous white noise plays near their bassinet. These womb-like sounds drown out other distracting noises and have a profoundly lulling effect. As with swaddling, the mere addition of white noise to your baby's nursery may extend his sleep by an hour or two.

4. Swing—

The movement of a swing (and to a lesser extent, a vibrating seat) can help your baby nap better and sleep longer at night. Not all babies need to swing to sleep well, but I know many parents whose babies sleep well only when they are allowed to swing all night during their first four months of life.

5. Suck—

Sucking on a breast or pacifier may help your baby fall asleep, but it won't really help him stay in deep sleep.

Even babies who have never experienced the 5 "S's" can benefit from their sleep-enhancing effects. Don't be concerned if your baby initially resists them. If you patiently persist, you'll be surprised by your success.

Weaning Your Sleeping Baby Off the 5 "S's"

All children eventually must learn to fall asleep on their own and to put themselves back to sleep when they wake during the night. In my experience, by three months most babies are ready to learn how to do this and should be placed in the crib sleepy but semi-awake.

I know that the parents of infants under three months are warned by some baby book authors that using nighttime sleep aids like the 5 "S's" will spoil their babies and make them abnormally dependent. I couldn't disagree more! For nine months before your baby was born, your womb surrounded him with sensations like the 5 "S's" every second of every day. That's why all babies sleep better and longer with a couple of "S's" to keep them company during the long night. But don't worry—by the time your baby is three to four months old, you will be able to wean him off them without difficulty.

The first "S" I advise you to wean is sucking. I like babies to get used to falling asleep without something in their mouths as early as one month of age. Don't misunderstand me: I think it's fine for your baby to fall asleep sucking your breast, bottle, or pacifier, but a minute or two after he conks out I recommend you wake him up—just a tiny bit—as you put him down. This lets him start learning how to put himself to sleep. (If he begins to cry, just soothe him with shushing and rocking.)

Another good reason for weaning your baby from a bedtime pacifier is because they fall out so often they aren't a reliable sleep tool. You're in control of the wrapping and can easily keep your baby wrapped till morning, but you have no control over the paci, which he can spit out anytime he wants.

The next "S" I phase out is swinging. At two to three months you can reduce the swing speed to the slowest setting. A few days later, if your baby is still sleeping well, let him sleep in the nonmoving swing. Finally, a few days later, if he still is sleeping soundly, move him to the bassinet.

Next, many parents wean the swaddling. After four months, try wrapping your baby tightly—with one arm out. He should be able to suck his fingers and soothe himself. If he sleeps just as well that way, try putting him to bed with no bundling. However, if he starts waking up more, take a step back and return to the wrapping.

Lastly, wean the shhhhing sound. Over a period of two weeks you can gradually lower the white-noise volume until it is so low you can turn it off.

In general, my little patients are out of their swings by three to four months, out of the swaddle by three to six months (a handful have continued until nine months), and sleeping in a quiet room by three to twelve months. (The shhhh noise is the last "S" to be dropped because it is so easy, effective, and simple to control.)

When your sweet baby goes all night without any of the "S's," give him a diploma. He's now graduated from the fourth trimester and is ready to start his life adventure!

The Truth About Putting Your Baby on a Schedule

New parents are often confused about the importance of putting their baby on a schedule. Should schedules be avoided or embraced? Like so many other child-rearing issues, there's more than one right answer.

Toddlers and young children love routines. They feel secure and safe when they know what's going to happen. In another year or two, you'll probably have a bedtime ritual: "blankie," warm milk, and *Goodnight Moon* to guide your sweet child into peaceful sleep—every night.

Similarly, flexible eating/sleeping schedules can be a great help to young babies and their parents. That's especially true if you have twins, older children, if you're working out of the house, and/or you're a single parent.

But before you try to put your new baby on a schedule, you should know that scheduling is a fairly new parenting concept. Mothers in the past didn't feed their babies according to the time on the sundial. And many moms today don't feel right trying to fit their baby into a preset mold.

I am not saying it is wrong to try to put your one-month-old baby on a schedule. Just as long as you understand that babies have only been "asked" to bend themselves to our clock-driven schedules over the past hundred years, and many babies are simply too immature to do it.

Your baby's receptiveness to being put on a schedule depends upon his ability to handle delayed gratification. In other words, how good is he at holding off his need for food or sleep? Some newborns are easily dis-

tracted, but others take months before they can ignore their brain's demands for milk or rest. The parents of these babies must patiently delay their desire to get their infants on a schedule until their babies are ready for one.

That said, if you want to try your baby on a schedule after one to two months, the best way to begin is by increasing the time between his daytime feedings to three hours. Of course, if he's hungry before two hours are up (and you can't soothe him any other way) forget the schedule and feed him. Also, wake him up and feed him if he goes more than four hours without crying for food. Babies who go too long without food during the day often wake up and feed more at night.

The next step in scheduling is to train your infant to fall asleep without a nipple in his mouth. After his feeding, play with him for a little while before you put him to sleep. That will begin to teach him he can put himself to sleep. If he immediately passes out after you fill his belly with warm milk, that's okay, just jostle him until he opens his eyes. Then lay him down and let him float back into sleep. With patience over the next month or two, this will help your baby develop the ability to put himself to sleep.

Most infants automatically fall into a regular pattern after a month or

It's easier to establish a schedule if you follow the same pattern every day. After your baby is a month old, start this reassuring nighttime routine:

low lights

toasty bath

loving massage with heated oil

some warm milk

cozy swaddle

a lullaby . . . softly sung

and

gentle white noise playing in the background

Within a short period of time, the constant association of these experiences to your baby's sleep time will work almost like hypnosis. As soon as you start the routine he'll say to himself, "Wow, I feel sleepy already!"

two; however, if you can't wait to establish a more predictable routine, feel free to give scheduling a try.

If, on the other hand, he seems to resist being molded to your schedule, I encourage you to respond to your tiny baby's needs with promptness and love; you can always try the schedule again in a week. The bottom line is that your job as a parent is to adapt to the needs of your newborn, not the other way around.

A Few More Helpful Sleep Tips

Here are a few more tips to help your baby sleep longer:

Feed Your Baby More During the Day

These steps can increase your baby's daytime eating and nighttime sleeping as he reaches the end of the fourth trimester:

- Wake him for a feeding if he naps for more than four hours.
- Feed him in a quiet room so he doesn't get distracted and refuse to eat.
- Give him "cluster feedings" (several meals given every two hours in the late afternoon and early evening to load him up with calories).
- "Top off the tank" by waking him for a midnight feeding.

One thing that will not help your baby sleep better is feeding him rice cereal at bedtime. While it is true that some nighttime formula can help a breast-fed baby sleep longer, repeated scientific studies have proved that rice cereal does not prolong a baby's sleep. And why should it? From a nutritional point of view, it makes no sense that four to six ounces of milk (with all its fat and protein) would leave a baby hungry but a few spoons of rice starch would keep him satisfied all night.

If you have any doubts at all that your infant is getting enough to eat, ask your doctor to weigh him to make sure that he's thriving.

Hold and Rock Your Baby During the Day

Parents are often told to keep their baby awake during the day in the hope of getting him tired and making him want to sleep longer at night.

Although this sounds logical, keeping a tired baby awake often makes him miserable, overtired, and thus *worsens* his sleep at night. In fact, not only should you let your newborn sleep during the day but you should give him motion while he naps (in a swing, a bouncy chair, or on you in a baby sling). In my experience, babies who are carried ("fed" with nourishing touch and motion) throughout the day are often calmer (less "hungry" for that stimulation) at night.

Turn the Lights Down

Reducing the lights in your house as evening comes also gives your baby the signal it's time for sleep. Low lights quiet a baby's nervous system and prepare him to relax. Many hospital nurseries have an evening routine of dimming the lights and covering the incubators of premature babies to block the light and help them get into their parents' day/night rhythm.

> Mabel, the mother of four daughters, piqued my curiosity when she mentioned that her pet theory about the cause of colic was <u>electricity!</u> She said, "I noticed my kids are more stimulated and have a harder time falling asleep when we keep the house well lit in the evening. I think the artificially long 'daytime' we create with electric lights tricks them into believing it's still time to play. Our kids consistently sleep better when we dim the lights at night or use candles."

Co-sleeping: "I Just Got Evicted— Can I Sleep at Your Place?"

Thou shalt sleep with thy fathers.
Deuteronomy 31:16

Since mankind's earliest days, parents and babies have slept together for mutual protection, warmth, and to make nighttime feedings convenient. Japanese parents traditionally sleep with their baby between them, safe as a valley protected by two great mountain ranges. They don't question whether a mother and infant should be together all night; they consider themselves to be two parts of one person and therefore they should be sep-

arated as little as possible. Mayan families are very social and for them the shared bed is a time to be together. These parents believe making their baby sleep alone is an unfair hardship.

Until the late 1800s, American children also slept in bed with their parents. However, at the turn of the century, U.S. parents were frightened away from co-sleeping. They were warned it could spread illness, spoil children, or cause them to suffocate. So we moved our babies to their own cribs and eventually to their own rooms. Today, we Americans see our children's sleep as a time for privacy and to begin learning about self-reliance. Many now view sharing the bed as a sacrifice or a bad habit. (Oddly, many of these same parents nap with their babies during the day without harboring similar concerns.)

This resistance to co-sleeping is slowly changing. As breast-feeding continues its rise in popularity, nursing mothers are realizing the cozy convenience of having their baby nearby. In addition, the immigration of non-Europeans into the U.S. has introduced a potpourri of cultural traditions—most of which encourage the intimacy of co-sleeping.

However, like so many other prehistoric customs, co-sleeping doesn't always fit the needs and lifestyles of contemporary parents. One mother in my practice said, "I can't sleep in bed with my four-week-old baby. I just keep worrying about him." Other parents get frustrated because co-sleeping babies wake up more during the night. My nurse practitioner, Dana Entin, explains the frequent night feedings that co-sleeping babies request as a case of temptation. "If I had a piece of chocolate cake in bed next to me, I would wake up all night and want a little nibble too!"

If you decide not to co-sleep, don't feel guilty! As Shakespeare wrote, "To thine own self be true." You certainly don't need to co-sleep to be a good parent. You have the wonderful alternative of keeping your baby all swaddled and cuddly in a cradle or bassinet.

On the other hand, if bringing your baby into bed with you feels right, trust your instincts. Sleeping with your baby is a natural continuation of the womb experience. Your baby enjoys your body's companionship and its help in molding his breathing, temperature stability, and sleep pattern. Additionally, after the rigors of pregnancy it's an abrupt change for *you* to be all the way down the hall from your infant, connected to him by an intercom only. One mother who worked long hours shared, "Sleeping with my baby lets me make up some time I couldn't spend with her during the day."

As long as you and your baby are happy with co-sleeping, enjoy this sweet, fleeting opportunity. If you are planning to move your baby out of your bed, it's easiest to do so by four to five months of age, before he gets used to this bedtime routine. You can still end co-sleeping after that time, but in general, the longer you wait the tougher it is for your baby to make the switch.

One additional bonus of co-sleeping may be prevention of SIDS. Researchers like James McKenna of Notre Dame University believe the lighter level of sleep of co-sleeping babies may lessen their risk of SIDS.

Is Co-sleeping Dangerous to Your Baby's Health?

In 1999, the U.S. Consumer Product Safety Commission (CPSC) issued a disturbing warning to parents about the possible dangers of co-sleeping. They reported an average of sixty-four infant deaths (children less than two years old) each year related to a baby being in an adult's bed. Their conclusion? Parents should never place infants in their beds.

Unfortunately, their recommendation was as off-target as someone suggesting we try to prevent the fifty thousand fatal car accidents each year *by not driving*. Obviously, a more constructive answer to traffic deaths is for all of us to drive better. Likewise, the vast majority of infant deaths in bed are preventable by taking a few reasonable precautions. For example, eighty percent of the deaths noted by the CPSC could have been avoided by filling the spaces around the bed to keep babies from getting wedged in and by never sleeping on waterbeds. Most of the remaining twenty percent of deaths could have been prevented by using a co-sleeper attachment (a small baby bed with raised rails that fits right next to a parent's bed).

Nine Ways to Keep Your Baby Safe in Bed With You

Any parent co-sleeping with their infant *must* protect him in the following ways:

1. Avoid pillows, toys, or loose bedding that could smother your baby.
2. Never put your baby to sleep on a waterbed.
3. Eliminate spaces between the mattress and the wall, or the mattress and the headboard, where your baby's head might get trapped.
4. Use a co-sleeper attachment on your bed so your baby can't fall off or get rolled on.
5. Don't sleep on the sofa with your baby.
6. Keep your baby swaddled tightly all night long so that he doesn't move into a dangerous position during the night.
7. Let your baby sleep only on his back.
8. Give up smoking! Babies are more likely to die of SIDS if their mom is a smoker.
9. Always go to bed sober.

The Whys About the "S's":
Questions Parents Ask
About Sleeping

1. *Every time I put my sleeping baby down, he's up and yelling in minutes. Why?*

Even though your baby is asleep when you put him down, he still has some awareness of his surroundings. To him there's too big a difference between your arms and a quiet, still bassinet.

Try using the 5 "S's" to help your baby make the transition to his crib. Swaddling, white noise, and swinging lessen the abrupt change from your cuddle to his cradle and can eliminate one or two night wakings.

2. *When my baby falls asleep after a feeding, should I burp him and risk waking him up?*

Yes. You should burp him, to keep him from spitting up in his sleep, and change his diaper too, to prevent a diaper rash. After a feeding, most babies feel a little "drunk" and usually go back to sleep quickly, especially if you're using the 5 "S's."

By the way, it is also a good idea to put ointment on your baby's bottom at night to protect his skin from any pee or poop that comes out while he's asleep.

3. *I worry about overbundling my baby in the warm weather. How can I tell if he's getting overheated at night?*

It's quite easy to know if your baby is overbundled: feel his ears and toes. If they are red, sweaty, or very warm, he's too hot; if they are cold and bluish, he's too chilly; and if they feel "fresh" (not hot, not cold, but a tiny bit on the cool side), his body temperature is just right.

Even on the hottest summer days, your baby will benefit from swaddling. Dress him in a diaper only and wrap him in a very light cotton blanket.

*For summertime, Talia's grandmother made some ultralight
blankets by cutting a sheet in quarters and hemming the edges.*

**4. Can a baby have trouble sleeping because he's going through a growth
spurt?**

Yes. Babies grow tremendously fast during the first few months,
doubling their weight in about six months. Some babies do all this
growing at an even, steady pace, but many babies grow in fits and
starts (growth spurts and plateaus). In the midst of a growth spurt,
your baby may wake up more frequently and yell for a meal. (That's
really *demand* feeding!)

**5. Will my baby sleep better if he takes both breasts or just one, so he
gets the hindmilk?**

Unlike formula, which doesn't change from the first drop to the
last, breast milk changes greatly during the course of a feeding.
The milk that spurts out for the first five minutes is loaded with
protein and antibodies, and it's more watery to satisfy your baby's
thirst. By the time the breast is almost empty (after ten to fifteen
minutes) the milk slowly dripping out is as rich as half and half.
This creamy, sweet dessert is called the hindmilk.

Some experts tell mothers not to switch their breasts during a
feeding. They worry that feeding just a few minutes on each side
will deprive a baby of the hindmilk, which they consider nature's
way of making babies satisfied and sleepy (like the drowsiness we
feel after a heavy meal).

Other experts believe babies get more milk if their moms switch
breasts during a meal. They advise mothers to feed for about seven
minutes on one side and then, after that breast has released its
quick, easy milk, switch to the other side, which is full and waiting
to be emptied.

I recommend this to my patients: Experiment to find what's best
for you and your baby. If one breast keeps him happy for two hours
in the day and sleeping four hours at night, then there is no need
for switching. However, if he feeds too often or is gaining weight
too slowly, try giving him seven minutes on one side and then let
him suck for ten to fifteen minutes, or longer, on the second side

(that's enough for him to fill up with the early milk from both breasts and still get the hindmilk from the second side).

6. *Why does my baby always get up at the crack of dawn?*

Even when babies are asleep they still feel, hear—and see! For many babies, the early-morning light filters through their closed eyes and thin skull and acts like an alarm clock. Fortunately, many of these babies can be coaxed to sleep a little longer by using black-out curtains to shut out the sun's first rays; white-noise machines to help obscure the early-morning sounds of birds, dogs, traffic, and neighbors; or, by bringing them into bed with you for some cozy time.

Parents who can't charm their infants back to sleep are often forced to wave good-bye to their warm beds and take their little "rooster babies" out for an early-morning constitutional. (Believe it or not, these strolls may become some of your most treasured memories of when your baby was little.)

7. *Is it wrong to let my baby get used to sleeping in his infant carrier?*

It's almost impossible to *keep* your baby from falling asleep when you tote him around outside in an infant carrier. That's because putting your baby in a carrier or a sling and taking him for a walk gives him three of his favorite sensations: jiggly motion, cuddling, and the rhythmic, soothing sound of your breathing. These devices are great ways to treat our babies to a sweet reminder of the fourth trimester.

So, don't worry about accidentally teaching him bad habits. After the fourth trimester ends, your four-month-old baby will be able to entertain himself and it will be relatively easy to get him used to less contact—if that's what you really want. (Truthfully, by then many parents love their carrier so much they want to "wear" their baby more and more.)

8. *Is it okay to let my baby sleep on my chest?*

In general, I don't recommend this position. I once had a couple call me in the middle of the night when their four-week-old baby fell off his father's chest and hit the wall next to the bed. (The exhausted duo had slipped into a sound sleep.) Fortunately, he wasn't hurt, but a fall like that could have caused a serious injury.

A Parent's Perspective: Memoirs from the Mattress

We went through fire and water almost in trying to procure for him a natural sleep. We swung him in blankets, wheeled him in little carts, walked the room with him by the hour, etc., etc., but it was wonderful how little sleep he obtained after all. He always looked wide awake and as if he did not need sleep.

G. L. Prentiss, *The Life and Letters of Elizabeth Prentiss*, 1822

Poor Elizabeth Prentiss could have learned a thing or two from the parents whose stories below reveal how they transformed their nighttime experience with their babies from getting "nickel and dimed" to money in the bank:

Debra and Andrew swaddled their twins, Audrey and Sophia, from the very first days in their lives. Swaddling prolonged their children's nighttime sleep. Even at four months old, the twins still preferred being swaddled. It helped them sleep a full eight hours every night.

Debra, Andrew, Audrey, and Sophia

As she reached the four-week mark, our daughter Eve became more wakeful and more distressed with the world around her. When she wasn't eating or sleeping, she was fussing—and at times she screamed inconsolably. One night she yelled so much her nose got stuffed and she began to snort. I called Dr. Karp's office for advice. As I spoke with his nurse, Louise, I cradled Eve in my arms and rested them on top of the dryer. The noise, vibration, and warmth of the dryer calmed her, allowing me to talk for a few minutes.

Over the next couple of weeks, as I became skilled at using the "S's" Nurse Louise had described that night, Eve rewarded us with six-to-eight-hour periods of uninterrupted sleep every night. At six months, we were still swaddling Eve at night but by then we would let one of her arms stay out so she could suck her fingers.

Shari, Michael, Hillary, Noah, and Eve

Didi and Richard were exhausted from Cameron's hourly waking—all night long. They tried keeping their six-week-old up more during the day in the hope he would sleep better at night, but that

just seemed to get him overtired and make him cry even more. At night, they tried to calm him with a bath, the vacuum, or a ride in the car, all of which worked for a while but Cameron would get upset again as soon as the "entertainment" stopped.

Then, they discovered their son liked to sleep tightly wrapped and seated in the swing next to a white-noise machine with the sound cranked up loud. However, they worried about leaving him in there, so after he fell asleep they would put him back into his bassinet. Cameron slept better that way, but still awoke every three or four hours.

Finally, Didi and Richard stumbled onto the secret for getting Cameron to sleep longer. One night when he was in the swing his exhausted parents fell asleep and let him stay in the swing, with white noise, all night long. It made a huge difference. With that nighttime assistance he began to sleep a six-hour stretch, eat, and then go back down for another three hours!

When Wyatt was two months old, his parents—Lise, a nurse, and Aaron, a physician—noticed he would sleep five hours at night when wrapped and serenaded by white noise but only three hours when his arms were free and the room was quiet.

Lise said, "I was happy to see how well our son did with swaddling. But I still worried he would get 'addicted' to it and have trouble sleeping unwrapped when he got older. So as soon as he turned three months, I began putting him to bed unwrapped.

"Everything seemed fine, until a month later when Wyatt turned four months. Out of the blue, he began waking every two hours through the night—screaming! One friend told me he was teething, but Tylenol didn't help. My husband guessed he was going through a growth spurt, but rice cereal didn't help either. At Wyatt's four-month checkup, I told Dr. Karp about my frustration and fatigue. He suggested I stop the medicine and cereal and try the wrapping and white noise again. To be honest, I thought Wyatt was too old for swaddling, but I was desperate.

"Within two nights, he went from waking up and shrieking five times a night to waking once, chowing down his milk, and then immediately sacking out again until 6 AM! He loved the waterfall sound of our sound machine. I played it loud for him for the first hour and then kept it turned on medium all night long. (It helped me to sleep, too!)

Everything worked so well that I continued the routine until one night, when Wyatt was six months old, I skipped putting him in his cocoon and still enjoyed a deep, beautiful sleep."

Lise, Aaron, Wyatt, and Rachel

I never would have believed it, but wrapping was the key to everything! Our first son, Eli, never resisted being bundled up, but Benji fought it with all his strength. However, only after he was tightly swaddled did the rocking, pacifier, and shushing calm him.

After a few days of practicing the 5 "S's," I could put Benji down for hours at a time with no problem. Now at six weeks of age, and at the peak of what should be his worst time, he's a pretty easy baby. He takes long naps and sleeps for seven to nine hours at night (with one very brief feeding).

For naps, I let him sleep in the swing on the fast speed and keep the noise machine on pretty loud.

I let him nap frequently because I've noticed that Ben gets overstimulated and has a hard time settling himself if I let him have long awake periods during the day. So, when he starts getting cranky, I take that as my cue to put him back in the swing and do my womb imitation.

I recommend this method for anyone with a "difficult" baby. I can't imagine what my mental state would be if I were still carrying him all day and rocking him all night. It has made an enormous difference for both me and Benji, as well as my first guys, Steve and Eli!

Wendy, Steve, Eli, and Benji

Conclusion

The Rainbow at the End of the Tunnel:
Finally Your Baby Is Ready to Be Born!

He's starting to love us back a little.
Francie about four-month-old Jackson

*At birth, Esmé was a pudgy, sweet-smelling baby who needed
to use all her concentration to gaze into her mother's eyes. Yet, by
four months, she could shoot broad grins out at anyone in the
room, as if to say, "Ain't I great!"*

Hooray! After months of fuzzy stares and long sleeps, your four-month-old's laugh and gurgle announce to the world: "Dress rehearsals are over . . . I'm ready for my Grand Premiere!"

It has been three long months since you cut the umbilical cord, but finally your baby is *really* ready to be born. He has weathered the challenging transition from your womb to the world and is no longer trapped inside his immature body. Now the rapidly increasing control he has over his actions offers him many new ways to handle his upsets without having to resort to crying.

Please don't underestimate what your baby has achieved during his brief lifetime. It truly is amazing. In essence, he has zipped through millions of years of evolution in a mere ninety days. He may have started out as helpless as a mouse yet now he's well on his way to mastering the most important skills of our species—the ability to reach out both manually and socially. His relaxed and open hands now allow him to latch on to his rattle (or your nose) and, like Esmé, he's already learning how to use his adorable, toothless grin to make everyone he meets fall in love with him!

Like a child on the first day of school, your scrubbed-cheeked, four-month-old baby's happy jabberings bubble forth energetically. Now, there's no question he's ready to learn and start making friends. And, as a direct consequence of your baby's increasing curiosity, you'll probably notice his sudden dislike for being put on his stomach. While newborns enjoy "tummy time" because it's calming and helps them ignore the chaos of the world, your four-month-old baby demands to be placed on his back so he can see the world. Now, he's *interested* in the chaos . . . he's ready to play.

Your infant isn't the only one ready for this next chapter of life. I'm sure you too are ready for a little more play . . . and rest. For the past three months, you've unselfishly accepted pain, fatigue, and anxiety. Now, *you've* become one of the experienced parents on the block and you've learned enough to earn an advanced degree in "Baby-ology." It is my sincere hope that this book has been a useful part of that education in helping you see the world through your baby's eyes and in helping you master the ancient techniques of infant soothing and comforting.

At last, there *is* a light at the end of the arduous tunnel that was the fourth trimester and happily, far from being an oncoming train, that light is . . . a glorious rainbow. All your love and hard work have paid off and the real fun is just beginning. So congratulations! Your baby is now well on the way to becoming *one of the happiest babies on the block!*

Appendix A

Red Flags and Red Alerts:
When You Should Call the Doctor

Fortunately, most colicky babies aren't physically sick. Rather, they're sort of "homesick"—struggling to cope with life outside Mama's womb. But how can you know when your infant's cries *are* a sign of sickness?

Here's a primer of the ten red flags that doctors look for to decide when a baby's cry signals illness, plus a review of the ten red-alert medical conditions that these red flags may indicate.

The Ten Red Flags Your Doctor Will Ask You About

Whenever you're worried about your baby, you should, of course, contact your doctor for guidance. When you do, he'll likely ask you these two questions to help him decide if your baby has colic or something more serious:

1. Is your baby growing well and acting normal in all other ways?
2. Is your baby calm for long periods of the day?

If you answer no to either question, then your doctor will ask you how your baby acts when she isn't crying. He is looking for these ten red flags:

1. *Persistent moaning* (groans and weak cries that continue for hours)
2. *Supershrill cry* (unlike any cry your baby has made before)
3. *Vomiting* (any green or yellow vomit or vomiting more than one ounce per episode and more than five episodes a day)

4. *Change in stool* (constipation or diarrhea, especially with blood)
5. *Fussing during eating* (twisting, arching, crying that begins during or shortly after a feed)
6. *Abnormal temperature* (a rectal temperature of more than 100.2°F or less than 97.0°F)
7. *Irritability* (crying all the time with almost no calm periods in between)
8. *Lethargy* (a baby sleeping twice as long as usual, acting "out of it," or not sucking well over an eight- to twelve-hour period)
9. *Bulging soft spot on the head* (even when your baby is sitting up)
10. *Poor weight gain* (gaining less than a half ounce a day)

The Ten Medical Red Alerts Your Doctor Will Consider

Whenever a doctor sees a crying baby who exhibits any red-flag symptoms, she tries to determine whether this indicates one of these ten serious—but treatable—medical conditions. Please remember, most of these conditions are *very, very* rare. (Excluding babies who cry because of food sensitivity or acid reflux less than one percent of infants with severe, persistent crying are affected by the problems listed below.)

1. **Infection: From Ear Infections to Appendicitis**

   You might think the best way to tell if your baby has an infection is to take her temperature, but many sick newborns don't get fevers. So even if your crying baby doesn't have fever, you should consider that her fussiness may be a sign of infection if she acts lethargic or irritable for more than a few hours. Call your doctor immediately. He may check her for:

   > **Ear Infection**—These babies may just get fussy and upset; they rarely pull on their ears.
   > **Urine Infection**—These babies can have smelly urine, but usually *don't.*
   > **Brain Infection (meningitis)**—These infants have bulging soft spots, vomiting, lethargy, and irritability that rapidly worsens over just a day or two.

Appendicitis—Extremely rare in infants, it may cause a hard stomach, poor appetite, and constant irritability.

Intestinal Infection—A baby with "stomach flu" vomits, has diarrhea, and usually has been in contact with a sick relative.

2. **Intestinal Pain: From Intestinal Blockages to Stomach Acid Reflux**

Some stomach problems cause pain and may explain crying in ten to fifteen percent of colicky infants (in descending order of seriousness):

> **Intestinal Blockage**—This is an extremely rare medical emergency that may occur right after birth or weeks later. Babies suffer from waves of severe painful spasms plus vomiting and/or the cessation of pooping. With intestinal blockages, the vomit often has a distinct yellow or green tint. (During the first days of life, a breast-fed baby's vomit may also be yellow, because that is the color of colostrum. However, if your baby has yellow vomit, *never* assume it's from your milk. Immediately consult your doctor to make sure it isn't the sign of a more serious condition.)
>
> **Stomach Acid Reflux**—This cause of burning pain occurs in approximately one to three percent of fussy babies.

A "Pain in the Rear": Can an Overly Tight Anus Block a Baby's Intestines?

In 100 A.D. the physician Soranus opined that a tight anus could block a baby's intestines, leading to spasms. He recommended stretching the anus to relieve a baby's crying. Over the next two thousand years, medical practitioners followed his advice and routinely stuck fingers up the behinds of crying babies. Today, however, we know this problem is extremely rare and probably never causes colic.

Food Sensitivity—Five to ten percent of fussy babies get better with a change in diet and so presumably have this condition. Besides crying, it may cause vomiting, diarrhea, rash, or mucousy blood in the stools.

(For a complete discussion of reflux and food sensitivities see Chapters 4 and 14.)

Crying before, during, and after feeding

Immediately before a feeding: hunger, thirst, challenging temperament

During a feeding: the gastro-colic reflex, the milk flow is too slow or too fast, the milk has a strange taste, stomach acid reflux

Immediately after a feeding: continued hunger, the gastro-colic reflex, needing to burp, needing to poop, wanting to suck more, food allergy, stomach acid reflux

---

3. **Breathing Trouble: From Blocked Nostrils to Oversize Tongues**

The most common cause of breathing trouble is a condition where a baby's tiny nostrils are blocked. Babies don't know how to breathe through their mouths, except when they're crying. That's why babies who are born with tight nostrils, or who have noses swollen shut from allergies or colds, get so frantic.

If you want to check for blockage, place the tip of your little finger snugly over one of your baby's nostrils, closing it off for a few seconds. She should easily be able to breathe through the open nostril. Then repeat this test on the other side.

If your baby can't breathe or gets agitated when you do this test, call your physician. If it seems the nostril is blocked from mucus, ask the best ways to clear it. And do your best to rid your home of dust, molds, sprays, perfumes, cigarette smoke, and anything else that might make her nose congested.

Very rarely, an infant will have trouble breathing if her tongue is too big for her mouth so it falls back into the throat and chokes her when she lies on her back. This problem is obvious from the moment of birth because her tongue will always stick out of her mouth.

4. **Increased Brain Pressure**

   When pressure builds up inside a baby's head, it also causes:

   - Irritability and crying from a headache
   - Vomiting
   - An unusual high-pitched cry
   - A bulging fontanelle (soft spot) even when the baby is seated
   - Swollen veins on the forehead
   - A head that's growing too rapidly (your doctor should measure your baby's head size at every well-baby checkup)
   - Sunset sign (a big-eyed stare with a crescent of the white of the eye displayed over the colored iris, making the eye look like a setting sun)

   If your baby fits the symptoms described above, contact your doctor immediately.

5. **Skin Pain: A Thread or Hair Twisted Around a Finger, Toe, or Penis**

   In years past, the sudden onset of sharp screaming in an otherwise calm baby made parents search for an open safety pin inside the diaper. Today, however, thanks to pin-less diapers, that no longer happens. Now a parent who hears that type of abrupt, shrill cry should look for a fine hair or thread wrapped tightly around their baby's finger, toe, or penis. This problem requires immediate medical attention. (Doctors often treat this problem by applying a dab of hair-removal cream to dissolve the hair.)

6. **Mouth Pain: From Thrush to Teething**

   Thrush, a yeast infection in the mouth, is easy to recognize because it causes a milky white residue on the lips and inside of the mouth that cannot be wiped away. Thrush may also cause a bumpy red rash in a baby's diaper area and/or itchy, red nipples in a breast-feeding mom.

Thrush rarely causes fussiness, but on occasion it can cause crying from an irritated mouth. Fortunately it is easy to treat, and recovery is rapid.

Many parents ask if teething causes their baby's crying. This is extremely unlikely, because teething two-month-olds are as rare as hen's teeth. However, if you think your baby is having teething pain, give her some acetaminophen drops and see if it gives any relief (ask your doctor for the correct dosage). This medicine won't help colic, but it may reduce mild teething pain.

7. Kidney Pain: Blockage of the Urinary System

A blockage of the kidney is a very rare cause of persistent crying that occurs any time, day or night. Unlike classic colic, which begins improving after two months, crying from kidney pain gets worse and worse.

8. Eye Pain: From Glaucoma to a Corneal Abrasion

Eye pain, also very rare, may come from glaucoma (high pressure inside the eyeball), an accidental scratch of the cornea, or even from a tiny, irritating object stuck underneath a baby's eyelid (such as an eyelash). Your doctor should consider these problems if your crying baby has red, tearful eyes and severe pain that lasts through the day and night.

9. Overdose: From Excessive Sodium to Vitamin A

Persistent, severe crying can result from giving babies excessive amounts of sodium (salt). This may occur when a parent mixes formula with too little water. It has also rarely been described after the first week of life if a breast-feeding woman is making so little milk that her breast milk becomes very salty. These babies are easily diagnosed because they are losing weight, not drinking any other liquids, and are both irritable and lethargic all day long.

Excess Vitamin A is an extremely rare cause of infant crying. It only occurs in babies who are given high doses of supplemental vitamins or fish oil.

10. Others: From Migraines to Heart Failure

Some extraordinarily rare conditions that have been reported as the cause of unstoppable crying in young infants include: a bone fracture, sugar intolerance in babies fed fruit or fruit juice, migraine headache, hyperthyroidism, and heart failure. These babies don't merely cry for three hours a day—they act poorly all day long.

Appendix B

A New Parents' Survival Guide:
The Top Ten Survival Tips for Parents of New Babies

Now that we've talked all about the baby's crying, let's talk about yours! All new parents know that if you ask five people for their advice (not that people even wait for you to ask), you'll get ten different opinions. So, even though you didn't ask *me* for my opinion, here is my list of ten sanity-saving survival tips to help you endure the challenges of your baby's first months a little more gracefully.

1. **Trust Yourself: You Are the Latest in the Unbroken Chain of the World's Top Parents**

    > *Leslie, still in her hospital bed with four-day old Gabriel, told me: "I'm usually such an optimist, yet I've had weird dreams of dropping him and leaving him places. My husband jokes that some special 'inexperienced-parent' alarm will go off when we take Gabe home from the hospital!"*

    Trust yourself. You know more than you think you do.
    Dr. Benjamin Spock

    If you're like most new parents, you probably alternate between feeling like a major-league pro and an amateur. It's enough to give a person "parental whiplash!" And, the conflicting advice given by many baby experts can deepen the confusion.

But before you lose confidence, please remember this: You are part of an unbroken chain of successful parents that stretches all the way back to the beginning of time. You and your baby have survived because you are descended from the best mothers, most protective fathers, and strongest children in the world. That's why Dr. Spock's advice to parents to trust themselves is so correct.

Trust your feelings. Relax and remember that all your baby really needs from you is milk and your nourishing love. And all you really need is patience, support, a little information, and perhaps a massage every once in a while.

2. Lower Your Expectations

> *You'll see. Having a baby is like going to sleep in your own bed and waking up in Zimbabwe!*
>
> Sonya to her daughter Denise a month before
> Denise gave birth to Aidan

Becoming a parent is filled with all sorts of misconceptions and surprises. And perhaps the biggest misconception of all is

that you'll automatically know what to do the moment your baby is born. Yet even after giving birth to her third child, Beth quipped, "At the end of my first pregnancy about the only thing I was really prepared to do was filling out forms and buying maternity dresses!"

Parenting requires some practical experience (especially when caring for challenging babies). Yet many pregnant couples today have never even touched a newborn. Despite this lack of experience, they expect themselves to instantly be able to care for the babies *and* manage the household *and* have a job *and* be lovers.

Unfortunately, these unrealistic expectations have been growing in our culture for at least the past fifty years. Even though people warned you when you were pregnant, "Your life will never be the same!" you probably shrugged it off. Few believe *their* baby will be tough. For most women, being pregnant is so close to their regular life that they get lulled into a false sense of security. Before delivery, you can still linger in a hot shower and think, "I'm ready. I'm on top of this." It's so automatic that many women are tricked into believing that taking care of their newborns would be just as natural, but as you now know, that couldn't be further from the truth. It's only after your baby is born that you begin to see the demands of parenthood more accurately. Suddenly, that long hot shower you took a month before the baby came looks like a Caribbean vacation.

Another expectation that may not immediately materialize is loving your baby the moment you see her. Of course, many parents *do* instantly fall in love with their new infant; however, one of the little-told truths about becoming a parent is that many new moms and dads *don't* feel smitten right away. It makes sense that falling in love might take a little time. After all, few of us experience love at first sight. Don't worry, like the song says, "You can't hurry love."

And that's not all. You may soon notice your brain has also unexpectedly changed. Memory loss is one more proof that your life is temporarily out of your control. One new mom told me, "My best guess is that during the delivery a piece of my brain came out with the placenta."

Lots of moms feel that giving birth turns them into complete "boobs"—and in a way it does! Lactation makes your body awash with prolactin which, along with the other massive hormonal changes going on inside you, probably is the basis for this new forgetfulness. Finally, you'll notice your ditziness is made ten times worse by exhaustion. Clear thinking is terribly hard to hold on to in the face of prolonged sleep deprivation.

So be patient and kind to yourself. In a few short months you'll have your feet on the ground again and, what's more, you'll know your baby better than anyone else in the world!

3. Accept All the Help You Can Get

> When I moved to California from Florida, I was happy
> to be independent from my family. But when my baby
> was born, I missed them in a way I had never felt before.
> I suddenly wanted and needed my family around me.
>
> Kathleen, mother of two-month-old Ella Rose

Never in history were a mother and a father expected to care for their baby *all by themselves.* The idea of a nuclear family—one mother and one father to do it all—is one of mankind's most recent, and riskiest, experiments, attempted only over the last two or three generations. (That's a mere sixty years out of the 60,000 years since the modern human era began.) In the past, a couple's family and community always pitched in to help, and later the couple would return the favor.

> Sharon, mother of Noah and Ariel, was a work-at-home
> mom, a thousand miles away from her family, with no
> baby-sitters or nanny. Sharon's goal was to make sure her
> kids were happy and healthy—even if she was dead on
> her feet. She described feeling like an old tomato plant,
> where the fruit looks plump and delicious even though
> the plant that nourishes it looks scraggly and anemic.

I'm always telling the parents of my patients: Get help and don't feel guilty about asking—or paying—for it. Enlist your friends to bring you a frozen casserole, do some cleaning, or watch your baby while you nap. Just as you are giving so much of yourself to take care of your new child, lean on your support network to help take care of *you*—you'll pay it back later. The extra pair of "hands" of a niece, neighbor, nanny, or swing is neither an extravagance nor a sign of failure. It's the bare minimum that most new moms have had throughout time.

4. Get Your Priorities Straight: Should You Take a Break or Do the Dishes?

> *On the few occasions that my crying baby fell asleep before I did, I used the time for me! I soaked in a bubble bath, relaxed with a drink, read a book, and prayed that she would sleep a little longer.*
>
> Frances Wells Burck, *Babysense*

As I just said, I encourage you to get some help, but if you don't have access to help, don't worry: Your job is doable—as long as you put your priorities in order. The time will come to achieve everything you want, but that time isn't right after having a baby.

One of your top priorities is: Don't try to do too much. For example, the week after having your baby is not the time for you to host your family from out of town. As my mother used to say, "Don't be stupid polite!" A few well-wishers are fine, but only if they're healthy and helpful. Visitors who can't cook or clean take up your precious time and, what's worse, *they can carry germs into your home.* People you keep away may call you paranoid but, in truth, you never had a better reason for being neurotic and overprotective!

Another good idea is to leave a sweet announcement on your answering machine, giving your baby's important statistics and telling everyone that you won't be returning calls for a few weeks. Of course, you can always return calls if you want, but this at least frees up enough time to accomplish even higher priorities—like soaking in a hot tub.

Rest: The Essential Nutrient for New Parents

> *Sometimes the most urgent and vital thing you can do . . . is take a nap.*
>
> Ashley Brilliant

When we were teenagers, we were "dying" to stay up all night. Now, we're "dying" **if** we stay up all night!

The extreme fatigue that goes along with being a new parent can make you feel depressed, irritable, inept, and distort your perceptions of the world like a fun-house mirror. (Some countries torture people by waking them up every time they fall asleep!)

So please nap when your baby does, sleep when your mom comes, and, however you have to do it—get some rest!

5. Be Flexible: It's Much Better to Bend Than to Snap

> *You just have to accept that some days you're the pigeon and some days you're the statue.*
>
> Roger Anderson

There may be a few times in life when an unwillingness to compromise is admirable—but after becoming a new parent *isn't* one of them. That's why I believe the official bumper-sticker slogan for all new parents should read, *Be flexible—or die!*

Part of the fun, and responsibility, of being a mom or dad is to be able to choose which parenting options make sense to *you* and works for *your* child. However, it's also important to be able to throw your choices out the window and start all over again when things are not going the way you planned.

If you're a person who enjoyed being organized, on time, and having a spotless house, this new flexibility may require practice—and deep breathing. But you may as well take it all with a sense of humor because the time has come when your milk will gush down the front of your favorite blouse and when your little darling will empty her diaper load on your white sofa!

If you can, throw away your to-do list for a few months. Accept that the clock on your wall has been temporarily transformed from a time-management tool to a decoration. And know that for a while, day and night will cease to have any true relevance.

You've "bought your ticket," so let go and open yourself to the marvel, awe, and exhilaration of one of the greatest adventures of life!

6. Know Thyself: How Do Your Baby's Cries Make You Feel?

When your baby screams in your face, are you able to calmly think, *He must be having a bad day?* Or do you think, *Oh, my God, I'm doing something wrong!* or *I don't deserve to be a mother!* Or even, *Who the hell does she think she is?*

There's no question your baby's screams may trigger a flood of upsetting feelings from the past. You may suddenly remember voices of anger, criticism, and ridicule directed at you long ago. And you may begin to get angry or defensive. Of course, your newborn's cries can't possibly have a connection to your past traumas. She's much too young to feel anger or to be able to criticize or manipulate you. However, fatigue and stress can sometimes fool your mind and make these innocent cries feel like stinging attacks.

This, too, is a normal part of being a new parent. When these emotions well up inside you, take the opportunity to be brave and share your feelings with your spouse or someone else who truly cares about you. The more you discuss your past pains and your current fears, the more clearly you'll see how unrelated your baby's cries are to those old experiences.

7. Don't Rock the Cradle Too Hard: Babies, Frustration, and Child Abuse

David suddenly felt a wave of anger blow across him like a hot wind. After weeks and weeks of colicky screaming

*by his twin sons, Sam and Ben, he got so angry he
punched his hand through the door. "I was so frustrated
and exhausted I couldn't control myself. I would never
hurt my boys, but for the first time in my life I understood how a parent could be driven to such desperation."*

Few things feel better than when we can easily calm our baby's screams, but when everything we do fails, few things can make us feel worse.

Remember, your baby can belt out a shriek that is louder than a vacuum cleaner. That's why it is so difficult to take when she's on your shoulder and blasting right next to your ear. The sound of her cry also sets off a "red alert" reflex inside your nervous system that makes your heart race and your skin cringe, creating an urgent desire to stop it. This crying can become almost intolerable when it's coupled with fatigue, depression, financial stress, hormonal chaos, family conflict, and a history of being abused. When these stressful forces combine, they can sometimes push even a loving parent over the edge into the dark abyss of child abuse.

A mild-mannered father I know told me that he once shocked himself, in the middle of the night, when his daughter's cries started to "get to him" and he found himself rocking her cradle "a little too hard." "I felt like such a terrible parent. My little Marlo was so unhappy, yet nothing I did seemed to help. I felt so incompetent."

Another great frustration for parents is when a technique that usually calms their baby suddenly does nothing. It's like getting mugged in broad daylight when you least expect it.

However, no matter how desperate you feel, always remember that there's a big difference between feelings and actions. When you are exhausted, you can joke all you want to about leaving your baby on someone's doorstep but, needless to say, you're not allowed to do it.

What should you do when you are feeling like you're near your breaking point?

- Lighten your workload and get some help to clean the house and watch the baby.
- Do something physical to vent your energy: dig a hole, hammer nails, beat the sofa, scream into a pillow, sob into a towel, or just go out and run!
- Talk to someone: a friend, a relative, or even a crisis hotline. (The National Child Abuse Hotline—800 4-A-CHILD—has counselors available every day, all day.)

8. Keep Your Sense of Humor Handy

He who laughs . . . lasts! Mary Pettibone Poole

There are times when parenthood seems like nothing but feeding the mouth that bites you. Peter de Vries

The only normal families are the ones you don't know very well. Joe Ancis

Babies are always more trouble than you thought . . . and more wonderful. Charles Osgood

It's not easy for me to take my problems one at a time when they refuse to get in line. Ashley Brilliant

Raising a child is a constant series of tasks and challenges. You don't want to make mistakes, but you will. Remember, perfection is found only in the dictionary. So, forget dignity . . . forget organization . . . be gentle with yourself . . . and *laugh, laugh, laugh.*

Laughter is exactly what this doctor orders. Rent some funny movies or watch reruns of *I Love Lucy.* Try imagining Cleopatra burping her baby and getting a giant spit-up down *her* back.

Laugh at your hair, laugh at your baby, laugh at your messy house. Laugh at the fact that you are now one of those women you used to avoid who gets into heated discussions at parties about burping and the color of her baby's poop.

9. **Take Care of Your Spouse (S/he Just Might Come in Handy Someday)**

> When Curtis, Cheryl and Jeff's second child, was four
> weeks old, Jeff said "We haven't even had sex once yet."
> Cheryl shot back, "What do you expect? Every sexual
> part of my body is either oozing, bruised, or throbbing!"

Taking care of a new baby is so demanding and time-consuming that it's easy for a parent to start feeling like they're giving a hundred and ten percent effort (usually true) and their partner is giving only seventy-five percent (usually false).

- "I work all day and still come home and give the baby a bath." *vs.* "I take care of the baby all day and still make him dinner and scratch his back."

- "She's so lucky to lounge around the house, watch soaps, and hang out with the baby all day." *vs.* "He's so lucky to go to work and see different people."

The truth is, being new parents is a joint effort. There is so much to do that the only way to do it all, and still be friends, is to work as a team.

Your baby's world balances on the two of you. That's why she would never want to hear you say, "I gave up everything for you. I even put you ahead of my relationship with your father/mother." In fact, if your baby could, she would sit you down and tell you, "Don't you worry about me. I'm fine, but I'm really gonna need you later. So, for right now, have some fun, see a movie . . . but please take care of yourselves."

Caring for your baby is only half your job; the other half is giving each other some TLC. Dads must support and adore their wives, moms must nurture and caress their husbands, and you both have to cut each other some extra slack and avoid harsh criticisms. (Of course, in any given situation your reactions will be different from your spouse's. You're separate individuals with unique life experiences.)

Make the time to take walks together, to give each other ten-minute massages, back scratches, or sexual pleasure. Try to never take your partner for granted and never go to bed angry. These first months are the hardest part of the first year, but the great news is, if you work together, your marriage can emerge from this period stronger than ever.

To Dads: Appreciate Your Wife—The Great Goddess of Creation

Can you imagine how embarrassed you would be if *your* "bag of waters" broke open in the middle of a business meeting? While a new dad has spent the past nine months going about his life in a fairly normal way, his wife has been stretched in a surreal kind of mind-body "taffy pull." Let's face it, any guy who has watched his wife give birth knows the real truth about who the weaker sex is.

Mothers are great heroes! When it comes to making babies, we men chip in a sperm while our wives essentially *pull a dog sled from Alaska to the Gulf of Mexico.* In fact, except for your 23 chromosomes, every single molecule of your baby was individually carried to her through your wife's body. It's almost as if each cell should carry a little tag that reads, *Inspected by Mom.*

And, after your child is born, your wife has another awesome responsibility on her shoulders. While you get to go to work, she's at home dealing with leaking breasts, sore nipples, an extra thirty pounds, and a frantic, red-faced person yelling at her—all after little or no training.

And then there's sex (or no sex)! You may be interested in having sex after abstaining for the last part of the pregnancy, but for many new moms, sex is the last thing on their mind. Women often have "pelvic exhaustion" after the delivery, and although your wife may look like she had a "boob job," she may not feel very erotic. (Remember those are really for the baby now.)

What should you do? Rethink your priorities. Remember, no one on his deathbed ever said, "My only regret is that I didn't spend more time at the office." Now is the time your wife needs your attention, support, and tenderness the most. (It's no accident researchers find the best predictor of breast-feeding success to be the spouse's support.) Bring home flowers, change some diapers, and give her a break to go out with friends—now, that's the type of "child support" she needs!

Another way to really help your wife is to take over the job of calming your baby. Men are superb at soothing babies when they learn the Cuddle Cure. Frank, a construction worker and father of colicky two-month-old Angela, said, "I love being able to soothe my screaming baby in seconds."

To Moms: Appreciate Your Husband—The Man Who Put the Us in Uterus

Okay, it's true: You *have* had to do all the hard work and "heavy lifting" so far, and you're so busy you barely get the chance to pee—but it's not easy being a new dad either.

Remember, your husband is descended from the world's most successful cavemen, and he probably has dinosaur-size expectations of himself. He may not have to protect you from saber-toothed tigers, but most men still feel a huge pressure to go out into the world and compete in order to provide for their families.

If your husband is quiet, don't think he doesn't feel things as deeply as you do. Men shown crying babies responded with less talking than their wives, but they had exactly the same sharp increase in sweating, heart rate, and blood pressure.

There's no doubt that many new dads feel as nervous handling their infants as the first time they asked a girl to the prom. So be patient with your sweetie. Be available if he needs you, but don't rescue him right away when he's fumbling around trying to figure out how to calm your baby—just remind him of the 5 "S's." He'll sense your confidence in him and he'll feel great when he can do it on his own. Then, rather than seeing himself as an outsider with the baby, he'll feel like a "star player on the team."

10. Don't Ignore Depression: The Uninvited Guest

My whole world suddenly turned black. My emotions jumped from guilt to rage to despair to such utter anxiety that I thought I would either jump out of my skin or lose my mind. I had terrible visions of hurting myself so I could be taken to the hospital and rescued from all this.

I felt like I was being punished for thinking I could be a good mother. I felt like I didn't deserve to have a child . . . and I cried for hours.

Louisa, mother of three-week-old Georgia

As shocking as it sounds, approximately forty percent of new moms experience unhappy feelings intruding upon their joy during the days and weeks after the birth of their babies. You may notice yourself suddenly being tearful, worried, or exhausted yet unable to sleep—all of which may be early signs of postpartum depression.

Shortly after delivery, women may experience three different levels of depression: *the baby blues*—mild weepiness, anxiety, and insomnia; *true postpartum depression*—a bruising, more debilitating type of grief; or *postpartum psychosis*—a severe and rare condition including hallucinations, incoherent statements, and bizarre behavior.

The Baby Blues

The baby blues usually start a few days after the baby is born and last at least several days. No one knows exactly why they occur, but some scientists think they're triggered by the dramatic changes in a woman's hormones after delivery. In addition, the blues can certainly be worsened by all the other stressful situations going on in a new mom's life—including having a very fussy baby.

The blues are so common that many doctors consider them a normal part of giving birth. Nonetheless, the fatigue, fear, and unanticipated sorrow can be very distressing while you're experiencing them.

> *Feeling dejected and rejected Sarah called me. She had just about had it with her four-week-old daughter, Julie. Sarah said, "She's fussy and demanding all the time; I feel robbed of my joy. I dread her crying because I never know if it will last five minutes or four hours! And on top of that, I have insomnia. I'm a light sleeper by nature, but now I'm so attuned to Julie's cry that I can't sleep for longer than a cat-nap. I'm anxious, exhausted . . . falling apart.*
>
> *"I watched my babysitter act so calmly around Julie and I couldn't help but feel that I was making her worse with my awkward attempts at calming her."*

I asked Sarah and Tom to come in so I could teach them the Cuddle. I hoped much of Sarah's problem stemmed from her exhaustion, but I was also concerned about her having the baby blues. After teaching them the 5 "S's," I encouraged Sarah to make an appointment with a psychologist, just in case the techniques didn't help. Fortunately, the Cuddle made a dramatic improvement in Julie's screaming. Sarah quickly mastered the skills of calming her and getting her to sleep longer. As Julie slept more, Sarah began to feel like a better mom.

"Yesterday, I calmed my little baby in less than five minutes! I was so proud! Within a week, I felt like the darkness lifted and my life had turned around."

True Postpartum Depression

One of the least discussed secrets about having a baby is depression. During the first weeks of what should be the greatest bliss of their lives, about five percent of normal moms (estimates range from three to twenty percent) experience strong feelings of sorrow and anxiety. If mild sadness after birth is called the baby blues, then this more severe depression should be called the baby "black-and-blues," because it is a bruising assault on a woman's psychological health.

Crashing waves of emotion knock these women off their feet and make them feel like they are drowning in sadness, shame, anger, anxiety, pain, fear, apathy, exhaustion, and hopelessness. It can take all the energy a mother has just to make a sandwich. Oftentimes they have fantasies of hurting themselves or their babies. These symptoms can occur at any time after delivery and last from a few weeks to several months.

A woman who feels this way can become so fragile that almost anything makes her think, *Every other woman would make a better mother.* Or, *I'm sure she's crying because she hates me.* No matter what words of support her loved ones offer, she feels totally adrift and thinks it's impossible for them to really understand how she feels.

This black hole sucks away a woman's optimism and self-confidence. Yet, at the same time, the shame and isolation accompanying postpartum depression lead most of these moms to keep their suffering a secret from their doctors.

However, depression *is* a medical illness. Although these mothers often feel responsible for their condition, they should have no more guilt than people suffering from allergies. Like its milder version, the baby blues, postpartum depression is believed to be caused by a temporary hormonal imbalance. It, too, is made worse by the stress of fatigue, financial pressures, family problems, and colic.

If you are feeling like this, you're not alone. Many women have experienced what you are going through. Fortunately, there are some very effective treatments that can help you feel better. Please, call your doctor. You may not even have postpartum depression—low thyroid levels after delivery mimic depression. And if you do have it, you can be greatly helped by any one of a dozen excellent new medicines, hypnosis, light therapy, or psychotherapy.

Postpartum Psychosis

This severe reaction to the physical, emotional, and hormonal shifts occurring around birth may affect as many as one in one thousand women (usually within two weeks of delivery). Typically, these distraught new mothers hear voices and see things that other people can't; their statements become irrational and preoccupied with bizarre trivia; and, they may refuse to eat and become frantically active and extremely confused.

Postpartum psychosis is treatable, but it's an absolute medical emergency! If you think you or someone you know may be suffering from this extremely serious condition, seek medical help *immediately.*

To get help with any level of postpartum depression, contact:

Postpartum Support International:
(805) 967-7636 or www.postpartum.net

Depression After Delivery:
(800) 944-4PPD or www.depressionafterdelivery.com.

Index

Page numbers of illustrations appear in italics.

Breast-feeding, (*cont.*)
  Supplemental Nursing System
    (SNS), 205
  supplementing, 205
  tooth-decay and, 182
  topping off the tank, 221
  underfeeding, 202–3
Burping
  GER and, 207
  how to, 34, *34*
  sleeping baby and, 226
Burping drops, 35, 193

C

Caffeine, 41–42
Calming reflex, 3, 10, 67, 92–103
  fetus and, 10, 92–93
  jiggling to trigger, 158
  side/stomach position and, 130
  sucking and, 174
  top ten ways you can imitate the
    uterus, 93
  turning on (5 "S's"), 3, 10–11,
    93–103 (*see also* 5 "S's")
  vigorous motion to trigger, 169
Care and Feeding of Children (Holt),
  155–56
Child Abuse. *See* Abuse
Colic, 25–32
  causes, top five theories, 32,
    33–60
  chiropractic, 208–9
  cultures where babies never get
    colic, 32, 39, 44, 53, 60, 68, 75,
    84–85
  fourth trimester (missing), 61–75
    (*see also* Fourth trimester)
  gas and poop and, 35, 36, 37, 74,
    105–6
  herbal teas, 207–8

homeopathy, 208
massage for, 194–97
medical problem, serious, 186,
  238–43 (*see also* Appendix A)
myths and ancient theories,
  28–29
osteopathy for, 208–9
pain and, 27–28, 31, 32, 48,
  73–74
preemies and, 31, 38–39, 44, 48,
  53, 60, 73
"Rule of Threes," 27
ten universal facts, 31–32, 43–44
timing of occurrence, 31, 39, 44,
  74
total hours of fussing, 26–27, *26*
walks outside, 197–98
warmth to soothe, 198–99
See also Gastro-esophageal Reflux
  (GER)
Constipation, 35, 36–7, 196, 201
  serious problem indicated, 202
Crying, 5–6, 17–24, 240
  cycles, 102–3
  distinct sounds of, 21–24
  emotional effect on parent,
    20–21, 251–53
  letting baby "cry it out," 30–31
  medical problem, 186, 200–7,
    238–43,
  myth of blowing off steam (or
    crying is good for baby),
    29–31
  overstimulation and, 11, 23, 50,
    51–52
  understimulation and, 52–53
  See also Colic; Cuddle cure; 5
    "S's"; Sleep
Crying reflex, 17–20, *19*
Cuddle Cure, 3, 11–14, 185–92
  keeping baby calm after you
    soothe crying, 189

D

Depression, 257–60
  baby blues, 258–59
  postpartum depression, 258–60
  postpartum psychosis, 260

E

Ear infections and pacifiers, 179
Efé tribe, Zaire, 133, 176

F

Fatigue or overtired cries, 23,
  221–22
Feces
  blood in, 41, 238
  normal appearance, 36
Feeding. *See* Breast-feeding; Bottle-
  feeding; Hunger
Fetal position, 9, 38, 130
Fetus
  calming reflex and, *9*, 10
  life in the womb, 62–63, 141
  missing fourth trimester, 8–9, 14,
   61–75, 194–95
5 "S's," 3, 10–11, *12*, 94
  finding your baby's favorite technique, 187
  how to switch off your baby's crying with, 126–27, *126–27*
  Shushing (shhhhing), 11, 12,
   93, 96–97, 100, 127, 139–51,
   217
  Side/Stomach position, 11, 12,
   93, 95–96, 126, *126*, 129–37,
   190, 216
  Sucking, 11, 12, 93, 98, 127,
   173–84, 191–92, 217

Swaddling, 11, 93, 94–95,
  105–26, 190, 199, 216
Swinging, 11, 12, 93, 97,
  127, *127*, 153–72, 191,
  217
  three reasons for a delayed
   response, 101–3
  vigor, 99–100, 169
  See also Cuddle Cure; Shushing;
   Side/Stomach position;
   Sucking; Swaddling; Swinging
Field, Tiffany, 195
Food sensitivity, 39–42, 72,
  199–201, 204
  bottle-fed babies (milk or soy
   allergy), 38, 40–41, 43–44,
   200–1, 207
  breast-fed babies, 39, 40–42,
   43
  caffeine, 41–42
Fourth trimester (missing), 8–9, 14,
  61–75
  colic and, 70–75, *71*
  parenting and, 67–70
  sucking and, 174, 175
  touch and, 194–95
  what it is, 62–67
  why baby needs, 66–67
Fussy baby, xiv, *xiv*, 5, 7, 9, 23, 54,
  89
  See also Temperament

G

Gala (milk), 175
Gas, 33–34, 38–40, 105–6
  colicky babies, 37
  massage for, 196
Gastro-colic reflex, 36–37, 240
Gastro-esophageal Reflux (GER),
  42–44, 72, 206–7, 239

Gaze aversion, 57
Girlfriend's Guide to Surviving the First Year of Motherhood, The (Iovine), 7
Gripe water, 208
Grunting, 35
Gynecology, 155

H

Habituation, 50
Heartburn. *See* Gastro-esophageal Reflux
Herbal teas, 204, 207–8
Hiccups, 23, 82
Hirschsprung's disease, 202
Holt, Emmett, 155
Hunger
  amount of milk consumed daily, 174
  cries, 23
  hints to watch for, 122, 179
  sucking satisfies,174
  underfeeding, 202–5, 240
Hypothyroidism, 202

I

Illington, Ronald, 35
Indonesia, 133
Infant carrier, 228
Infant swings, 166–71, *167*
  Karp's Law of Swings, 168
  parents' concerns, 166–68, 170
  sleeping and, 217–18
  swaddling in, 168
  weaning from, 166–67
  white noise while using, 169
Iovine, Vicki, 7
Iran, 155

J

Jell-O head movement, 158, 161, *162*

K

!Kung San tribe, 3–4, 75, 84–85, 132, 212

L

La Leche League, 203
Lapp people of Greenland, 132
Laughing, 18
Lullabies, 162–63

M

Manali tribesman, 75
Massage, 194–97
Maternal anxiety (as colic cause), 44–48, 72
McClure, Vimala, 197
McKenna, James, 224
Milk Shake, 157, *157*

N

Native Americans
  childrearing, 70
  swaddling, 109
"Neck nestle," 147
Newborn babies, 4–6, 8–9, 79–84, *80*
  abilities, 49, 82
  brains of, 8, 101–3
  crying at birth, 17–20

four-day-old babies vs. four-month-old babies, 80–82, *81*
head size, 65
hearing of (sound-damping factors), 141
"kangaroo" treatment, 85
physiological characteristics, 82
reflexes, 90–93
state control, 49–51, *50*
See also Temperament

O

Overactive intestines, 36–37
Overeating, 180–81, 205–6, 207
Overheated babies, 121–22
  cautions, 199
  SIDS and, 131, 132, 199
  sleeping, 226–27
Overstimulation, 11, 23, 50, 51–52

P

Pacifier, 98, 112, 127, 166, 174, 176–84, 191–92
  "dummies," 176
  ear infections and, 179
  nipple confusion, 177–78
  preemies and, 175
  reverse psychology to keep from falling out, 177
  SIDS and, 179–80
  weaning from, 178, 180, 218
Pain
  colic, 27–28, 31, 32, 48, 73–74
  gas, 105–6
  gastro-colic reflex, 37
  gastro-intestinal reflux (GER), 43, 44, 206–7

medical problem, 186, 238–43
visual clues, 23
Parenting
  experience of the fourth trimester (what your baby needs), 67–68
  instinctual response to crying, 20–21
  maternal anxiety (as colic cause), 44–48, 72
  new mothers, difficulties and top ten stressors, 45–47
  response to crying, immediate and consistent, 20, 30–31, 84–85
  spoiling a baby, 14, 20, 68–70, 112
  temperament clashes, 59
  survival guide, 245–60, 246 (*see also* Appendix B)
  See also 5 "S's"
Parmelee, Arthur H., xiv
Postpartum depression, 257–60
Preemies
  colic in, 31, 38–39, 44, 53, 60, 73
  massage, effect of, 195
  sucking pacifiers and, 175

R

Reflexes, 49, 90–93
  calming. *See* Calming reflex
  crying, 17–20, 90
  gastro-colic. *See* Gastro-colic reflux
  grasping, 91
  Moro, 91–92, 130–31, 158
  rooting, 91
  sneezing, 90–91
  step, 91
  sucking, 91, 173–74

S

About the Author

Harvey Karp, M.D., perfected his approach to crying babies during his twenty-five years of experience as a pediatrician and child development specialist. Trained by some of America's top pediatricians, including Dr. T. Berry Brazelton, in 1981 Dr. Karp received the prestigious Ehrmann Fellowship to study crying and colic. Dr. Karp is an assistant professor of pediatrics at the UCLA School of Medicine, with a private practice in Santa Monica. He is also a nationally renowned expert on children's health and the environment and an authority on breastfeeding. He lives with his wife and daughter in California.

For further information please contact: *www.thehappiestbaby.com*